UNIVERSITY OF NORTH CAROLINA AT CHAPEL HILL
DEPARTMENT OF ROMANCE LANGUAGES

NORTH CAROLINA STUDIES
IN THE ROMANCE LANGUAGES AND LITERATURES

Founder: URBAN TIGNER HOLMES

Editor: CAROL L. SHERMAN

Distributed by:

UNIVERSITY OF NORTH CAROLINA PRESS

CHAPEL HILL
North Carolina 27515-2288
U.S.A.

NORTH CAROLINA STUDIES IN THE
ROMANCE LANGUAGES AND LITERATURES
Number 257

RONSARD'S CONTENTIOUS SISTERS

RONSARD'S CONTENTIOUS SISTERS

The Paragone between Poetry and Painting in the Works of Pierre de Ronsard

BY

ROBERTO E. CAMPO

CHAPEL HILL

NORTH CAROLINA STUDIES IN THE ROMANCE
LANGUAGES AND LITERATURES
U.N.C. DEPARTMENT OF ROMANCE LANGUAGES

1998

Library of Congress Cataloging-in-Publication Data

Campo, Roberto E., 1954-
    Ronsard's contentious sisters: the paragone between poetry and painting in the works of Pierre de Ronsard / by Roberto E. Campo.
        p. – cm. – (North Carolina Studies in the Romance Languages & Literatures; no. 257).
        Includes bibliographical references and indexes.
        ISBN 0-8078-9261-0 (pbk.)
        1. Ronsard, Pierre de, 1524-1585 – Knowledge – Arts. 2. Ut pictura poesis (Aesthetics). 3. Art and literature – France. I. Title. II. Series.

PQ1678.C36   1998   98-29034
841'.3 – DC21   CIP

Cover: Vasari, *Poetry and Painting*, by permission of the Archivi OCTAVO, Florence

Cover design: Shelley Greundler

ISBN 0-8078-9261-0

IMPRESO EN ESPAÑA

PRINTED IN SPAIN

DEPÓSITO LEGAL: V. 4.195 - 1998

ARTES GRÁFICAS SOLER, S. A. - LA OLIVERETA, 28 - 46018 VALENCIA

TABLE OF CONTENTS

To Diane

Pour vous montrer que j'ay parfaitte envie
De vous servir tout le temps de ma vie,
Je vous supply vouloir prendre de moy
Ce seul present, le tesmoing de ma foy,
Vous le donnant d'affections extresme
Avecq' mon coeur, ma peinture, & moymesme.

(*Elegie* for Diane, 1:170, vv. 1-6)

ILLUSTRATIONS

ACKNOWLEDGEMENTS

Many have contributed their support and wisdom throughout the preparation of this book. I would first like to acknowledge the editors of *French Forum, Romance Quarterly,* and *The Sixteenth Century Journal* for kindly allowing me to reproduce, with multiple refinements and additions, my earlier articles on Ronsard's poetry about painting. I am similarly grateful to the libraries, museums, art collections, and agencies that have granted permission to replicate the photographic illustrations enriching the *dehors* and *dedans* of this volume. Sincere thanks are also due to the National Endowment for the Humanities and the Research Council of the University of North Carolina at Greensboro, without whose financial support, by way of a summer stipend and a summer research excellence award, this project would have taken far longer to complete.

On a more personal note, I would like to express my deep appreciation to the colleagues, past and present, who have so generously given of their scholarly expertise at various stages in the development of this book. I would especially like to recognize Professors G. Mallary Masters, Lance K. Donaldson-Evans, David Fein, Roch Smith, Kathleen Kish, Mark Smith-Soto, Shirley Whitaker, and among my art historian friends, Professors Carl Goldstein and Paul Watson. A special word of thanks likewise belongs to the two anonymous editorial readers who painstakingly reviewed the book manuscript in typescript. Their thoughtful comments and advice were invaluable in making the following pages both more informative and more readable. I am also obliged to Dr. Anna Pani McLin and Mr. Marco Caproni for their assistance in procuring the prints of Vasari's wonderful frescos of the sister arts.

Finally, I shall be forever grateful to my wife Diane, to whom this book is lovingly dedicated as a testimony to her unfailing encouragement and affection.

NOTE ON EDITIONS

The ancient, medieval, and early modern works quoted in this book belong to the most reputable scholarly editions available. For convenience, citations of the Greek, Latin, and Italian sources are presented, first, in English translation (taken from published parallel-text or English versions of demonstrated critical reliability), and, second, in the original language (either immediately following the translation, for shorter quotations, or in an endnote, for longer ones). French texts remain untranslated unless otherwise required for the purposes of the discussion (in which case the translations are my own). In the interest of authenticity, all spellings and features of punctuation coincide with the editions of origin. The reader should therefore allow for inconsistencies in these regards.

For details of publication, the reader is invited to consult the relevant entries in the select bibliography. In general, the translated and original citations of Plato, Aristotle, Plotinus, and Longinus are from the works published in the Loeb Classical Library series (unless indicated differently). Similarly, the quotations of Aquinas' *Summa Theologiae* originate in the Blackfriars version; and the citations of Dante's *Divina Commedia* derive from Charles S. Singleton's critical edition for the Bollingen Series, while those of his *Convivio* (*Banquet*) are taken from the editions by Christopher Ryan (for the English) and by Maria Simonelli (for the Italian). Passages from Leonardo da Vinci's *Trattato della pittura* correspond to the excerpts provided in Jean Paul Richter's *The Literary Works of Leonardo da Vinci*; and quotations of Alberti's *Della pittura* originate in John R. Spencer's *On Painting* (for the English) and Cecil Grayson's third volume of the *Opere Volgari* (for the Italian).

Henceforth, locations of citations will be identified parenthetically, as necessary, in two parts separated by a semicolon. The first segment indicates the conventionally sanctioned manuscript reference; the second entry designates the precise location (typically volume and page) in the relevant scholarly edition employed. Footnotes are supplied wherever ambiguities are anticipated (as in the cases of Proclus, Ficino, and Pico).

The principal source for Ronsard's works is the twenty volume *Œuvres complètes* by Paul Laumonier (et al.). Citation locations are described parenthetically, as appropriate, by volume, page, and verse in this edition. Again, footnotes serve to identify quotations from (or references to) other scholarly editions.

INTRODUCTION

Scholars of sixteenth-century French literature have found a favorite object of study in the poems on painting of Pierre de Ronsard (1524-85). Besides shedding light on the dynamic relations between this preeminent poet of Renaissance France and the many painters and pictorial artworks he came to know as a favorite of the kings and nobles of his day, these works have provided insights into his own poetic genius and the principles of the Pléiade school of poetry he helped to found and lead during the second half of the century. They have also done much to exemplify and elucidate the dynamics of Renaissance philosophy and aesthetic theory. Throughout these extraordinary verses Ronsard directly engages prevailing conceptions of human knowledge and metaphysical ontology, beauty and artistic affectivity.

The richness of these implications is doubtless behind the diversity that has come to characterize the critical approaches to this poetry. To date these approaches have followed three principal paths. One mode of criticism has given priority to the extra-verbal plastic models. While recognizing Ronsard's obligation toward literary antecedents and the strongly autoreflexive nature of all his writing,[1] researchers with this point of view have supposed that the poet fully embraced the popular Renaissance understanding of *ut pictura poesis* ("as is painting, so is poetry"). Loosely borrowed from Horace's *Epistola ad Pisones* (361-65), this phrase was commonly taken to say that poetry and painting are (or ought to be) reciprocally de-

---

[1] On the reflexivity of Ronsard's poetry, see Terence Cave, *The Cornucopian Text* (Oxford: Clarendon Press, 1979), esp. 223-70.

pendent for subject matter and equally (if differently) capable of conveying ideas and stimulating emotions, that they are (or ought to be) veritable "sisters" in the hierarchy of human endeavors, as Giorgio Vasari depicted them in the spandrels of the chamber of Fame and the Arts (1542) at his home in Arezzo (figs. 1-2).[2] In supporting this position, the critics have typically cited Ronsard's many collaborations with contemporary painters. It is well known, for example, that he contributed substantially to the multi-media extravaganza marking the entry of Charles IX into Paris in 1571,[3] and more obliquely, that he furnished the *Epitaphe* for Jean Martin's 1553 translation of the treatise on architecture, *De Re Aedificatoria*, by the famous fifteenth-century Italian art theorist, Leon Battista Alberti.[4] In the same spirit, these commentators have made common currency of his early modern explicators and biographers. Among the latter, Claude Binet furnished the most memorable testimony when, in his 1586 *Vie de Pierre de Ronsard*, he announced that painting and other non-verbal artforms "estoient à singulier plaisir" to our poet.[5] In this case the evocations of pictures would signify Ronsard's eminently plastic imagination.[6] Not only would

---

[2] For the history and application of the principle of *ut pictura poesis*, see especially Rensselaer Lee, *Ut Pictura Poesis: The Humanistic Theory of Painting* (New York: Norton, 1967). See also, W. J. Thomas Mitchell, *Iconology: Image, Text, Ideology* (Chicago: University of Chicago Press, 1986), esp. 48; Wesley Trimpi, "The Meaning of Horace's 'Ut Pictura Poesis'," *Warburg and Courtauld Institutes* 36 (1973): 1-34; Jean H. Hagstrum, *The Sister Arts: The Tradition of Literary Pictorialism and English Poetry from Dryden to Gray* (Chicago: University of Chicago Press, 1958), 57-92. On Vasari's *Camera della Fama e delle Arti*, see Patricia Lee Rubin, *Giorgio Vasari: Art and History* (New Haven: Yale University Press, 1995), 137, and Plates 58-60, 164-65.

[3] Cf. Margaret McGowan, *Ideal Forms in the Age of Ronsard* (Berkeley: University of California Press, 1985), 65-68.

[4] Laumonier, *Œuvres complètes*, 5:252-58. Another significant collaboration may be seen in Ronsard's quatrains for Baptiste Pellerin's 1579 *Les Figures et portraicts des sept aages de l'homme* (18:335-38). For more on the latter project, see Isidore Silver's note in the Laumonier edition (18:335-36) and Georges Wildenstein, "La Collection de tableaux d'un admirateur de Ronsard," *Gazette des Beaux-Arts* 51 (1958): 5-8.

[5] Claude Binet, *La Vie de P. de Ronsard* (1586), ed. Paul Laumonier (1909; rpt. Geneva: Slatkine, 1969), 45 n. 12. Certain remarks that appear in Marc Antoine de Muret's commentaries on the *Amours* likewise make allusion to Ronsard's admiration for his painter counterparts (notably, the portraitist "Janet," or François Clouet). For more on these testimonials, see Chapter Three.

[6] See Michel Dassonville's comments on Ronsard's "imagination éminemment plastique": *Ronsard: Etude historique et littéraire*, 5 vols. (Geneva: Librairie Droz, 1985), 4:139-58, esp. 153.

FIG. 1: Giorgio Vasari, *Poetry*, Arezzo, Casa Vasari Camera della Fama e delle Arti (Archivi OCTAVO-Firenze)

FIG. 2: Giorgio Vasari, *Painting*, Arezzo, Casa Vasari Camera della Fama e delle Arti (Archivi OCTAVO-Firenze)

his poetry betoken a belief in the formal and conceptual relatedness of poems and paintings (frequently in connection with the period-style concept of "mannerism"), but in a few instances of shortsighted hyperbole, it would also denote our laureate's unqualified acceptance of the ontological parity between words and images.[7]

Consonant with a conclusion drawn by Jean Plattard in his seminal 1914 article on the reaction of major sixteenth-century French writers to the plastic arts and artists of their time,[8] a second brand of scholarship has minimized or utterly dismissed any debt the Pléiade laureate might have owed to extra-verbal realities. This viewpoint has prompted many commentators to adduce the poems about painting to Ronsard's desire to imitate and outdo the bards of Antiquity. His verses are exclusively the products of a quest to emulate Greek and Roman masters such as Homer, Virgil, and Anacreon, whose fondness for discussing and describing pictorial works of art is incidental to our poet's first concern. Still other readers have imputed these works solely to the rhetorical tradition of *ekphrasis*, the representation in words of a real or imagined work of art,[9] codified by late-classical Sophists like Philostratus the Elder, Philostra-

---

[7] The principal proponents of this critical perspective include Henri Chamard, *Joachim du Bellay* (Lille: University of Lille, 1900), esp. 86-87; Helmut A. Hatzfeld, *Literature Through Art: A New Approach to French Literature* (Chapel Hill: University of North Carolina Press, 1952), 60-61; Jean Adhémar, "Ronsard et l'Ecole de Fontainebleau," *Bibliothèque d'Humanisme et Renaissance* 20 (1958): 344-48; Richard A. Sayce, "Ronsard and Mannerism: The Elégie à Janet," *L'Esprit Créateur* 6 (1966): 234-47; Marcel Raymond, *Etre et dire* (Neuchâtel: Editions de la Baconnière, 1970), 63-112; Dassonville, *Ronsard*, 4.

[8] Jean Plattard, "Les Arts et les artistes de la Renaissance française jugés par les écrivains du temps," *Revue d'Histoire littéraire de la France* 21 (1914): 481-502. As the title of his essay suggests, Plattard does not confine this opinion to Ronsard. In the end, the eminent *seiziémiste* judges that none of the major French Renaissance authors seriously sought to imitate the works or workings of their contemporary counterparts in the pictorial arts (489).

[9] This working definition coincides with the one proposed by Murray Krieger in his groundbreaking 1967 article, "The Ekphrastic Principle and the Still Movement of Poetry; or Laokoön Revisited," in *The Play and Place of Criticism* (Baltimore: The Johns Hopkins Press, 1967), 105-28. For a more thorough examination of this notion, see Krieger's recent book, *Ekphrasis: The Illusion of the Natural Sign* (Baltimore: The Johns Hopkins University Press, 1992). It is important to note that Krieger's definition is at once broader than Jean Hagstrum's, whereby the words must ascribe a "voice and language to the otherwise mute art object" (*Sister Arts*, 18, n. 34), and narrower than Doranne Fenoaltea's, according to which the words must merely "faire voir" (*Du palais au jardin: L'architecture des 'Odes' de Ronsard*, *Etudes Ronsardiennes* 3 [Geneva: Librairie Droz, 1990], 28).

tus the Younger, and Callistratus. In general, then, advocates of the second critical direction have primarily interpreted Ronsard's painting evocations in figurative terms, as metaphors operating to crystalize the poet's experiences of love and beauty and, above all, to reify the possibilities of verbal description or verbal "semiosis," the signification process destined to continue *ad infinitum* because it involves signs whose signifieds are always other signs. [10]

Distinct from both of these approaches is the manner of reading that has begun to measure Ronsard's place in the *paragone* debate over the relative values of the arts of architecture, sculpture, music and, most importantly, the proverbial sisters, poetry and painting. [11]

---

[10] Advocates of these views include Raymond Lebègue, "La Pléiade et les Beaux-Arts," *International Federation for Modern Languages and Literatures: Atti del Quinto Congresso Internazionale di Lingue e Letterature Moderne* (Florence, 1951): 115-24, esp. 122-23; Yvonne Bellenger, "Les poètes français et la peinture: la ressemblance comme critère esthétique au XVIe siècle," *Mélanges à la mémoire de Franco Simone* 1 (Geneva: Slatkine, 1980), 427-48; and Philip Ford, as in his "Ronsard the Painter: a Reading of 'Des Peintures contenues dedans un tableau'," *French Studies* 40 (1986): 32-44; his "La Fonction de l'ekphrasis chez Ronsard," *Ronsard en son IVe Centenaire*, eds. Yvonne Bellenger et al., 2 vols. (Geneva: Droz, 1989), 2:81-89; and most recently, his *Ronsard's "Hymnes:" A Literary and Iconographical Study* (Tempe, Arizona: MRTS, 1997). In the last work, Ford applies the findings of his earlier articles to an analysis of the *Hymnes*, where he again relates Ronsard's poetic commentaries on the visual arts less to the theoretical discourse of the paragone rivals than to the rhetorical and metaphysical principles laid out by Aristotle (in the earlier hymns) and the Neoplatonists (in the later pieces). Among the critics who have emphasized the Sophistic models are Brian Barron, " 'Ut Pictura poesis': un lieu commun de la Renaissance et son importance dans l'oeuvre de Ronsard" (Ph.D. diss., University of Edinburgh, 1981); and, in sixteenth-century French literature beyond Ronsard, Perrine Galand-Hallyn, " 'Enargeia' maniériste, 'enargeia' visionnaire des prophéties du Tibre au songe d'océan," *Bibliothèque d'Humanisme et Renaissance* 53 (1991): 305-28. On the verbal semiosis underlying Ronsard's ekphrastic poetry, see Jerry C. Nash, " 'Fantastiquant mille monstres bossus': Poetic Incongruities, Poetic Epiphanies, and the Writerly Semiosis of Pierre de Ronsard," *Romanic Review* 84 (1993): 143-62. The definition of semiosis I propose here is based upon Maryann Ayim's article on the concept in the *Encyclopedic Dictionary of Semiotics*, eds. Thomas A. Sebeok et al., 2 vols. (Berlin: Mouton de Gruyter, 1986), 2:887-93; Michael Riffaterre, *Fictional Truth* (Baltimore: Johns Hopkins University Press, 1990), 130; and especially, Umberto Eco, *The Limits of Interpretation* (Bloomington: Indiana University Press, 1990), 23-32. We shall return to Eco's theories below.

[11] Our operative understanding of the paragone reflects the research of several scholars, especially (in order of importance): Jean Paul Richter, ed., *The Literary Works of Leonardo da Vinci*, 3rd ed., 2 vols. (New York: Phaidon Press, 1970), esp. 1:13-22 and 1:41-68; Jean H. Hagstrum, *Sister Arts*, esp. 66-70; Leatrice Mendelsohn, *Paragoni: Benedetto Varchi's Due Lezzioni and Cinquecento Art Theory* (Ann Arbor: University of Michigan Research Press, 1982); Erwin Panofsky, *Galileo as a Critic of the Arts* (The Hague: Nijhoff, 1954).

This age-old polemic, or "contest," [12] grew especially heated during the Renaissance. As the visual media advanced in technological and theoretical sophistication–thanks, for example, to the innovations of Filippo Brunelleschi in the science of optics, and to the art treatises of Alberti and Leonardo da Vinci during the Quattrocento– they also gained significant ground on poetry, whose early inclusion among the seven "liberal arts" had sustained its first-place position in the hierarchy of aesthetic endeavors throughout much of Western history. [13] In fact, as the popularity of the parity-centered Renaissance principle of ut pictura poesis clearly signals, the plastic artist (notably the painter) even became the full-fledged equal of the poet. This equivalence was hardly a source of equilibrium, however. It was as if the new regime only accentuated actual and imagined polarities and thereby precipitated the centrifugal forces of dissension. In the perspective of Margaret McGowan, "[i]t was inevitable that arts which claimed the same purpose and attempted the same rousing effects should see themselves sometimes as complementing each other and sometimes as rivals." [14]

Of course this paradoxical development was further fueled by the practical considerations of patronage. Art benefactors of the period increasingly recognized the prestige to be gained by commissioning a portrait or funding a building. In France this new awareness was exquisitely apparent in the munificence of François I toward the artists at Fontainebleau, and in the generosity of Henri II toward the designers of Diane de Poitiers' castle at Anet. The result was an environment of competition in which the poets soon realized that their best hopes for financial and social success depended

---

[12] The proper translation of the Italian term *paragone* is "comparison." Given the history of its application in the inter-art rivalry debates, however, I adopt the more figurative meaning, "contest," introduced by Hagstrum (*Sister Arts*, 66) and reprised by James V. Mirollo (*Mannerism and Renaissance Poetry: Concept, Mode, Inner Design* [New Haven: Yale University Press, 1984], 78 and 184, nn. 15, 23).

[13] The elevated status of poetry is generally attributed to Aristotle and his recognition of the poet's ability to give "general truth" ($\kappa\alpha\theta\delta\lambda o\nu$) (cf. *Poetics* 9.1451a-b.1-4). This is not to say, however, that poetry was thereafter to enjoy the highest place in the ranking of the arts. In truth, there was considerable instability in this hierarchy (cf. the eminence accorded to painters by Pliny in the *Natural History* 35). At times Aristotle himself seems to have preferred plastic artworks to verbal ones (cf. his praise for the ability of visual images to instruct the sense of sight: *Politics* 8.1338a.18).

[14] McGowan, *Ideal Forms*, 57.

on establishing the unique merits of their poems. [15] They had to convince the ranks of potential patrons that verses offered a better guarantee of glory than paint or stones because, in the end, verbal artworks are superior to plastic creations in terms of the physical and metaphysical insight, didactic comprehensibility, and temporal durability that derive from their semiotic versatility and ontological eminence.

While successfully synthesizing the more worthwhile contribu-. tions of the previous two approaches, the third mode of criticism has done surprisingly little to identify the precise points at which the author's remarks intersect the main theoretical lines of this rivalry. François Lecercle has even hinted that such a pursuit would be fundamentally spurious since poets such as Ronsard "avaient sans doute fort peu lu" the theoretical writings that stirred this early modern polemic. [16] Thus, despite their eagerness to include a chapter or section that would outline these foundations, investigators have been content, like Margaret McGowan, to speak broadly of Ronsard's "fiercely antagonistic" tone toward the plastic arts, or like Françoise Joukovsky, to acknowledge vaguely the poet's "besoin de dépasser cet art de la surface qu'est la peinture." [17] A similar evasiveness is apparent in a recent study of the *Odes* by Doranne Fenoaltea. Here, Ronsard's participation in the paragone is once more cast in largely metaphorical terms. Reminiscent of the scholars who have stressed the poet's debt to the ancient sophists, Fenoaltea has isolated Ronsard's attacks on the plastic arts (especially architecture) from the intellectual milieu of aesthetic rivalries in which they developed. Instead, she has read this opposition as a metaphor for the laureate's revolt against highly structured modes of writing,

---

[15] As Henri Weber has noted, this need was felt by virtually all sixteenth-century poets, whether or not they were of noble lineage, since at that time "la noblesse ne peut plus qu'exceptionnellement vivre du revenu de ses terres": *La Création poétique au XVIe siècle en France* (Paris: Librairie Nizet, 1955), 63. For more on the tensions stirred by the generosity of French Renaissance kings toward plastic artists, see Doranne Fenoaltea, *Du palais au jardin: L'architecture des 'Odes' de Ronsard*, Etudes Ronsardiennes 3 (Geneva: Librairie Droz, 1990), esp. 13-26 and 100-05. For a sample of how this spending was conducted, see Pierre Désiré Roussel, *Histoire et description du château d'Anet* (Paris: D. Jouaust, 1875).

[16] François Lecercle, *La Chimère de Zeuxis: Portrait poétique et portrait peint en France et en Italie à la Renaissance* (Tübingen: Gunter Narr Verlag, 1987), 172.

[17] McGowan, *Ideal Forms*, 80; Françoise Joukovsky, *Le Bel objet: Les Paradis artificiels de la Pléiade* (Paris: Librairie Honoré Champion, 1991), 106.

typified by the architectonic principles of "emboîtement" (inter-
locking) and "imbrication" (overlapping), in favor of a natural poetic–i.e., one that is more personal and botanically unsymmetrical. [18]

On another level, this research has also tended to oversimplify
Ronsard's posture in this polemic. The aforementioned critics have
unanimously portrayed the poet as a steadfast partisan of the primacy of poetry. Notwithstanding Ronsard's frequent praises for the
verisimilitude of portraits, and despite the inherently oculocentric
basis of his preoccupation with the visual arts, these readers have
identified no significant ambivalence in his attitude toward the plastic media.

In a broad sense, the study to follow continues the prior investigations of Ronsard's place in the paragone debate. As its title indicates, the present book shall again probe the contentious relations
between the sister arts of poetry and painting as those relations are
defined and perpetuated by the foremost poet of Renaissance
France. In other regards, however, this investigation enters domains
that the previous studies have left largely or wholly uncharted. For
example, different from McGowan and Joukovsky, who have out-
lined our laureate's reactions to all the major modes of plastic expression, or Fenoaltea, who has emphasized his responses to architecture, this book takes up the particular relations between poetry
and the art of "painting"–a term that shall henceforth designate
every manner of visual picture, be it painted, drawn, embroidered,
etched, or engraved. The object of interest thereby coincides with
the matter that most absorbs Ronsard's commentaries on the visual
media, indeed all the paragone literature of the day: the similarities
and differences between words and *pictorial images*. What is more,
it centers on the most fundamental preoccupation of virtually every
theoretical and practical discussion about the arts during the Renaissance: how or whether a poet or painter can imitate natural realities and metaphysical truths.

In order best to delineate these concerns, the ensuing pages
concentrate on Ronsard's many and varied evocations of the two
principal painting genres of the Renaissance. Unlike Lecercle's
study, which stops at the poet's treatment of portraits, the present
book investigates Ronsard's responses to both portraiture and nar-

---

[18] Fenoaltea, *Du palais*, esp. 36 and 106-19.

rative painting. Exemplified by the elaborate historical, biblical, and mythological tableaux of Giovanni Battista Rosso, Francesco Primaticcio, and Nicolò dell'Abate that adorn the galleries and chambers of the castle at Fontainebleau, artworks of the latter type comprise the most highly esteemed pictorial category of the period. [19] In addition, rather than inspect only one form of poetry, as Lecercle has done by restricting his inquiries to the sonnets produced between 1549 and 1561, [20] the following study explores a representative mixture of odes, elegies, sonnets, hymns, and other poetic pieces from various points in Ronsard's career. It thereby affords a perspective that is more comprehensive than any view heretofore provided.

This is not to say that Ronsard's allusions to painting are always of equal interest. Notwithstanding the prevalence of terms like "peinture," "tableau," "portrait," and "peintre" throughout his poetry, [21] on occasion these words have only a tangential relevance to the pictorial arts. At times the verb *peindre* denotes more "to depict" (in the broadest sense) than "to paint" (in the narrow sense examined here); and occasionally a *portrait* is not a "portrait," but rather a "model" or "example." [22] Such cases are marginal to the present investigation, whose main focus is the most explicit and sustained reflections that Ronsard has to offer on painters and painting. In all instances, the poems selected for examination make

---

[19] While occasionally in dispute by modern art historians, this hierarchy is convincingly corroborated by contemporary royal account books. As Louis Dimier has noted (and as we shall discuss at greater length in our Conclusion), the imported Italian narrative painters, Giovanni Battista Rosso and Francesco Primaticcio, typically received salaries three to six times greater than the best portraitists of the day (*Portrait*, 24). Although the reasons for preferring narrative painting to portraiture are difficult to reconstruct, the seeds of this ranking might well have been sown by the early Neoplatonists. In *Ennead* 1.6.8-9, for example, Plotinus clearly attacks portraits as servile imitations of visible particulars (γεγονός) while praising more complex narrative-type images for being drawn from ideas (νοητόν). For more on the status and history of narrative painting in sixteenth-century France, see Plattard, "Les Arts," 490-93; and Louis Dimier, *French Painting in the Sixteenth Century*, trans. Harold Child (London: Duckworth & Co., 1904), esp. 50-193.

[20] Lecercle, *La Chimère*, 1-2.

[21] See the relevant entries in Alvin Emerson Creore, *A Word-Index to the Poetic Works of Ronsard*, 2 vols. (Leeds: W. S. Maney, 1972).

[22] In the first case, see the 1555 *Hymne du roy Henri II*: "ces Chevaliers qu'Homere nous *a peints* / Si vaillans devant Troie" (8:9-10, vv. 85-86; my emphasis). In the second case, see sonnet III of the *Sonnets pour Helene* (*Second livre*): "Voy son corps, des beautez *le portrait* & *l'exemple*" (17:249, v. 5; my emphasis).

unequivocal reference to painting as an autonomous artistic enterprise, and they often contain or comprise at least one ekphrasis
(plural: ekphraseis).

Lastly, by defining the object and corpus of study in these ways,
this book takes an important step toward filling the two lacunae
noted previously. On the one hand, it exposes the narrow and
broad-reaching issues that combine to fuel Ronsard's conflict with
painting. A careful probe of the textual evidence reveals not only
the precise paragone-related arguments that preoccupy our author,
but also the deeper philosophical assumptions that intrigue this
major sixteenth-century French poet and virtually all contributors
to the aesthetic discourse before and during the early modern period. In the last regard, for example, we discover that Ronsard's observations regularly reflect and manipulate existing notions about
the relative presence (or absence) of meaning and truth in verbal
and visual signs–notions derived from the semiotic, hermeneutic,
epistemological, and metaphysical theories of the predominant
philosophical systems propelling the vortex of French Renaissance
thought: Platonism, Aristotelianism, Scholasticism, and Neoplatonism.

Naturally, this pursuit must respect certain limits. Never, for example, can the catalysts of Ronsard's thinking be identified with absolute certainty. At no time does our author pay open homage to his
intellectual sources in this debate. In fact, Ronsard gives the same
anonymous treatment to the Italian *trattisti* who led the Renaissance paragone as he does to the Italian artists whose contributions
to the elevated prestige of painting cannot have failed to affect his
engagement in the dispute. He is similarly reticent about the philosophical systems that prompted his poetic remarks on painting.
Nowhere does he name the theorists who shaped his conception of
the philosophical distinctions between the verbal and visual arts.
For this reason the pages to follow aspire only to indicate some *possible* connections between Ronsard's paragone-related comments
and the relevant theories of Plato, Aristotle, and their Scholastic
and Neoplatonic heirs.

In respect to the second critical lacuna, close textual analysis
also restores important nuances to Ronsard's participation in the
inter-art contest. The evidence shows a poet who is far more ambivalent about painting than the researchers of this question have
hitherto admitted. In a sense, the investigation at hand recalls the

paradoxical attitude intuited by Plattard before he moved to dis-
miss the extra-literary dimensions of Ronsard's poetry on painting.
However, where Plattard identifies a preference for narrative pictures above portraits,[23] the present study evinces the reverse to be
true. Distinct from the poetry about narrative painting, where Ronsard's overarching emphasis remains the weaknesses of pictorial
representation, the evocations of portraiture encode a noticeably
more sympathetic point of view. Our laureate manifests a deference
toward certain extraordinary expressive capabilities of figure painting. Thus, beyond examining the cases in which Ronsard maneu-
vers primarily to exalt the poet, this book considers when he does
not, and as far as possible, the reasons why. It therefore presents a
more exact idea of the complexity in Ronsard's approach and,
again, the intellectual debt he owes to the major philosophical traditions of the ancient, pre-modern, and early modern periods.

To meet these numerous goals, the following study is divided
into three chapters and a conclusion. The first chapter outlines the
complicated theoretical background against which the findings of
the subsequent chapters assume their sharpest definition. While
substantially indebted to the wealth of existing scholarship on the
tenets of early modern poetic and art theory, this discussion stands
apart for the clarity it brings to two key truths about the Renaissance paragone. To start, it reaffirms that the inter-art rivalry is in
fact a perennial phenomenon. The paragone is ultimately a contest
of converging desires for semantic and socio-economic presence;
and like all converging desires, it invariably activates what the modern literary critic, René Girard, has characterized as the perpetual
"primary impulse" to contention of nearly all living creatures.[24]
Further, this chapter confirms that this perennial "impulse" is detectable from the earliest poetic evocations of painting, in the ambivalence that defines Western ekphrastic literature since as early as
Homer's famous representation of Achilles' shield in *Iliad* 18.

The opening chapter also goes beyond the previous essays in
detailing the influences on the paragone of the predominant pro-
genitors of French Renaissance philosophical thought. Its inspec-

---

[23] Plattard, "Les Arts," 490-92.
[24] René Girard, *Violence and the Sacred*, trans. Patrick Gregory (Baltimore:
Johns Hopkins University Press, 1977), 147. We shall return to Girard's socio-psychological theories in Chapter One.

tion of the paragone-related theoretical discourse plainly shows that Plato, Aristotle, Thomas Aquinas, Dante Alighieri, Plotinus, Proclus, Marsilio Ficino, and Pico della Mirandola all left indelible marks on the multiple facets of this debate. What is more, this chapter demonstrates that virtually all of the contributors expressed paradoxical or contradictory positions on the relations between the arts. As we shall see, they are these same paradoxes and contradictions that set the initial contours of the discourses on poetry and painting by 'paragonists' like Leonardo da Vinci and ultimately Ronsard himself.

Surprisingly, this last fact has gone largely unexplored. Although scholars such as Jean Hagstrum, Erwin Panofsky, Umberto Eco, David Summers, and Murray Krieger have often acknowledged and described similar incongruities, they have done little to explain how the very existence of these problems may have shaped early modern aesthetic theory and the treatment of the inter-art relations by individual Renaissance authors. [25] Nowhere have they read them as a recurrent, even defining, feature of the paragone-related literature. Chapter One attempts to rectify this oversight and, in so doing, to lay the foundation for a better understanding of Ronsard's paragone poetry and French Renaissance aesthetic theory in general.

Chapters Two and Three are the practical complements of the opening theoretical discussion. Here the attention turns to the textual evidence of Ronsard's engagement in the inter-art contest, and especially to his responses to the Italian trattisti and the philosophical currents on which they drew.

Chapter Two investigates Ronsard's poetic commentaries on historical, biblical, and mythological pictures. Borrowing from the terminology employed by Erwin and Dora Panofsky in their memorable study of the Galerie François I at Fontainebleau, we shall hereafter designate these artworks as *narrative paintings*.[26] Although

---

[25] See Jean Hagstrum, *Sister Arts*; Erwin Panofsky, *Idea: A Concept in Art Theory*, trans. Joseph J. S. Peake (Columbia: University of South Carolina Press, 1968); Umberto Eco, *Art and Beauty in the Middle Ages* (New Haven: Yale University Press, 1986) and *Limits*, esp. 8-21; David Summers, *The Judgment of Sense: Renaissance Naturalism and the Rise of Aesthetics* (Cambridge: Cambridge University Press, 1987); and Murray Krieger, *Ekphrasis*.

[26] Erwin Panofsky and Dora Panofsky, "The Iconography of the Galérie François Ier at Fontainebleau," *Gazette des Beaux-Arts* 52 (1958): 113-90.

the Panofskys never explicitly define this generic label, their usage allows that a picture should qualify as "narrative" when (a) it is moderately *naturalistic* (i.e., reasonably comparable to the optical experience of objective reality[27]); (b) it features at least one human figure; and (c) the figure(s) in question appear(s) in a scene or scenes portraying a biblical, historical, or mythological *event* (i.e., an incident with causal links to prior and subsequent incidents).[28]

Contrary to Plattard's long-standing assumption that Ronsard had only the highest regard for narrative tableaux, Chapter Two reveals a poet who is bent on discrediting these pictures and exalting the status of poetry. He accomplishes this goal in two correlative ways. On the one hand, he refutes the most compelling early modern arguments for the supremacy of painting. These arguments –which would most closely resemble those that Leonardo da Vinci forcefully advances in the paragone passages of his late-fifteenth-century *Trattato della pittura*–are rooted in the Neoplatonic notion that the painted image presents imitations of physical and metaphysical truths that are at once more intelligible and more moving than the written (or spoken) word. Paradoxically, however, Ronsard's refutation would appear to rely on a conflicting Neoplatonic assumption: the Hermetic idea according to which no sign may attain full semantic presence. Insofar as any given truth necessarily recalls every other, any attempt to signify that truth is doomed to continue indefinitely in pursuit of meaning, to multiply signs that forever imply an *absence*, a truth deferred. In his most recent collection of essays on semiotic theories from the Middle

---

[27] Cf. David Summers, *Judgment*, esp. 3-9. See also, Claude-Gilbert Dubois, "Problems of 'Representation' in the Sixteenth Century," trans. Monique Briand-Walker, *Poetics Today* 5 (1984): 462.

[28] In the end, this definition of narrative painting closely resembles the one advanced by Wendy Steiner in her critically acclaimed *Pictures of Romance* (Chicago: University of Chicago Press, 1988), esp. 1-42. For Steiner, a painting would qualify as "narrative" when: (a) it depicts more than one temporal moment; (b) a subject is repeated from one moment to another; and (c) the subject is embedded in a minimally realistic setting (2). The definition offered in the present study purposely understates the requirement to repeat the same figure in multiple moments since, as Steiner herself has conceded, Renaissance rules of pictorial naturalism typically forbid such repetitions (*Pictures*, 23-24). For more on these standards, see Alberti's comments on "Historia" ("istoria" or "storia") in his *Della pittura*, in *Opere Volgari*, ed. Cecil Grayson, vol. 3 (Bari: G. Laterza & Figli, 1973), esp. 69-75 (¶ 40-42); and Leonardo's remarks on *storia* in the *Trattato della pittura*: Richter, *Literary Works* 1, esp. 340-41.

Ages to the present, *The Limits of Interpretation*, Umberto Eco has described this process as a "labyrinthine web of mutual referrals," the culmination of which resides in the infinite Oneness of God. In Hermetic thought, Eco explains, all truths are trapped in the endless "drift" of semiosis by virtue of the world to which they belong. Being "perfused with signatures" and "ruled . . . by the principle of universal significance," this world produces "a perennial shift and deferral of any possible meaning," an environment in which the "meaning of a given word or of a given thing [is] another word or another thing," and "everything that [is] said is in fact nothing else but an ambiguous allusion to something else." [29] For Ronsard, narrative painting would be caught in just such a semiosic drift, tied to just such a world: a point the poet drives poignantly home by highlighting the semantic instability of that artform, the inability of the narrative picture to produce a unified (and unifying) meaning. [30]

To assert the superior status of poetry, on the other hand, Ronsard would seem to depend on a premise grounded in Scholastic hermeneutics. While allowing the existence of a metaphysical realm of semiotically slippery, Platonic and Neoplatonic (Hermetic) ideal truths, Ronsard appears to join Aquinas and (especially) Dante in supposing that the best verbal signs can substantially reduce that slippage. Rather than suspend meaning, the carefully combined words of a good poem can contain it in a way that is at least immanently, but often actually, understandable to the reader. In contrast to the painter, the poet can therefore subdue the flow of the infinite semiosic drift. [31]

Chapter Three assesses the applications of this strategy in the poetry about portraiture–i.e., pictures of historically verifiable or imaginably plausible men and women, whether alone or in small groups, that swiftly became the second most popular genre among

---

[29] Eco, *Limits*, 23-32, esp. 27.

[30] Here and throughout this book, I apply the logicians' sense of "semantics" (and the adjective "semantic"), which Alain Rey (following Charles Morris) defines as the "'relationship between signs and their referents'," or meanings (*Encyclopedic Dictionary*, 899).

[31] The following study does not deny a desire for "writerly semiosis" in Ronsard's poetry of the kind identified by Jerry Nash ("'Fantastiquant'") and Claude-Gilbert Dubois ("Problems of 'Representation'," 461-78). Rather, it posits a simultaneous, conflicting, and frankly more ambitious desire to tame the semiosis, particularly in the paragone-related poems.

early modern painters and their patrons.[32] Once more Ronsard displays his faith in the expressive strengths of words. Beginning with his most famous portrait poem, the ekphrastic *Elegie à Janet, peintre du roi*, this chapter presents further evidence of Ronsard's deeply held confidence in the ability of poetry to contain and communicate meanings. In this instance, however, a compelling deference toward the semantic capabilities of the painter is also identified. Despite the many expressive shortcomings of Janet's painted portrait–faults which remain a locus of interest throughout most of the *Elegie*–this artwork achieves a presence that the poet cannot help but acknowledge and admire. The result is an ambivalence in Ronsard's otherwise disapproving attitude toward the pictorial arts that never quite emerges in the verses on narrative pictures.

The remainder of the chapter explores additional instances of this ambivalence. The extended survey bears out our findings in the *Elegie à Janet*: Ronsard is distinctly more sanguine about painted portraits than he is about narrative paintings. More importantly, it reveals that this opinion has something to do with the emotive power of portraits, the ability of such pictures to stir emotions at least as effectively as the greatest pieces of poetry. For Ronsard, portrait paintings would seem to enjoy a quality of *ekplexis* (εκπλ-ηξις) like the one promoted by Longinus in his literary treatise of the first century A.D., *On the Sublime* (Περὶ Ὕψους) (Chap. 15.2): an ability to excite a surprise or fear that 'knocks you out', that enthralls and astounds the very soul.

---

[32] By so defining our corpus of study, I leave aside the numerous poems that evoke paintings of individual mythological figures and allegorical subjects: cf. sonnet VI of the 1555 *Continuation des Amours*, "E, n'esse, mon Pasquier, é n'esse pas grand cas" (7:122-23), and the *Stances*, "J'ay quitté le rempart," in *Les Amours d'Eurymedon et de Callirée* of the 1578 *Œuvres* (17:144-48, esp. vv. 55-60). This exclusion is justifiable on two grounds. First, pictures of this type are not, strictly speaking, "portraits." Modern art historians employ this designation as I am doing, to denote pictures of historically authentic or imaginably conceivable mortal human beings: cf. Lorne Campbell's portrait criteria of individualization, characterization, and idealization in *Renaissance Portraits: European Portrait-Painting in the 14th, 15th and 16th Centuries* (New Haven: Yale University Press, 1990), 9-39; and John Pope-Hennessy, *The Portrait in the Renaissance* (Washington: Pantheon Books, 1966). Second, even if we were to examine the marginalized poems, we would find that they duplicate the ambivalence of the pieces on 'real'-people portraits. Thus their absence here in no way biases the results of this investigation. On the popularity of portraiture in Renaissance France, see Louis Dimier, *Histoire de la peinture de portrait en France au XVIe siècle*, 2 vols. (Paris: Librairie Nationale d'Art et d'Histoire, 1924-25), 1:6, and below, Chapter Three.

In his latest thought-provoking statement on the manifestations
and aspirations of the ekphrastic impulse in literature, *Ekphrasis:
The Illusion of the Natural Sign*, Murray Krieger has folded this
quality into "enargeia II"–the counterpart of the naturalistic
"enargeia I" (vivid physical representation) and the ultimate goal of
artists who would escape the moorings of Platonic and Aristotelian
mimesis:

> What we are seeing in the difference between what I am terming
> *enargeia I* and *enargeia II* is the difference between the cool aes-
> thetic based on distance between audience and object and the
> heated aesthetic founded on fusion, or empathy, between audi-
> ence and the object into which they enter (feel themselves into)
> as imaginary subjects. This becomes the basis of a strikingly dif-
> ferent aesthetic, one that is emotionalist rather than mimetic,
> that dissolves the dimensions of a structured object into the free-
> ranging consciousness of the reader. . . .[33]

The present book emphasizes the idea of 'ekplexis' over "enargeia
II" because the latter concept goes beyond what Ronsard would
allow in his poems on portraiture. Far from finding "any suggestion
of the natural sign undesirable," as required in the aesthetic of
enargeia II,[34] the Pléiade laureate finds the naturalistic mimesis of
certain painted portraits a cause of profound–and wholly envi-
able–astonishment.

The fourth chapter, our Conclusion, takes up the additional implications of the preceding findings. It focuses especially on the
overarching reasons for Ronsard's ambivalence toward portraiture,
the contradictory sentiment which seriously calls into question the
sincerity and legitimacy of his claims for the supremacy of poetry.
The motives considered range from the philosophical to the personal while touching on both the poetic and the aesthetic. On one
level, this ambiloquy may be ascribed to the paradoxical commentaries that serve as Ronsard's philosophical antecedents throughout
his paragone poetry; on another level, it may relate to our laureate's
mannerist mentality, a correlate of the impulse to contention that
drives all his paragone pieces and otherwise corresponds to the "al-

---

[33] Krieger, *Ekphrasis*, 67-112, esp. 94.
[34] Krieger, *Ekphrasis*, 94.

légeance subversive" embedded in the "attitude maniériste" as Claude-Gilbert Dubois has defined it in his masterful study, *Le Maniérisme.*[35] On the personal plane, the same equivocation may be linked to our laureate's close acquaintance with the figure painters and paintings of his day and, specifically regarding his partiality for portraits over story pictures, to his national chauvinism and practical jealousies, since most major portraitists were modestly paid Frenchmen while the leading narrative painters were generously rewarded expatriates from Italy. Further, this ambivalence may be affiliated with the heightened physicality of portrait paintings, a quality that might have inspired Ronsard's admiration for its affinity with the principle of sensuality that distinguishes his poetic representations of love. Finally, it may be imputed to a previously underrated emotionalist inflection in our laureate's poetic and aesthetic theory—one that parallels or fully invokes the notion of ekplexis promoted by Longinus and, in so doing, brings Ronsard into uneasy agreement with paragone arch-adversaries like Leonardo da Vinci, who promoted a similar aesthetic of enthrallment, and with the basic tenets of ut pictura poesis.

In general terms, this book is devoted to the idea that Ronsard's pronouncements on the paragone between poetry and painting have a far greater complexity and significance than the previous scholarship has revealed. One might well say that his paragone-related poems become a lodestone for many of the most important philosophical, semiotic, poetic, and aesthetic issues of concern to Ronsard and the intellectual elite of Renaissance Europe.

---

[35] Claude-Gilbert Dubois, *Le Maniérisme* (Paris: Presses Universitaires de France, 1979).

CHAPTER ONE

THE PARAGONE IN FOCUS

> Two desires converging on the same object are bound to clash. Thus, mimesis coupled with desire leads automatically to conflict. . . .
>
> The mimetic aspects of desire must correspond to a primary impulse of most living creatures. . . . Man cannot respond to that universal human injunction, "imitate me!" without almost immediately encountering an inexplicable counterorder: "Don't imitate me!". . . . Man and his desires thus perpetually transmit contradictory signals to one another. . . . Far from being restricted to a limited number of pathological cases, . . . the *double bind*—a contradictory double imperative, or rather a whole network of contradictory imperatives—is an extremely common phenomenon. In fact, it is so common that it might be said to form the basis of all human relationships. (René Girard, *Violence and the Sacred* [1972/1977] [1])

I. A PERENNIALLY AMBIVALENT CONTEST FOR PRESENCE

By many accounts poetry and painting first began to compete in reaction to the aesthetic pronouncements of Plato during the fifth and fourth centuries B.C. In Book Ten of his *Republic*, the ancient philosopher peremptorily banishes both arts from the garden of the well-ordered state. This treatment, he insists, is the only admissible response to their one-sided devotion to mimesis ($\mu\acute{\iota}\mu\eta\sigma\iota\varsigma$), the im-

---

[1] René Girard, *Violence and the Sacred*, trans. Patrick Gregory (Baltimore: Johns Hopkins Press, 1977), 146-47.

itation of material objects and physical experiences that are but the shadows of the 'real' world of ideal essences and truths. In Plato's view, poetry and painting can never present more than the appearance ($\phi\alpha\nu\tau\acute{\alpha}\sigma\mu\alpha\tau o\varsigma$) of those shadows, a deceptive simulacrum that is thrice removed from the realm of reality and ideas and, thus, stands fundamentally opposed to the noblest human faculty of reason (*Republic* 10.595-608). The consequence, it has been argued, was a formidable double challenge to the poet and the painter. On the one hand, both imitators would thereafter need to reclaim a 'presence' in legitimate society, to regain the prestige and advantages they had lost in the wake of Plato's denunciations. On the other hand, as a requirement for achieving that redemption, they would have to certify their ability to transcend the domain of appearances, to affirm their compatibility with reason by giving 'presence' to ideal reality. For many commentators, these two compelling needs forever drove the poet and the painter from a state of harmonious coexistence to a condition of hostile competition, from a congenial partnership to an acrimonious confrontation, presumably because the philosopher ignited desires whose objects of social inclusion and expressive plenitude are somehow inherently unsharable.

In truth, however, the poet and the painter never knew such a prelapsarian bliss. Rather, they have perpetually faced off in the quest to fulfill their desires for presence, and that pursuit was, and would remain, a perennial source of conflict. W. J. T. Mitchell was among the first to make this critical correction in his milestone contribution to sister-arts studies, *Iconology: Image, Text, Ideology.* Based upon the commentaries of aesthetic theorists and philosophers from Simonides of Ceos to Edmund Burke, Karl Marx and Nelson Goodman, Mitchell has advanced that the perennity of this conflict ultimately relates to the intrinsic oppositeness of words and images and to a culture that depends on such a contrariety "to sort out the distinctive qualities of its ensemble of signs and symbols." It derives at once from a set of fundamental conceptual and semiotic dualities:

(words)	(images)
sound	sight
convention	nature
time	space
motion	stasis
idea	material

and from a society that "wants to embrace or repudiate" these and "all the antithetical values" with which it is "riddled."[2]

Although Mitchell's dualities are eminently well founded, his reading of the cultural substructure that drives these cognitive and linguistic dichotomies—a substructure conceived about the Marxian mind-body axis of ideology and commodity—leaves us to wonder whether a more fundamental mechanism might also be at work. Could there be a deeper psychological basis for the word-image op-position—one that influences or fully causes all the oppositions that define our multifarious relations with ourselves, our society, and the world?

While this matter extends well beyond our interest in the peren-nial rivalry between poetry and painting, it also strikes at the very heart of that issue. This relevance becomes clear on reconsidering the broad-reaching insights into the dynamics of human contention offered by René Girard in his literary-critical and socio-psycholog-ical disquisitions, *Mensonge romantique et vérité romanesque* (1961) and *La Violence et le sacré* (1972).[3] Especially significant is his the-ory of "mimetic desire"[4] and the revolt against the "monstrous dou-ble." Inspired by Lévi-Strauss' notion of the dualistically organized "savage mind" and, above all, by Freud's concept of the Oedipus complex, Girard's thesis may be summarized to say that "all human relationships" are defined by conflict and that this conflict is the necessary consequence of perpetually converging human desires. More specifically, it holds that society is a battleground upon which subjects ('children' and 'fathers') continuously compete among and within themselves *to be alike* in the 'possession' of the same objects ('mothers'), where the "I" ('child-disciple') constantly struggles (outwardly and inwardly) *to resemble* the "Other" ('father-model'). Once achieved, however, this resemblance is hardly a desirable quality to maintain. It is in fact "a formless and grotesque mixture

[2] W. J. T. Mitchell, *Iconology*, 47-49.

[3] *Deceit, Desire, and the Novel*, trans. Yvonne Freccerro (Baltimore: Johns Hop-kins Press, 1965); *Violence and the Sacred*, trans. Patrick Gregory. All citations of these works are from their English translations.

[4] In fact the notion of "mimetic desire," which Girard proposed in 1972, is a broader and more useful formulation of the idea of "triangular desire" introduced in 1961. It should also be noted that Girard's concept of mimesis is only marginally related to Plato's. As we shall see, the theory of "mimetic desire" is more intimately influenced by the writings of Lévi-Strauss and Freud.

of things that are normally separate," a veritable "monster" against which the subject is compelled to revolt in order to unmake the mixture and restore authentic alterity. For Girard, this compulsion to rebel is otherwise adducible to the endemic psychological predicament of the "contradictory double imperative," or "double bind." This is the "primary impulse" to rivalry that eternally enjoins beings with intersecting wants to fight both inter- and intra-personally to establish mutual resemblance as they simultaneously strive for individual difference.[5]

From this perspective, it might then be said that the perennity of the sister arts' contest for presence pertains not only to the inherent conceptual and semiotic contrariety of words and images, as Mitchell reaffirms, but also to the contradictory imperative that defines all human relationships. This perennity–whose inscription is already apparent in Homer's prototypical ekphrasis of Achilles' shield in *Iliad* 18,[6] hence well before Plato's deprecations–is a concomitant of the conflict-centered double bind that follows whenever desires converge, as they do about the objects of 'presence' in this case. Thus again it is clear that Plato can hardly be impugned as the cause of the inter-art rivalry. Whereas his comments almost certainly did much to intensify the duel between the poet and the painter (if only by equating their respective arts, and thus sparking their irrepressible urge to reassert original alterity), this contention is ineluctably tied to the conflict endemic to the human condition and psyche in general. Furthermore, although the shareability–or rather unshareability–of the objects desired may well have made those objects more elusive, and so more desirable within the psycho-economic logic of supply and demand, the (un-)shareability of the *desires* themselves provides a more significant catalyst for the competition between poetry and painting.

---

[5] René Girard, *Violence*, 143-68, esp. 144-47. An insightful assessment of Girard's important contribution to the study of human conflict is presented by Burton Mack, "Religion and Ritual," "Introduction" in *Violent Origins*, ed. Robert G. Hamerton-Kelly (Stanford: Stanford University Press, 1987), 1-70, esp. 6-22.

[6] For related interpretations of the Achilles' shield episode, see Jean H. Hagstrum, *Sister Arts*, 19-22; Krieger, *Ekphrasis*, 17-18; James A. W. Heffernan, *Museum of Words: The Poetics of Ekphrasis from Homer to Ashbery* (Chicago: University of Chicago Press, 1993), 10-22, esp. 17. See also, Samuel Eliot Bassett, *The Poetry of Homer* (Berkeley: University of California Press, 1938), 94-99; Malcolm Willcock, *A Companion to the "Iliad"* (Chicago: University of Chicago Press, 1976), 212; Kenneth John Atchity, *Homer's 'Iliad': The Shield of Memory* (Carbondale and Edwardsville: Southern Illinois University Press, 1978), 158-87, esp. 173-74.

This contest is otherwise embedded in the ekphrastic gesture it-self, where the verbal text aspires paradoxically to be both like and unlike a picture and, thus, reveals its inscription of the double bind at the base of all human rivalries. While a verbal description might strive, on the illusory level, to become a pictorial work of art by placing a representational emphasis on natural signs, those that would denote static physical entities (e.g., Achilles' shield) and qualities (e.g., material, chromatic, and spatial properties) perceiv-able to the eye, on the ontologically authentic level, it does so via the "conventional signs" of words, whose properly acoustic, tempo-ral, and noetic essence necessarily contravenes the illusory pursuit, eternally defers the attainment of that identity in a peremptory reaf-firmation of poetic alterity.

In his recent book on ekphrasis, Murray Krieger indicates that this contradictory ambition would again be a feature of language it-self. With W. J. T. Mitchell and his own earlier thinking on the "ekphrastic principle"[7] firmly in mind, Krieger proclaims that "the ekphrastic aspiration in the poet and the reader must come to terms with two opposed impulses, two opposed feelings, about language: one is exhilarated by the notion of ekphrasis and one is exasperated by it." "Ekphrasis," he concludes, "arises out of the first, which craves the spatial fix, while the second yearns for the freedom of the temporal flow."[8] Although Krieger's statement is replete with allusions to a psychological basis for this linguistic duality, those al-lusions are never referentially fulfilled. Words like "aspiration," "impulses," "feelings," "exhilarated" and "exasperated" are never linked to any defined psychological substructure. Thanks to René Girard's theory of conflict, however, it is now possible to imagine that missing foundation. Like Mitchell's word-image duality, Krieger's linguistic antithesis might finally be tied to the underlying psychological imperative that enjoins imitating subjects to deny all difference as they simultaneously and paradoxically strain to affirm it–the double bind that compels the poet and his poetic words to be concurrently *one with* and *other than* the painter and his pictori-al images.

We ought not to conclude, of course, that the paragone be-tween the poet and the painter resides exclusively in the ekphrastic

---

[7] Krieger, "The Ekphrastic Principle," 105-28 (reprinted in *Ekphrasis*, 263-88).
[8] Krieger, *Ekphrasis*, 10.

discourses of the former. While ekphraseis invariably inscribe many aspects of the contest, that contest is scarcely reducible to those ekphraseis. There are other significant voices in the competition –the discourses of philosophers, aesthetic theorists, and visual artists who likewise take a profound interest in delineating the complex and contentious relations between words and images.

II. CONTENTION WITHIN AND AMONG THE THEORIES

By the time the paragone between poetry and painting reaches Pierre de Ronsard in mid-sixteenth-century France, it has already assumed a degree of antagonism without equal either before or since the Renaissance. This unprecedented animosity grew not only from recent changes in the technology of artistic and literary repro- duction,[9] but above all from the 'scientification' of the painter's en- terprise in the sophisticated arithmetic and geometric theories of pictorial perspective and proportion produced in Quattrocento Italy. Thanks especially to theorizing artists like Filippo Brunelleschi, Leon Battista Alberti, and Leonardo da Vinci,[10] painting had charged inexorably closer to its long-sought goal of presence–by then understood as inclusion among the all-prestigious seven Liber- al Arts (particularly the mathematical sciences of the Quadrivium, but eventually the Trivium as well),[11] and thus among the pursuits deemed worthy of the financial, political, and intellectual backing of the Court, the Church, and the humanist litterati. It had also caught up with and threatened to overtake poetry, which had made consid- erable gains in these regards very early on, with the help of Aris- totle's *Poetics* and subsequent Greek, Roman, and medieval treatises

---

[9] Cf. Claude-Gilbert Dubois, "Problems of 'Representation'."

[10] This rise occurred most rapidly between 1430 and 1540: see Panofsky, *Galileo*, 3; Mendelsohn, *Paragoni*, xv. This is not to say that painting did not make headway earlier (cf. Aristotle's commendations of the didactic potential of the visu- al arts in *Politics* 8 1338a, 18). By comparison, such support only modestly im- proved the relative prestige of the painter's art. For more on the rise of painting be- fore Leonardo da Vinci see Richter, *Leonardo*, 1: esp. 13-22; and Eco, *Art*, 92-115. The status of painting since Antiquity will be reconsidered in relation to specific au- thors and theorists, including Leonardo da Vinci, in the pages to follow.

[11] In fact, thanks to Pliny's *Historia naturalis* (35.77), painting had attained a tentative place among the Liberal Arts much earlier. The rise of painting into the Trivium is reconsidered in the discussion of Leonardo da Vinci that follows.

on rhetoric and literature (as we shall see). The resulting equalization stimulated an unparalleled interest in the similitude between
poetry and painting that supplied the conceptual basis for the popular, analogical interpretation of Horace's "ut pictura poesis" dic-
tum. [12] At the same time, however, it had the opposite effect of
prompting the poet and the painter to stress their underlying dis-
similarity. They set forth as never before to confirm the alterity of
their respective art forms. Hence, in the end that equalization
brought an unprecedented intensity to the poet's and the painter's
experience and expression of their psychological double bind, to
their conflictual desire to be different in spite of their resemblance.
In a related regard, the paragone of Ronsard's day has also already
acquired a theoretical infrastructure whose extraordinary intricacy
is matched only by its often overt inconsistency. As an aesthetic
matter that engages the most vital issues of metaphysics, epistemology, semiotics, hermeneutics, and ethics, the inter-art contest has attracted the explicit or implied consideration of the foremost
spokesmen of the major philosophical systems of the pre-modern
and early modern periods. In addition to Plato and Aristotle, its
primary theoretical contributors included Scholastics such as
Thomas Aquinas and Dante Alighieri and Neoplatonists like Plotinus, Proclus, Marsilio Ficino and Giovanni Pico della Mirandola.
Moreover–and of special interest in the present investigation–this
contest frequently assumed a highly confusing contour. Thanks inevitably to its multiple nature and wide appeal, the paragone fos-
tered a set of discussions and conclusions among and within the
major philosophical systems that syncretic-minded, sixteenth-century humanists like Pierre de Ronsard were bound to judge unruly, if
not (on many occasions) wholly contradictory.

On inspection, virtually all of these deliberations and their inconsistencies are found to turn around three principal aspects of
each art form. In broadest terms, these aspects would correspond
to the three main factors identified by Roman Jakobson in any mes-
sage-communication act (of which poetry and painting have always
been considered model examples, however much or little 'pres-

---

[12] Jean Hagstrum explains that, although this interpretation may be traced to
the Pseudo-Acron, it gained its most faithful following during the mid-sixteenth
century, in the literary commentaries of Pomponius Gauricus (1541), Robortello
(1548), and Luisinus (1554) (*Sister Arts*, 61, 66).

ence'–i.e., meaning in the most general sense–either art would transmit or allow).[13] First, there is the *addresser*, or message sender: in this case, the poet or the painter who 'conceives' (i.e., finds or imagines) the message content of the artwork and initiates and conducts its transmission. Second, there is the *message* communicated, which is itself minimally reducible to the *code* of transmission and its *context*: i.e., the signifier (word or image) and its signified (objective and/or conceptual referent). Last, there is the *addressee*, or message receiver: the individual who would ideally perceive the message through one or more of the senses and process (i.e., decode and interpret or ascribe) its meaning.[14]

A. *Plato and Aristotle*

On the status of the poet and the painter as addressers, Plato presents a set of sharply discrepant commentaries. On the one hand, he expresses deep-seated misgivings about the epistemological reach of both mimetic artists. This conviction is most vigorously voiced in the politically focused discussions of the *Republic* (especially Book Ten) and the *Sophist*, where Plato takes a special interest in denouncing any person or activity that might threaten the principle of reason on which the ideal state would be founded. Unlike God and the carpenter, whom Plato extols for their primary and secondary contact with the real (as the creator of true nature and ideas, in the first case; as the maker who "fixes his eyes on" God's creative operation, in the second), the poet and the painter, who consider only "the thing which those others produce" (the creation itself), are at "three removes" from the realm of essences. Each artist is an imitator ($\mu\iota\mu\eta\tau\iota\kappa\acute{\eta}$) who "*knows* nothing of the reality" because, as the famous allegory of the cave in *Republic* 7 vividly illustrates, the worldly objects of his concern are themselves only shadowy projections on the chasm wall of the truth that resides forever in the light and forms just beyond the cavern's entrance.

---

[13] Cf. Eco, *Limits*, 11.

[14] Roman Jakobson, "Linguistics and Poetics," in *Roman Jakobson: Selected Writings*, vol. 3, *Poetry of Grammar and Grammar of Poetry*, ed. Stephen Rudy (The Hague: Mouton Publishers, 1981), 18-51, esp. 21-22.

Accordingly, on the semiotic level, the poet and the painter can never signify the real. However well the verbal and visual signs they employ might succeed in imitating nature–a success Plato grants willingly and in such a way that, while intending to underscore the illegitimacy of all mimetic pursuits, he unexpectedly lays the ground for the natural-sign aesthetic that has become the defining principle (or foil) of virtually every Western theory of poetry and painting since that time [15]–those imitations are condemned to remain the mere shadow of a shadow ($\sigma\kappa\iota\acute{\alpha}$), the appearance of an appearance ($\phi\alpha\nu\tau\acute{\alpha}\sigma\mu\alpha\tau o\varsigma$). What is more, on the ethical level, the poet and the painter are doomed to effect a moral corruption of the addressee. Being "far removed from truth" as they set about "in the accomplishment of [their] task," these imitators have "no sound and true purpose." They are the agents of public deception: "associates with the part in us that is [intrinsically] remote from intelligence," or reason, the loftiest faculty of the soul and the basis of the well-ordered state (*Republic* 10.596-98, 601-03; 2:420-31, 442-51). [16]

By contrast, outside of his political deliberations, Plato also ascribes certain exceptional privileges to the poet and painter. On these occasions, the philosopher typically regards each artist and art form in isolation from the other, in agreement with the traditional aesthetic theory of ancient Greece, which typically distinguished between poetry as an art of soothsaying and painting as an art of production. [17] According to the *Phaedrus* and the *Ion*, for example, certain *true* poets would enjoy the epistemological gift of divine madness ($\mu\alpha\nu\acute{\iota}\alpha\varsigma$). This admirable quality endows bards like Homer–among the 'maddest' of all poets–with an essentially unlimited access to the realm of ultimate truths. Paradoxically, however, it is assumed solely in the absence of reason, when the exceptional poet "has been inspired and is out of his senses, and the mind is no

---

[15] See *Republic* 3.392-98, *Cratylus* 428-35, and *Sophist* 219-43, 264-68. On the problems inscribed in Plato's natural-sign aesthetic, see Krieger, *Ekphrasis*, esp. 13-14, 32-41, 67-76.

[16] Although Plato's strongest and most influential statement on aesthetic theory is the one in *Republic* 10 considered here, it is true that he grants a positive value to mimesis in certain well-defined didactic circumstances (e.g., *Republic* 3:396; *Laws* 2:667-68). For more on the poet's and the painter's affinity with appearances, see the *Sophist* 236. On the prestige of reason, see *Republic* 6:511. For an overview of the notion of imitation in Antiquity, see Richard McKeon, "Literary Criticism and the Concept of Imitation in Antiquity," in *Critics and Criticism: Ancient and Modern*, ed. R. S. Crane (Chicago: University of Chicago Press, 1952), 147-75.

[17] Cf. Tatarkiewicz, *History*, 1:145.

longer in him." Then and only then does he join the "diviners and holy prophets," the few extraordinary mortals who become the "ministers" and "interpreters of the Gods" (*Phaedrus* 245 [1:249-50]; *Ion* 533-34 [3:420-25]). [18]

To the painter, on the other hand, Plato allows a privileged access to the Idea of beauty. Repeatedly in the *Phaedrus, Republic* 6, and three late-life dialogues, the *Timaeus,* the *Philebus,* and the *Laws,* the philosopher intimates that this access should relate to the particular operations and sensory origins of the painter's message. Not only does this message engage a carefully selected and arranged variety of shapes and colors, hence the most elemental properties of ideal beauty–proportion (συμμετρία), measure (μετριότης), and order (τάξεων)–but it does so to enhance good pleasure (ἡδονὰς), a primary aim in our experience of the beautiful. In addition, it achieves all of this through and for the faculty of sight, which Plato commonly esteems "the most piercing of our bodily senses," the sensory ability whose special affiliation with the sun (and thus with the divine light and the soul) assures it a uniquely intimate connection to both natural and celestial truths. [19]

* * *

Even though Aristotle's paragone-related commentaries are substantially more developed and (on balance) favorably disposed toward poetry and painting than Plato's, they too pose a number of deep-seated paradoxes. [20] As in Plato's case, the most significant

---

[18] Clearly we touch on another important paradox here, since such madness is also an object of scorn for Plato. This incongruity is most clearly staged in the ironic discussion of *mania* in Plato's comments to the rhapsode, Ion of Ephesus. For more on this paradox, see Stephen Halliwell, *Aristotle's Poetics* (Chapel Hill: University of North Carolina Press, 1986), 83-84.

[19] On the properties of beauty, see esp. *Philebus* 64, *Timaeus* 87, and *Laws* 653-54. On the relations between beauty and pleasure, see *Philebus* 51 and *Gorgias* 474. On the virtues of sight, see *Phaedrus* 250-51 and *Republic* 6:507-08. It should be noted that the elevated status of sight will also play an important part in validating Plato's unintended natural-sign aesthetic and in reinforcing theories that draw upon that aesthetic to raise the standing of natural-sign arts like painting (including drama and *enargeia*-poetry) (see note 15, above). For a more elaborate summary of Plato's aesthetic theories, see Tatarkiewicz, *History*, 1:112-27.

[20] Although Hagstrum makes the point that Aristotle's aesthetic remarks are in fact the basis of subsequent theories of literary pictorialism and the similitude among the arts in the spirit of *ut pictura poesis* (*Sister Arts*, 8), it is also true that Aristotle had much to do with their differentiation and consequently, as we shall see below, with their rivalry.

problems concern the addressers' access to the real and the status and locus of reality and ideas as referents ('contexts') of the addressers' message. It is well known, of course, that Aristotle does much to make this access virtually total by situating these referents in the perceivable world and in the recesses of our own mind and soul. Whereas Plato places all essences in the ontologically distinct domain beyond the cave of our common earthly experience and knowledge, the Stagirite decisively effaces the boundaries between these realms, thus relocating the essences (now 'forms') in physical matter and the particularized thoughts of individual human beings. [21] While often summoned by later aesthetic theorists to validate the practice and product of all mimetic art activity, [22] this fundamental redefinition of the nature and locus of the real in fact largely discourages such a forensic use. In the final analysis, it unleashes a surfeit of legitimate and attainable forms for imitation that thrusts mimetic artists into an intractable struggle to discriminate among the 'best' of possible objects (since although all would now appear more or less equal in value, certain objects are necessarily better than others), [23] and thus into a situation where their artistic legitimacy is as tenuous as Plato had left it.

These paradoxical consequences are among the main reasons why Aristotle puts such a heavy emphasis on rules in the *Poetics* and throughout his aesthetic and philosophical writings. [24] Because

---

[21] As Erwin Panofsky explains, "Aristotle had replaced, in the domain of epistemology, the antithetic dualism between the world of Ideas and the world of appearances [of Plato] by the synthetic interaction between the general concept and the single, particular notion; and, in the domain of natural philosophy and aesthetics, by the synthetic interaction between form and matter. . . . That is to say, whatsoever is formed by nature or the hand of man, is . . . formed . . . by the entrance of a definite form into a definite substance" (*Idea*, 17).

[22] To some degree, of course, this validation depends on the natural-sign aesthetic extracted from the theories of Plato. Among those who subsequently take advantage of Aristotle's reconception are Cicero and Seneca and, as we shall see below, the Scholastic philosophers and Renaissance art theorists like Leonardo da Vinci. For more on this influence, see Panofsky, *Idea*, 11-99.

[23] This sense of hierarchy is clearly inscribed throughout Aristotle's comments on beauty (see his idea of selection among the "best" parts in the *Politics* 1281b 10) and his notions about artistic "error" (e.g., *Poetics* 1460b 13).

[24] It is also true, of course, that Aristotle is reacting against the irrationalist view of artistic activity promoted by Plato. As Stephen Halliwell observes: "The *Poetics* creates an unmistakable impression, from the first sentence onwards, of a craft-based view of poetry and art. Again and again Aristotle flatly contradicts both the *Ion* and other germane Platonic passages by asserting and assuming that poetry is a complete *technê*, a rational productive activity whose methods can be both defined and justified" (*Aristotle's Poetics*, 84).

the poet and the painter can, indeed logically and ethically *must*, "always represent . . . either things as they were or are; or things as they are said and seem to be; or things as they should be" (*Poetics* 1460b 2; 100-01)–hence virtually everything that is in nature and/or their own idiosyncratic thoughts–they can and logically and ethically must follow a myriad of precepts if they hope to choose *what is best* to imitate and *how best* to do it. Even when an object already possesses a manifestly superior aesthetic worth in the world, the mimetic-artist addressers must adhere to certain strict precepts to stand any real chance of reproducing that worth in their artworks: "a painter would not let his animal have its foot of disproportionately large size, even though it was an exceptionally beautiful foot, nor would a shipbuilder make the stern or some other part of a ship disproportionately big . . ." (*Politics* 1284b 8; 244-45).

This redefinition implies and precipitates other paradoxes as well. For example, whereas aesthetic rules are also a key feature in Aristotle's anti-Platonic program to demystify all artists, their complexity and power serve only to compound that mystery. At the same time Aristotle recommends that the poet and the painter should depend less on the ephemeral inspiration of Plato's divinely bestowed irrational madness ($\mu\alpha\nu\iota\alpha\varsigma$) and more on the self-wrought "genius to madness near allied" ($\mu\alpha\nu\iota\kappa\acute{o}\varsigma$) (*Poetics* 1455a 30; 64-65, n. c)[25] obtained through the knowledge and skillful application of certain empirically grounded aesthetic codes, he posits conditions that make the compliance with those codes and the attainment of that "genius" virtually as exceptional–and hence mysterious–as the acquisition of the gods' inspiration. In the end, Aristotle's Homer enjoys a kind of rational madness that makes him qualitatively more divine than Plato's Homer.[26]

Furthermore, this reconception compromises the basis of one of the most important artistic rules: the principle that every art should

---

[25] Cf. S. H. Butcher: "a strain of madness" ("Aristotle's Poetics," in *Aristotle's Theory of Poetry and Fine Art*, 5-111 [New York: Dover Publications, 1951], 63); and Ingram Bywater: "a touch of madness" (*Aristotle on the Art of Poetry* [1920; reprint, Oxford: Oxford University Press, 1990], 61).

[26] This is not to suggest that Aristotle (or for that matter, Plato) believes in an early form of individualism or 'natural genius.' As Halliwell points out, such modern ideas are clearly out of place in ancient thought (*Aristotle's Poetics*, 82-92). Nevertheless, I disagree with Halliwell's sharper distinction between Aristotle and Plato on this point. When all is said and done, Aristotle identifies an otherness in Homer that parallels the divinity attributed to him by Plato.

achieve unity to be truly good. Aristotle advances this principle in a variety of ways and in a number of different treatises. In the *Politics*, for instance, it enters into the idea of superior beauty (a sign of true goodness), which may be artistically created only when "a number of scattered good points have been *collected together into one example*" (1281b 10; 222-23: my emphasis). Then again, in the *Poetics* it corresponds to the beauty obtained through the proper manipulation of size and order: "for beauty consists in magnitude and *ordered* [i.e., unified] arrangement" (1450b 38; 30-31: my emphasis). And in the same context, it motivates the call for a "natural limit" (πράγματος ὅρος) (1451a 11; 32-33) in dramatic action that will subsequently inspire the "règle des trois unités" of the seventeenth-century French theater. Relatedly, in the *Rhetoric* this principle is an implied concomitant of the notions of aesthetic perceptibility and pleasure (two more essential features of the beautiful and the good for Aristotle). These notions are raised simultaneously in his remarks on the periodic style of speech (the antithesis of the continuous style): "By a period I mean a sentence that has a beginning and end in itself and a magnitude *that can be easily grasped . . .* [and is therefore] pleasant because *it is the opposite of that which is unlimited*" (1409a 35; 386-87: my emphasis).[27]

However, by supposing a virtual infinity of proper objects of imitation, and so an endlessly multiple and multiplying universe (if only because each new mimetic artwork attains the status of a new objective form in its own right, and thus automatically reconstitutes and expands the universe to which it is added[28]), Aristotle lays a metaphysical foundation that this aesthetic principle can reasonably not abide.[29] It is logically impossible that a work of mimetic art should attain (or even attempt to achieve) unity to the degree that, by its mimetic charge, this artwork ought also to remain consistent with an objective reality that is inherently multiple. It is for this rea-

---

[27] For more on Aristotle's concept of artistic unity, see Halliwell, *Aristotle's Poetics*, 96-108; Butcher, *Theory of Poetry*, 274-301; Michael Davis, *Aristotle's "Poetics": The Poetry of Philosophy* (Lanham: Rowman & Littlefield Publishers, 1992), 49-63.

[28] See Aristotle's comments on the idea of art as 'production' in the *Nicomachean Ethics* 1140a 9 and the *Physics* 190b 5. See also Dubois' remarks on mimesis in "Problems of 'Representation'," 462.

[29] This foundation is reinforced in other ways as well. Aristotle's theories of multiple categories and causes might be taken to pose the same basic threat.

son that Aristotle moves progressively from an external, objectivist sense of mimesis (extrapolated from Plato) toward an internal, subjectivist mode of imitation, whose focus becomes the universalized–hence unified–judgments that result from the processing of worldly experiences in the artist's soul. As we learn from the *Posterior Analytics*, it is in these ideas that the philosopher is ultimately obliged, by the logic of his aesthetic of unity, to fix the "starting-point of art": "And experience, that is, the universal, when established as a whole in the soul–the One that corresponds to the Many, then unity that is identically present in them all–provides the starting-point of art" (100a 6; 258-59).

Notwithstanding this important conceptual shift (an idea likewise embedded in the concepts of artistic beauty and pleasure noted above),[30] the objectivist mode of mimesis is never fully eradicated from his–or our–thinking about art. As Aristotle reveals in his discussion of humanity's "natural instinct for representation" in the *Poetics*, there is still a sense in which the validity of mimesis is measured by its coincidence with the external objective world: "From childhood men have an instinct for representation, and in this respect man differs from the other animals that he is far more imitative and learns his first lessons *by representing things*" (1448b 5; 12-13: my emphasis).[31] Thus the paradox persists: outside of the soul the many are constrained to remain many, and Aristotle's artistic principle of unity is never fully reconciled with his metaphysical principle of objective plurality[32]

---

[30] Undoubtedly this shift is one of the first steps in what Erwin Panofsky calls (in a broader discussion of the evolution of ancient Greek aesthetic thought in general) "the increasing emphasis on an intellectual as opposed to a sensory approach" (*Idea*, 15).

[31] The same point might be inferred from the aesthetic privilege Aristotle accords to objective reality over the artistic imitation of universalized 'reality' in *Parts of Animals*: "If we study mere likenesses of these things and take pleasure in so doing, because then we are contemplating the painter's or the carver's Art which fashioned them, and yet fail to delight much more in studying the works of Nature themselves, though we have the ability to discern the actual causes–that would be a strange absurdity indeed" (645a 10-15; 98-99).

[32] Although Stephen Halliwell seems to anticipate the paradox I describe here, he prefers to follow the more traditional view (cf. Krieger, *Ekphrasis*, 42-43) to conclude that Aristotle's mimesis is "a fictional representation of the material of human life": *Aristotle's Poetics*, 21-25 (esp. 21-22), 109-37. Cf. Tatarkiewicz, *History*, 1:142-44. It is also important that Aristotle's artistic principle of unity never quite allows for the notions of *discordia concors* and *coincidentia oppositorum* embedded in the concepts of God and the One elaborated by Plato and his Neoplatonic fol-

Aristotle is likewise inconsistent on the driving concern of the paragone contest itself: the relative merits of the artist addressers and their messages. Although his redefinition of reality suggests a basic parity between poets and painters in regard to their intellectual access to the same real objects, it is clear that the former retain a distinct advantage over the latter in terms of the means of rendering those objects. This unstated preference is apparent not only in the significant fact the philosopher never seems to have written an *ars pictura* to complement his *ars poetica*, but also in the privilege he extends to the mimesis of human 'objects' as they act *in time* (regardless of whether that action is better than, worse than, or the same as it is in real life). For as Aristotle points out at the start of the *Poetics*, the prime "objects of representation" in the arts are "men *doing or experiencing* something" (πράττοντας) (1448a 1; 8-9, n. d: my emphasis). [33] It follows, then, that poets are necessarily superior to painters since their poetic messages employ a verbal code that can recreate space in the eye of the mind as it concurrently realizes its full potency ("energeia" [ἐνέργεια]) [34] in the stream of time. This last and most critical diachronic characteristic is inscribed in the representational means of poetry, in what Aristotle calls its "rhythm and language and tune," or "harmony" (ἁρμονία) (1447a 18; 6-7). By contrast, painted messages would be more or

---

lowers (see Plato: *Timeaus* 68, *Phaedrus* 266, *Symposium* 187, and *Parmenides* passim; Manilius: *Astronomicon* 1,142; Horace: *Epistula ad Iccium*; Ovid: *Metamorphoses* 1,433; Ficino: *Theologia Platonica*). For critical discussions of these ideas, see Erwin Panofsky, *Studies in Iconology: Humanistic Themes in the Art of the Renaissance* (rpt. 1939; New York: Harper & Row, 1972), 131; Robert Valentine Merrill and Robert J. Clements, *Platonism in French Renaissance Poetry* (New York: New York University Press, 1957), 1-4; Malcolm Quainton, *Ronsard's Ordered Chaos: Visions of Flux and Stability in the Poetry of Pierre de Ronsard* (Manchester: Manchester University Press, 1980), 1-30; John O'Brian, "Clio's 'Cabinet': Metaphorical Edifices in Ronsard's 'Hymnes' of 1555-1556," *Modern Language Review* 81 (1986): 37-50. On the "problem of relating the One and the Many . . . at the center of the methodological and epistemological preoccupations of the sixteenth century," see Dubois, "Problems of 'Representation'," 462 and esp. 469-71.

[33] Cf. S. H. Butcher: "the objects of imitation are men *in action*" (*Aristotle's Theory*, 11: my emphasis). Although this phrase has most often been taken as a comment on poetry alone, it is ambiguous enough to allow the broader interpretation I propose here. This reading is especially appropriate in light of the preference Aristotle subsequently expresses for drama, the most 'active' of 'poetic' artforms. See Krieger, *Ekphrasis*, esp. 41-42; and Moshe Barasch, *Theories of Art, from Plato to Winckelmann* (New York: New York University Press, 1985), 12-13.

[34] *Rhetoric* 3 111.1-2. For more on this concept, see Hagstrum, *Sister Arts*, 12, n. 20.

less completely confined to the spacial. As the Stagirite insinuates by his enduring, indeed exclusive, emphasis on painted portraiture,[35] the pictorial genre which has traditionally made a point of minimizing (if not eliminating) all sense of movement and spatial displacement (at least, that is, before the Dada and Cubist portraits of the twentieth century), visual artworks would have no appreciable power to encode the temporal flow. Thus despite his willingness to draw important analogies between verbal plot and visual line or poetic character and pictorial color elsewhere in the *Poetics* (e.g., 1450a 39), Aristotle leaves little doubt that poetry is the greater art because the poet, true to his name, is demonstrably the most effective "maker"–the one who fashions things (here imitations) most true to the dynamically *active* nature of life.[36]

B. *The Scholastics and Neoplatonists*

The Scholastic and Neoplatonic inheritors of Aristotle's and Plato's aesthetic thinking display a similar and often conceptually related penchant for paradox. However, while this propensity is likewise perceptible within the particular theories of individual representatives of each philosophical system, it is sometimes more acutely apparent in the differences between ideological brethren. Such is the case, for example, within the paragone-related remarks of the preeminent Scholastic philosopher of the Middle Ages, Thomas Aquinas, and in the contrast between his theories and those of his thirteenth-century contemporary, the foremost Scholastic poet, Dante Alighieri.

Perhaps the most striking paradox in Aquinas' many aesthetic commentaries is the conspicuous absence of any explicit discussion of painting. Nowhere in the voluminous *Summa Theologiae* or his other theological and philosophical writings (such as the many biblical and philosophical commentaries, the *Quaestiones quodlibetales*, and the *Summa Contra Gentiles*) does Aquinas openly acknowledge the strengths, the weaknesses, or, for that matter, the existence of painters and their pictures. This void is puzzling in part because

---

[35] *Poetics* 1448a 1, 1450a 39, 1461b 12; and *Politics* 1281b 10, 1284b 8.
[36] *Poetics* 1451b 27; 36-37. For more on Aristotle's concept of the poet as maker, see Barasch, *Theories of Art*, 9-10.

most major thinkers of the period are quite vocal on the topic. Authors like Robert Grosseteste, Bonaventure, and the liturgist William Durandus all play important roles in revitalizing and re-shaping the painting theories of Plato, Aristotle, and other ancient theorists. [37] It is also surprising because Aquinas has no pressing doctrinal or political motives for remaining silent. Whereas princi-ple or prudence might have persuaded him to suspend such pro-nouncements had he written during the eighth and ninth centuries, at the height of the Iconoclastic Controversy–the dispute over the truth, or falsehood, of religious and secular imagery instigated by the Byzantine emperor and 'Iconoclast' (image breaker) Leo III[38]–, by Aquinas' day this controversy is effectively resolved (though scarcely forgotten). With support from the art-related reflections of Church Fathers like St. Augustine and Gregory the Great, and the reasoned remarks of Charlemagne, Theodulf of Orleans (presumed author of the eighth-century *Libri Carolini*), and the delegates at the Synod of Arras in 1025, the 'Iconodules' (image worshipers) had succeeded in vindicating pictures for their enormous utility in the religious edification of the illiterate. In the words of the Church of-ficials of the Synod of Arras: "Illiterate men can contemplate in the lines of a picture what they cannot learn by means of the written word." [39]

Further and more textually pertinent, the theory of beauty that becomes one of Aquinas' most enduring philosophical and theolog-ical concerns relies prominently on the very perceptual and qualita-tive properties that have driven art theoretical discussions of paint-ing since Antiquity. In the *Summa Theologiae*, for example, the notion of 'vision' (*visio*) is at the center of his definition of the beau-tiful: "Beauty . . . has to do with knowledge, and we call a thing

---

[37] See especially, Grosseteste's *De unica forma omnium*, Bonaventure's com-mentaries on the *Sententiae* of Peter Lombard (D3 p. 1 a. 1 q. 2 and D31 p. 2 a. 2 q. 1), and Durandus' *Rationale Divinorum officiorum* (1, 3, 4). These texts are repro-duced and discussed in Tatarkiewicz, *History*, 2:225-29, 231 n. 13 (Grosseteste); 232-36, 239 nn. 14a, 15 (Bonaventure); 98, 145-46, 106 n. 32 (Durandus).

[38] Among the principal points of contention is the issue of 'truthfulness' in rep-resentation and, in the case of pictorial renderings of Christ, the danger of commit-ting the Monophysite heresy, the blasphemous reduction of Jesus' infinite essence to one nature. For more on the Iconoclastic Controversy, see Barasch, *Theories*, 47-60, 64; Tatarkiewicz, *History*, 2:97-99, 145-46.

[39] "Illiterati quod per scripturam non possunt intueri, hoc per quaedam pic-turae lineamenta contemplantur": Tatarkiewicz, *History*, 2:105, n. 27.

beautiful *when it pleases the eye* of the beholder." [40] Aquinas is similarly interested in 'proportion' (*proportio*) and the related notions of
'luminous brightness', or 'clarity' (*claritas*), and 'color' (*color*). With
such august authorities as Plato, Plotinus, Augustine, the Pseudo-
Dionysius, and Robert Grosseteste firmly in mind, the Scholastic
philosopher combines these qualities with the idea of 'integrity' (*integritas*), or 'proper wholeness' (a correlate of the Aristotelian concept of unity), to define the primary objective properties of beauty:
"Beauty must include three qualities: integrity or completeness
–since things that lack something are thereby ugly; right proportion
or harmony; and brightness–we call things bright in colour beautiful." [41]

In truth, however, Aquinas does not stop at the physical implications of these terms. Again in the *Summa Theologiae* he imbues
them with an abstract sense in order to delineate the proper epistemological operations of aesthetic perception. Accordingly, 'vision'
comes also to denote the intellectual results of the higher order cognitive processes: "This term, in view of the special nature and certi-
tude of the sense of sight, is extended in common usage to the
knowledge of all the senses . . . and it is even made to include intellectual knowledge. . . ." [42] Likewise, the terms 'proportion', 'brightness', and 'color' are applied metaphorically. The quantitative (physical) sense of *proportio* is supplanted by the qualitative (conceptual)
notion of appropriateness (*convenientia*), and the objectively visible
properties of *claritas* and *color* are abstracted to denote the spiritual
inner glow of all beautiful entities. Thus although Aquinas continues to take an interest in the sensual vision of the physical eye as the
starting point of aesthetic apprehension (*apprehensio*), his chief pre-

---

[40] "Pulchrum . . . respicit vim cognitivam, pulchra enim dicuntur *quae visa pla-
cent*" (*ST* 1a. 5, 4, 1; 2:72-73: my emphasis). It should be noted that this definition
receives a less 'sight'-specific formulation in *ST* 1a.2ae. 27, 1, 3: " 'beautiful' refers to
that which gives pleasure when it is perceived or contemplated" ("pulchrum autem
dicature id cujus ipsa apprehension placet") (19:76-77). The implications of this
broader understanding are considered below.

[41] "Nam ad pulchritudinem tria requiruntur. Primo quidem integritas, sive per-
fectio, quae enim diminuta sunt, hoc ipso turpia sunt; et debita proportio sive con-
sonantia; et iterum claritas, unde quae habent colorem nitidum pulchra esse dicuntur" (*ST* 1a. 39, 8; 7:132-33).

[42] "[S]ed propter dignitatem et certitudinem hujus sensus, extensum est hoc
nomen, secundum usum loquentium, ad omnem cognitionem aliorum sensuum . . .
et ulterius etiam ad cognitionem intellectus. . . ." (*ST* 1a. 67, 1; 10:54-55).

occupation is the cognitive and spiritual vision of the mind's eye (*visus interior*). As Umberto Eco concludes in his detailed analysis of the Thomistic *visio* theory of beauty, "aesthetic seeing [for Aquinas] does not occur before the act of abstraction, nor in the act, nor just after it . . . [i]t occurs instead at the end of the second operation of the intellect–that is, *in the judgment*." [43]

Accordingly, as regards the theory of beauty at least, Aquinas' silence on the painter's art seems somewhat less paradoxical than it appears initially. To the extent that this theory downplays the notions of physical sight and seeing that have helped define the discourse on painting since the time of the ancient Greeks, we could infer that it has little real bearing on pictorial images and image making and so presents no clear opportunity or motive for addressing that matter. In fact, however, the theory of beauty is but a subordinate consideration within Aquinas' primary quest to understand divine truth: a metaphysical, epistemological, and semiotic matter that inevitably intersects the issue of mimesis and, so, the *first* preoccupation of all traditional painting theory. In the end, then, Aquinas' reticence toward the pictorial arts proves to be all the more surprising. Given this overarching preoccupation with divine truth, we are all the more compelled to ask why Aquinas avoids any overt commentary on painting.

A definitive answer is forever lost in the textual void that provokes this query. Nevertheless, a likely solution might be found in Aquinas' thoughts on the verbal arts. It is well known that, like most Church philosophers of the Middle Ages, Aquinas regards all the universe as 'Word' (Λόγος, a metaphor for Christ in action), as a kind of infinitely complex 'sign', from its physical creations to its abstract divine truths and God the Creator Himself. He inherits this conception from the Gospel of St. John: "In the beginning was the Word, and the Word was with God, and the Word was God . . . ; all things were made through him [the Word], and without him was not anything made that was made" (John 1.1-3). [44] With Scripture as his supreme authority, Aquinas joins the ranks of past and contemporary Catholic intellectuals to extend a privileged

---

[43] Umberto Eco, *The Aesthetics of Thomas Aquinas*, trans. Hugh Bredin (Cambridge: Harvard University Press, 1988), 196.

[44] *The Holy Bible*, eds. Herbert G. May and Bruce M. Metzger (New York: Oxford University Press, 1962), 1284.

status to the words of verbal language. Like other medieval Church philosophers, he moves against the Plato of *Republic* 10 (with whom the Middle Ages was thoroughly familiar) and in step with the Aristotle of the *Poetics* (whose principles could only be inferred from the writings on logic, physics, and metaphysics actually available at the time) to assert that, in the most essential way, *all words* have the *capability* to inscribe and convey *the Word*, which is the infinite but real universe and God. They have the inherent *potential* to achieve the fullest possible presence–both *to imitate* and *to communicate* all truths, factual and spiritual (albeit in many instances only once they are veiled by figures for the benefit of the unrefined people who are unprepared to confront the divine truth directly[45]).

In a crucial refinement of his theory, however, Aquinas also makes clear that only the authors of the holy Scripture had genuinely realized that verbal potential. Rather like the divinely mad poets of Plato's *Phaedrus* and *Ion* and (ultimately) of Aristotle's *Poetics*, they alone were the beneficiaries of celestial revelation–those blessed to transmit the sacred Christian doctrine (*sacra doctrina*), to transcribe the Word-God: "Christian theology . . . flows from founts recognized in the light of a higher science, namely God's very own *which he shares with the blessed.*"[46]

These sanctified authors were able to employ words that, like the Word and its countless manifestations in the objective world,[47] enjoy a "superabundance of truth" ("excedentem veritatem") (*ST* 1a2ae. 101, 3; 29:120-21) yet manage to delimit, or 'tame', that superabundance into conformity with the univocality of the One God's one true message of faith.[48] For Aquinas, this semiotic power and versatility is particularly evident through the rich hermeneutic opportunities that the biblical authors make available to their readers. With St. Augustine's famous directions for the fourfold exegesis

---

[45] "In statu autem praesentis vitae, non possumus divinam veritatem in seipsa intueri . . . [e]t ideo utilius [est] ut sub quodam figurarum velamine divina mysteria rudi populo traderentur" (*ST* 1a2ae. 101, 2, 1; 29:118-19). See also Aquinas' discussion of metaphorical *veils*: *ST* 1a, 1, 9.

[46] "[S]acra doctrina . . . procedit ex principiis notis lumine superioris scientiae, *quae scilicet est Dei et beatorum*" (*ST* 1a. 1, 2; 1:10-11: my emphasis).

[47] On the multiplicity of meanings inscribed in the Word as the amalgam of all the things of the world, see *ST* 1a, 1, 10.

[48] Umberto Eco provides a fuller explanation of this concept, particularly in relation to the 'taming' of the Hermetic Platonists' pansemiotic metaphysics, in *Limits*, esp. 11-15. We shall return to the Hermetic view of language below.

of the Old Testament firmly in mind,[49] he drives this point home in
an important *sed contra* declaration of the *Summa Theologiae* that
borrows directly from St. Gregory's comment on Scriptural interpretation in the *Moralium* (20, 1): "'holy Scripture transcends all
other sciences by its very style of expression, in that one and the
same discourse, while narrating an event, transmits a mystery as
well'."[50] Thus the Scriptural addressers present a message that their
addressees are allowed to decode in two major ways. On the one
hand, they may read it as a report about things and events of the
world. Again following St. Augustine, Aquinas calls this the "historical or literal" meaning ("sensus historicus vel litteralis"), which he
otherwise defines as "that which the author [consciously] intends"
("quem auctor intendit") (*ST* 1a. 1, 10; 1:34-37). On the other
hand, they may read it as a report about what the things of the
world signify in God's grand design. This is the "spiritual sense"
("sensus spiritualis") which, while based on the literal signification,
inscribes three unifying meanings of a distinctly superior order–the
allegorical, the moral, and the anagogical:

> [T]he allegorical sense is brought into play when the things of
> the Old Law signify the things of the New Law; the moral sense
> when the things done in Christ and in those who prefigured him
> are signs of what we should carry out; and the anagogical sense
> when the things that lie ahead in eternal glory are signified.[51]

---

[49] Aquinas cites Augustine's directions for an exegesis "'according to history,
to etiology, to analogy, and to allegory'" ("'secundum historiam, secundum aetio-
logiam, secundum analogiam, secundum allegoriam'") in *ST* 1a. 1, 10 (1:36-37)
(cf. the earlier presentation of this procedure in the *De Doctrina Christiana* and the
De utilitate credendi). In their edition of the *ST* 1a1ae. 98-105 for the Blackfriars,
David Bourke and Arthur Littledale remind us that "the scheme of the senses of
scripture evolved by St. Thomas [and Augustine] is based on a formula which goes
back ultimately to Origen: *umbra-Imago-Veritas*, 'Shadow-Image-Truth'" (29:118-
119, n. a).

[50] "'Sacra Scriptura omnes scientias ipso locutionis suae more transcendit, quia
uno eodemque sermone, dum narrat gestum, prodit mysterium'" (*ST* 1a. 1, 10;
1:36-37).

[51] "[Q]uod ea quae sunt veteris legis significant ea quae sunt novae legis est sensus allegoricus; secundum vero quod ea quae in Christo sunt facta vel in his quae
Christum significant sunt signa eorum quae nos agere debemus est sensus moralis;
prout vero significant ea quae sunt in aeterna gloria est sensus anagogicus" (*ST* 1a.
1, 10; 1:38-39). In-depth analyses of these meanings also reveal the medieval theories of symbol and allegory that prompted Augustine and Aquinas to devise their
complex hermeneutic rules for a correct "disambiguation" of Scripture. See Eco:
Art, 52-64; *Aquinas*, 137-54; *Limits*, esp. 11-15.

In stark contrast to the divine addressers of the biblical message are the human addressers of profane poetry. Although he is himself a skilled medieval poet (or perhaps for that very reason), Aquinas believes that the practitioners of the poetic art employ words in a substantially inferior way. They can never realize the full potential of their medium of words because their knowledge is itself inferior in kind. Whereas the authors of Scripture enjoyed a certain pure knowledge mediated by the grace of God, poets must rely on their own human intelligence and intuition, which are attained and guided not by revelation, but by *work*. In this way, their art remains but a "judgment about things to be produced" ("ratio factibilium") (*ST* 1.2ae 57, 4; 23:50-51),[52] and their words suffer an inevitable "deficiency in truth" ("defectum veritatis") (*ST* 1a2ae. 101, 3; 29:120-21). In the final analysis, poets succeed in providing only "the most modest of all teaching methods," an *infima doctrina* (*ST* 1a. 1, 9; 1:32-33), which enjoys none of the spiritual plenitude of Scripture.

Certainly, Aquinas knows well that poets make considerable and effective use of *rhetorical* allegory, what Augustine and others call *allegoria in verbis*.[53] Yet *allegoria in verbis* is at best a source of "parabolical" meanings: *fictions* (*fictiones*)[54] beneath veils of similitudes, or metaphors (*metaphorae*), governed by conventional rhetorical rules and the labors of the human imagination that are mere subspecies of the literal signification ("sensus parabolicus sub litterali continetur") (*ST* 1a. 1, 9-10; 1:33-41). Thus again Aquinas recognizes no practical equivalencies between poets and the authors of Scripture. Whatever objective verisimilitude they may achieve, the sub-literal poetic words of the former attain nothing of the spiritual significance in the divine words of the latter. Whereas the addressers of Scripture are able to supply their addressees with knowledge of a properly useful kind, the addressers of poetry can at best hope to provide them ideas of a merely delightful sort: "Poetry employs metaphors for the sake of representation, in which we are born to take delight. Holy teaching, on the other hand, adopts them for their indispensable usefulness. . . ."[55]

---

[52] See Eco, *Aquinas*, 148. In drawing this conclusion Aquinas retains the classical notion of art as 'making' (τέχνης).

[53] See Eco, *Aquinas*, 144, 256 n. 44; and *Limits*, 13.

[54] See *Quaestiones quodlibetales* 7.6, 3 ad 2: cited in Eco, *Aquinas*, 152.

[55] "[P]oëtica utitur metaphoris propter repraesentationem, repraesentatio enim naturaliter homini delectabilis est. Sed sacra doctrina utitur metaphoris propter ne-

To return at last to Aquinas' paradoxical silence about painting, then, we may surmise that the matter is simply unworthy of his notice. In a philosophical system that privileges verbal language yet already finds the poem wanting in that regard, 'speechless' pictures cannot hope to merit serious attention. [56] Even though Aquinas openly acknowledges that "all art imitates nature" ("Ars imitatur naturam"), [57] and that imitating nature is less a question of copying the appearance of a visible form than representing it "in its workings" ("in sua operatione") (ST 1a. 117, 1; 15:132-33), i.e., in the way "nature is directed to its aim" ("natura ordinatur ad finem suum"), [58] the fact remains that the art of painting employs images not words. By virtue of its very signifiers painting has a smaller chance to present spiritual meaning than poetry. What is more, and for the same reason, it is less inclined or able to inspire adoration. Four and a half centuries earlier, the same basic notion allowed Theodulf of Orleans to argue with effective irony against the heretical 'glorifier' criticism of the Iconoclasts in his Libri Carolini: "O glorifier of pictures, gaze then at your pictures, and let us devote our attention to the Holy Scriptures. Be the venerator of artificial colours, and let us venerate and penetrate secret thoughts. Enjoy your painted pictures, and let us enjoy the words of God." [59]

It is a leap, of course, to suppose that Aquinas follows the eighth- and ninth-century Carolingian painting theory of Theodulf of Orleans. It is unclear, for example, how he would have reacted to the idea, also promoted in Theodulf's theory, that painting fulfills a useful mnemonic function in promoting the commemoration of sacred people and events ("ad memoriam rerum gestarum"). [60] However, since Aquinas expressly recognizes that most human learning depends on both memory and "corporeal similitudes" in the mind,

---

cessitatem et utilitatem . . ." (ST 1a. 1, 9; 1:34-35). For more on Aquinas' distinction between the useful (utile) and the delightful (delectabile), see ST 1a. 5, 6; 2:78-81.

[56] See, for example, Libri Carolini 1.2 and 4.16 (cited in Tatarkiewicz, History, 2:100, nn. 6a-7).

[57] Physics 2.4 (cited in Tatarkiewicz, History, 2:262, n. 23).

[58] Ibid.

[59] "O imaginum adorator . . . tu luminaribus perlustra picturas, nos frequentemus divinas Scripturas. Tu fucatorum venerator esto colorum, nos veneratores et capaces simus sensuum arcanorum. Tu depictis demulcere tabulis, nos divinis mulceamur alloquiis" (Libri Carolini, 3.30: cited in Tatarkiewicz, History, 2:102, n. 14).

[60] Libri Carolini, 3.16 (cited in Tatarkiewicz, History, 2:105-06, n. 30).

we may assume he would have accepted that notion as well. [61] Hence it seems reasonable that he would have judged the treatment of painting by the *Libri Carolini* to be consistent with his overall concept of the primacy of language. In fact, had he made a statement about painting, it would probably have resembled another important conclusion in the *Libri*: "Painters are . . . able in some way to commit events to the memory; but things which are perceptible only to the mind and expressible only in words cannot be grasped and shown by painters, but by writers and other similar people." [62]

* * *

On balance, then, the most salient paradox is the one between Aquinas and Dante Alighieri who, although a good Thomist in most regards, advances a very different idea of the poetic and pictorial arts. As Umberto Eco has reminded us, for example, Dante is far more generous toward poetry, believing that, contrary to Aquinas' characterization, "poets continue the work of the scriptures." [63] Like the addressers of Scripture, in other words, the addressers of poems are able to realize the full semantic plenitude of their verbal code for the benefit of their addressees.

Eco bases this conclusion on a number of explicit commentaries, including an oft-cited yet unauthenticated letter to Can Grande della Scala defending the psalm-like polysemy of the *Divina Commedia*, [64] exegetical prescriptions in *Il Convivio* (*The Banquet*), and praises for the epiphanic accomplishments of poets in the *Com-*

---

[61] See Summers, *Judgment*, 220-27; and Frances A. Yates, *The Art of Memory* (Chicago: University of Chicago Press, 1966), 62-81.

[62] "Pictores . . . rerum gestarum historias ad memoriam reducere quodammodo valent, res autem, quae sensibus tantummodo percipiuntur et verbis proferuntur, non a pictoribus, sed a scriptoribus comprehendi et aliorum relatibus demonstrari valent" (*Libri Carolini*, 3.23: cited in Tatarkiewicz, *History*, 2:102, n. 13).

[63] See Eco, *Aquinas*, 162; *Limits*, 11-15. See also Charles S. Singleton, *Commedia: Elements of Structure* (Cambridge: Harvard University Press, 1954), 1-17 (reprinted as "Allegory," in *Critical Essays on Dante*, ed. Giuseppe Mazzotta [Boston: G. K. Hall & Co., 1991], 139-51); and Thomas G. Bergin, *Dante* (New York: Orion Press, 1965), esp. 97-152, 250-64.

[64] This letter is reprinted in Robert S. Haller, *Literary Criticism of Dante Alighieri* (Lincoln: University of Nebraska Press, 1973), 95-111. Other discussions of the epistle appear in Charles S. Singleton, *Commedia*, 1-17; and Bergin, *Dante*, 195-212, esp. 204-08.

media itself. In the *Convivio*, for instance, Dante makes clear from the start that his writings carry much more than a literal meaning. Alluding to his *Vita Nuova* in the opening chapter, the Scholastic poet insists that "since the meaning I really intended to convey in the canzoni . . . was other than the obvious, *I intend to explain them according to their allegorical significance* after discussing the literal narrative . . . ." [65] As Eco astutely admits, such talk of intentions might well suggest that the "allegory" in question is merely the poetic *allegoria in verbis*. From Dante's elaboration at the beginning of Book Two, however, it is soon evident that this allegory actually corresponds to the spiritual senses identified by Aquinas:

> As I noted in the opening chapter, this commentary must be literal and allegorical. To indicate what this means it should be explained that texts can be interpreted, and must therefore be elucidated, principally in four senses. The first is called literal: . . . the overt meaning of the words of a fictitious story. . . . The second is called allegorical: this is the sense concealed under the cloak of these fables. . . . The third sense is called moral: this is the sense that teachers must be on the alert to notice . . . for their own [moral] benefit and that of their students. . . . The fourth sense is called anagogical . . . : this is brought out when a work is expounded with regard to its spiritual meaning. [66]

In *Purgatorio* 22 of the *Divina Commedia*, Dante likewise applauds the mystically prophetic, and hence superior spiritual, potential of 'profane' poetic discourse. He puts this idea into the

[65] "[C]on ciò sia cosa che la vera intenzione mia fosse altra che quella che di fuori mostrano le canzoni . . . , *per allegorica esposizione quelle intendo mostrare*, appresso la litterale istoria ragionata . . . " (*Il Convivio* 1.1.18; my emphasis). See Dante Alighieri, *Il Convivio*, ed. Maria Simonelli (Bologna: Casa Editrice Prof. Riccardo Pàtron, 1966), 3-4; *The Banquet*, trans. and ed. Christopher Ryan (Saratoga: Anma Libri, 1989), 15. Henceforth, these editions are identified as *C* and *B*, respectively.

[66] "Dico che, sì come nel primo capitolo è narrato, questa sposizione conviene essere litterale e allegorica. E a ciò dare a intendere, si vuol sapere che le scritture si possono intendere e deonsi esporre massimamente per quattro sensi. L'uno si chiama litterale . . . ciò che suona la parola fittizia, si come ne' le favole dei poeti. L'altro si chiama allegorico e questo è quello che si nasconde sotto 'l manto di queste favole. . . . Lo terzo senso si chiama morale, e questo è quello che li lettori deono intentamente andare . . . ad utilitade di loro e di loro discenti. . . . Lo quarto senso si chiama anagogico . . . e questo è quando spiritualmente si spone una scrittura" (2.1.2-8; *C* 31-32; *B* 42-43).

mouth of the Roman poet and reputed Christian convert, Publius Papinius Statius. Here Statius thanks Virgil (Dante's esteemed guide through Hell and Purgatory) for the poetic words that lighted his path not only to Parnassus, but all the way to the Christian faith and God:

> "You [Virgil] it was who first sent me [Statius] toward Parnassus to drink in its caves, and you who first did light me on to God. You were like one who goes by night and carries the light behind him and profits not himself, but makes those wise who follow him . . . . Through you I was a poet, through you a Christian." [67]

A departure from Aquinas is similarly apparent in Dante's approach to painting. Beyond his regular and explicit interest in pictorial artworks throughout the *Commedia* (especially in the *Purgatorio*, but also, in a more abstract way, in the *Paradiso*),[68] Dante seems willing to ascribe not only 'words' to the visual image, but also a potential to signify spiritually. Jean Hagstrum has done much to expose the first attribution in his examination of the three carvings ("intagli") of humility adorning the sheer marble cliffs above the terrace of pride in *Purgatorio* 10 (vv. 28-99; 100-05). For Hagstrum, there is a "crescendo" toward voice throughout the descriptions. Indeed, while alluding to the pilgrim's summation of this pictorial experience in verse 95, Hagstrum duly concludes that "in silent plastic art Dante has discovered visible speech ('visibile parlare')." [69]

---

[67] "Tu prima m'invïasti / verso Parnaso a ber ne le sue grotte, / e prima appresso Dio m'alluminasti. / Facesti come quei che va di notte, / che porta il lume dietro e sé non giova, / ma dopo sé fa le persone dotte . . . . / Per te poeta fui, per te cristiano" (22.64-73). This passage and the paradoxical status of Statius as a 'good' misreader of Virgil has been carefully examined elsewhere. See Marguerite Mills Chiarenza, *The Divine Comedy, Tracing God's Art* (Boston: Twayne Publishers, 1989), 72-78; and Jeffrey T. Schnapp, "Introduction to *Purgatorio*," *The Cambridge Companion to Dante*, ed. Rachel Jacoff (New York: Cambridge University Press, 1993), 192-207, esp. 200.

[68] While it is appropriate to restate Dorothy Sayers' observation that, in many ways, "[t]he *Divine Comedy* is an enchanting picture-book," it is essential to recall that this critic employs the words "picture" and "pictorial" to designate virtually all evocations of visual impressions ("Dante's Imagery: II–Pictorial," in *Introductory Papers on Dante* [New York: Harper & Brothers, 1954], 21-43, esp. 32). By contrast, the present study uses these terms to denote scenes or images ascribed explicitly to an autonomous pictorial artwork.

[69] Hagstrum, *Sister Arts*, 51-55, esp. 53.

In addition, Dante indicates that these visual 'words' are more than an *allegoria in verbis*. They attain a spiritual presence as well. As Dante makes clear in his poetic persona's affirmation that they come to be "images of humilities so great" ("imagini di tante umilitadi") (v. 98) for the pride-stained souls sufficiently cleansed to raise up their gaze to ponder them, pictures are fully able to teach spiritual virtues and truths. Further, there is the significant fact that Dante chooses to locate them in Purgatory. Not only is this the realm where "reality has become imagination," and thus image (as Francesco De Sanctis has remarked), where "everything speaks of renewal [and] regeneration" (as Marguerite Chiarenza has noted), and where "time lived" modulates into "liturgical time" (as Jeffrey Schnapp has observed), [70] but it is where all things, from human souls to pictorial engravings, inscribe the fullest range of their respective possible meanings, from the merely mundane to the magnificently divine. In locating them here, that is, Dante signals that each of these pictures–and by synecdoche, painting in general–may be read simultaneously on the literal and spiritual levels, as a record of historical reality and a promise of eternal truths to come.

The higher reading is not immediately accessible to everyone, however. For Dante, certain addressees can see readily through the veils of objective appearance, others cannot. Such is the idea that overlays and completes the humility lesson of the second (and central) *intaglio*, the scene of King David's revels before the Ark of the Covenant. For what the picture also includes, and which the author takes pains to point out, is the figure of an archetypal bad reader, David's first wife, Michal ("Micòl"): "Opposite, figured at a window of a great palace, was Michal looking on, like a woman vexed and scornful." [71] At first, the inclusion of this lady seems a simple concession to the biblical source for Dante's picture. She is presented in nearly identical terms in 2 Samuel 6.16: "As the ark of the Lord came into the city of David, Michal the daughter of Saul looked out of the window, and saw King David leaping and dancing before the Lord; and she despised him in her heart." In the *Purgatorio*, however, Michal assumes a role the Old Testament author

---

[70] Francesco De Sanctis, *History of Italian Literature*, trans. Joan Redfern (New York: Harcourt Brace, 1931), 1:220-21 (also cited in Hagstrum, *Sister Arts*, 52); Chiarenza, *Divine Comedy*, 56; Schnapp, "*Purgatorio*," 197.

[71] "Di contra, effigïata ad una vista / d'un gran palazzo, Micòl ammirava / sì come donna dispettosa e trista" (vv. 67-69; 102-03).

only begins to prepare. Looking from her "vista," i.e., window or opening,[72] she becomes a double for the poet-pilgrim and the chastened souls who gaze into the 'window' of the "story set in the rock" ("storia ne la roccia imposta") (v. 52). However, whereas the pilgrim and the purged have the requisite knowledge and purity of heart to decode the true message of the picture before them, to interpret David's ribald "dancing" with ephod "girt up" as the act of a truly "*humble* Psalmist" ("trescando alzato, l'*umile* salmista") (v. 65: my emphasis), Michal has no such wisdom or innocence. Unlike the former addressee-spectators, whom Dante thereby holds up as models to inspire our personal hermeneutic habits, the latter feels nothing but scorn and frustration because she is prevented from reading beyond the surface of her husband's comportment by her own prideful nature (which Gregory I clearly names and condemns in his comment on the biblical text in the *Moralium libri*[73]).

It might therefore appear that the Scholastic poet regards poetry and painting as equal partners rather than ill-matched rivals. Dante's conjunction of *visibile* and *parlare* in *Purgatorio* 10.95 ostensibly encourages such an assumption. Indeed, this affiliation and the proliferation of synaesthesia throughout the *Commedia* would suggest that the author is loath to privilege any of the senses. Rather, he appears to prefer a kind of "translinguistic perception" whose culmination occurs in the "synaesthetic drift" (the dissolution of all sensory distinctions) of the *Paradiso*[74] and, by extension, to be averse to granting supremacy to any sense-specific art form.

Three problems linger to cast doubt on this conclusion, however. On the theoretical level, the fact remains that Dante's carvings are ekphraseis, and as such, they inscribe contention by their very nature. While striving to reproduce synchronic natural signs both in and like the visible art objects under consideration, the *intagli*

---

[72] See Charles S. Singleton, *Divine Comedy: Purgatorio 2, Commentary* (Princeton: Princeton University Press, 1973), 210.

[73] See Gregory I, *Moralium libri*, 5:27.46, 77: "still mad with pride at her royal descent" ("ex tumore regii generis insana"). This comment is cited and translated by Charles S. Singleton, *Purgatorio 2*, 207-08.

[74] See Gino Casagrande, "'Esto Visibile Parlare': A Synaesthetic Approach to *Purgatorio* 10.55-63," in *Lectura Dantis Newberryana 2*, ed. Paolo Cherchi and Antonio C. Mastrobuono (Evanston: Northwestern University Press, 1990), 21-57, esp. 51; G. O'Malley, "Literary Synaesthesia," *Journal of Aesthetic and Art Criticism* 15 (1957): 391-411, esp. 409-10.

employ verbal signs that necessarily enact their diachronic and conventional difference. Thus any sense that these ekphraseis might acknowledge the sameness of the arts is, in theory at least, inherently countered by the equal and overriding sense that they must reaffirm artistic alterity.

Second and more textually explicit, it is impossible to ignore that the superbly gifted and all expressive poets of the *Convivio* (Dante) and *Purgatorio* 22 (Dante and Virgil) are eminently human, whereas the only spiritually communicative painter of *Purgatorio* 10 (and elsewhere) is "He who never beheld any new thing" ("Colui che mai non vide cosa nova") (v. 94), God the "Craftsman" ("fabbro") (v. 99). Paradoxically, then, at the same time the expression "visibile parlare" seems to announce the essential resemblance and parity between poetry and painting, Dante seems to deny that idea by intimating that the hand of God is required to make the pictorial arts spiritually meaningful. Accordingly, had Michal been looking at an 'image' portrayed by a mere mortal, we are left to suppose that her contemptuous reading would have been complete and legitimate since, in the end, mortal painters can render nothing but the literal surface.

Finally, to return to the idea of *visibile parlare*, we are obliged to recognize that, on a certain level, this expression inscribes a fundamental and constant, hierarchical opposition. Despite the synaesthesia-based theories that have posited this binary denomination as an essentially reversible "elementary semantic structure" (an expression in which the two terms must be taken as united and equal in the "semic nucleus" of "logos"),[75] grammatical logic not only upholds the inherent duality of the phrase, but it also guarantees the primacy of the second term, *parlare* ("speech"), and with it (by synecdoche) the verbal art of poetry. When all is said and done, *visibile* is a mere adjectival qualifier, an accidental quality of the substantial term *parlare*, which enjoys the distinction of being functionally triple: infinitive, noun, and nominalized infinitive.

Notwithstanding this subtle bias, one fact must always be kept in mind: unlike Aquinas, Dante remains conspicuously optimistic about the semantic reach of poetry and painting. Building upon Aristotle's redefinition of the real and the Scholastic philosopher's

---

[75] Casagrande, "Esto Visibile Parlare," 37.

empowerment of verbal language as revealed through Scriptural hermeneutics, the Scholastic poet leaves little doubt that profane words and images have a genuine or potential ability to give presence to historical (literal) and divine (spiritual) truths: each medium inscribes the actual or immanent power to tame the superabundant meanings infusing the one true Word-God.

* * *

For the Neoplatonists, on the other hand, any optimism is distinctly more tenuous. This is not to say that the latter follow Plato in distrusting and disallowing all mimetic modes of expression. On the contrary, against the primary teachings of their intellectual progenitor, philosophers like Plotinus, Proclus, Marsilio Ficino, and Pico della Mirandola greatly admire and value the verbal and visual makers and their products. They express considerable confidence in the conceptual reach of all poet/artist addressers (and, in principle, every human soul). Divine madness does not stop at the prophets and celestially anointed bards. Rather, all poets and painters possess notions or intuitions (Ficino: *formulas*[76]) of the ideal forms and truths (Plotinus: εἶδος; Ficino: *ideas*[77]); all poets and painters share in (or have access to) God's creative mind (Plotinus: Νοῦς). In fact, according to Plotinus in a section of the *Enneads* on the nature of "the intelligible beauty," their arts "do not simply imitate what they see, but they run back up to the forming principles [λόγοι] from which nature derives" (*En.* 5.8.1; 5:236-37). As Plotinus goes on to explain in a commonplace allusion to Phidias' colossal *Zeus* (the fifth-century B.C. chryselephantine world-wonder which, although a sculpture, stands broadly for any heuretic work of art, regardless of the medium): "Pheidias . . . did not make his Zeus from any model perceived by the senses, but un-

---

[76] See the *Commentum cum summis capitulorum* (Ch. 21, 25, 26), in *Marsilio Ficino and the Phaedran Charioteer*, ed. and trans. Michael J. B. Allen (Berkeley: University of California Press, 1981), 154-55, 172-75. See also the *Commentum in Phaedrum* 2, 1177 ff. as cited in Panofsky, *Idea*, 56-57.

[77] For Plotinus, see *Ennead* 5.8.1: "The stone which has been brought to beauty of form [εἴδους κάλλος] by art . . . did not have this form [εἶδος], but *it was in the man who had it in his mind even before it came into the stone*" (*En.* 5:236-37: my emphasis). For Ficino, see the citations indicated in note 76, above.

derstood what Zeus would look like if he wanted to make himself
visible" (*En.* 5.8.1; 5:238-41).[78]

In this respect, too, the 'madness' of the poet and the painter is
hardly the enemy of reason. When operating more symbolically
than mimetically this inspired delirium imparts an important, even
indispensable, didactic function to words and images. Beyond providing sensory pleasure, poems and pictures so conceived can instruct the intellect in the loftier realities, launch and sustain the soul
of the reader/viewer-addressee on its difficult journey back to the
Divine. Thanks to their special noetic and ontologically immediate
(or synchronic) qualities, for example, the ancient Egyptian hieroglyphs have the power to spark ecstatic memories of the soul's pre-
corporeal intercourse with the celestial essences. In an *Enneads* passage whose fifteenth-century reformulation by Ficino may well have
inspired Leonardo da Vinci's distinctive insistence on the virtues of
pictorial all-at-onceness in the *Trattato della pittura*, Plotinus unam-
biguously asserts that when "[t]he wise men of Egypt . . . wished to
signify something wisely, [they] did not use the forms of letters . . .
but by drawing images . . . *they manifested the non-discursiveness of
the intelligible world*, . . . a kind of knowledge and wisdom . . .
[that] is a subject of statements, *all together in one*, and not discourse or deliberation" (*En.* 5.8.6; 5:256-57: my emphasis).[79]

Poets and poetry may provide a similar enlightenment. In Book
Two of his lengthy *Commentary on the Republic*, Proclus adeptly argues that, despite his sustained criticisms, Plato in fact regards
Homer as a "master of all truth" and "a divinely inspired [man],
transported by the frenzy of the Muses . . . [who] gives us his in-
struction on divine and human things." [80] Likewise, in the context
of his mystical reflections on the soul's return to God through love,
Marsilio Ficino makes poetry the first of the "four divine frenzies"
("divini furores"). It is the activity of intellect and spirit whose harmonious musical effects inaugurate the divided soul's reunification

---

[78] For more on Phidias' *Zeus*, including its earliest celebration by the orator,
Dion Chrysostomus (c. AD 40-after 111), see Panofsky, *Idea*, 16, 184-85 nn. 19-20.
See also Tatarkiewicz, *History*, 1:293-96, and Lucian, *Essays in Portraiture Defended,*
ed. and trans. A. M. Harmon (London: William Heinemann Ltd., 1925), (¶ 14).

[79] The matter of Ficino's reformulation of Plotinus' hieroglyph passage and
Leonardo's possible debt to both Neoplatonists is taken up below.

[80] Proclus, *Commentaire sur la République*, trans. A. J. Festugière (Paris: Librairie Philosophique J. Vrin, 1970), 1:175-221; esp. 175, 178-79 (my translation of
the French).

and reascent to the heights of the super-essential One: "The soul cannot return to the One unless made one itself. . . . [s]o first the soul requires the poetic madness: it can arouse the torpid parts by way of musical sounds, soothe those that are perturbed by its harmonious sweetness, . . . and temper the soul's various parts." [81]

Paradoxically, however, the very same philosophers are far from sanguine about the ability of poetry and painting to convey the divine truths in a substantially *complete* way. In contradiction to the aforementioned concessions, the Neoplatonists firmly reject that these art forms, or any others, can truly fulfill what Panofsky calls "the thoroughly metaphysical task of re-establishing and re-affirming the principles buried beneath the given appearance" [82]–i.e., of giving an adequate measure of presence to the divine ideas and truths that lie beyond the stretch of our bodily senses.

There are two main reasons for this failing. The first relates precisely to the status of the signifiers employed in poetic and pictorial messages. Words, for example, are fundamentally disposed to ambiguity. Being both conventionally arbitrary and inherently diachronic, they lack the univocity and immediate accessibility required for an *efficient* communication of truth, be it mundane or divine. In a sense, verbal language is fallen and forever condemned to try in vain to rise to semantic plenitude. [83]

This concern is implicitly yet unmistakably inscribed in the *Heptaplus*, or *Sevenfold Narration of the Six Days of Genesis*, of Ficino's Florentine Academy colleague, Pico della Mirandola. Recog-

---

[81] "Redire quippe ad unum animus nequit nisi ipse unum efficiatur . . . [p]oetico ergo furore primum opus est, qui per musicos tonos que torpent suscitet, per harmonicam suavitatem que turbantur mulceat, . . . et varias partes animi temperet": Ficino, *De Amore* 7.14, in *Phaedran Charioteer*, 220-23. For extensive discussions of Ficino's theory of love and poetic madness, see Paul Oskar Kristeller, *The Philosophy of Marsilio Ficino*, trans. Virginia Conant (New York: Columbia University Press, 1943), esp. 256-88; Erwin Panofsky, *Studies in Iconology*, 140-46; André Chastel, *Marsile Ficin et l'art* (Geneva: Librairie E. Droz, 1975), 118-35, esp. 129-35; Michael J. B. Allen, *The Platonism of Marsilio Ficino: A Study of His "Phaedrus" Commentary, Its Sources and Genesis* (Berkeley: University of California Press, 1984), 41-67.

[82] Panofsky, *Idea*, 95.

[83] Of course, the correction of this perception will be one of the principal preoccupations of the Neoplatonic evangelical humanist, Desiderius Erasmus: cf. Terence Cave, "*Enargeia*: Erasmus and the Rhetoric of Presence in the Sixteenth Century," *L'Esprit Créateur* 16 (1976): 5-19. See below for more on the concept of *enargeia* (though primarily in the Longinian sense of 'enthrallment' introduced by Murray Krieger).

nizing that the (supposedly) definitive fourfold approach to textual exegesis proposed by St. Augustine and Aquinas is inadequate to tame all the ambiguities of Scripture, Pico boldly offers his own "self-consistent and coherent course of interpretation." Specifically, he proposes to interpret Genesis from seven complementary perspectives. The first four perspectives present meanings that correspond to the four worlds of known existence (the sublunary and corruptible world, the celestial world, the angelic and invisible world, and, most originally for Pico, the world of man himself, the synthesis of the preceding three); the fifth meaning, to the principle of multiplicity, or discordant concord (*discordia concors*); the sixth, to the concept that all things are related in one or more of fifteen different ways; the seventh, to the notion that biblical texts always supply insights into the eternal felicity of God.[84] This extraordinary proposition is significant for the challenge it poses to the sanctioned hermeneutic model of the Scholastics: a challenge the Church quickly meets by (once again) condemning Pico and his treatise for heresy. More important here, however, is the insight it provides into Pico's and the Neoplatonists' underlying distrust of verbal language. The proliferation of possible exegetical approaches in the *Heptaplus* is clearly symptomatic of their commonly held fear that words are inherently ambiguous, that even the most spiritually determined *verba* of Scripture may be irremediably doomed to semantic openness.[85]

Ficino is equally distrustful of verbal ambiguities, though his principal concern is the inherent temporality, or diachrony, of words. This quality not only delays, and thus diminishes, the comprehension of all verbal messages, but in cases where words would aim to denote a divine truth, it also precludes the success of that attempt because diachrony is fundamentally antithetical to the perfectly comprehensive, synchronous mode of knowing and revealing of God, who "*has knowledge of things not by way of multiple*

---

[84] The contours of this theory are sketched out in the first and second proems. See Pico della Mirandola, *Heptaplus*, trans. Douglas Carmichael (New York: Bobbs-Merrill Co., 1965), 67-84, esp. 73, 78-81. On the *Heptaplus* and its relation to the writings of other Florentine Neoplatonists, see Chastel, *Ficin*, 141-50. Pico's original conception of man as the juncture of the traditionally accepted elemental, celestial and angelic worlds is considered by Kristeller in *Ficino*, 408-10.

[85] A more thorough examination of this anxiety may be found in Chastel, *Ficin*, 141-50.

thought but like the pure and firm shape of the thing itself." Ficino elaborates on this position in a passage inspired by the hieroglyph commentary of Plotinus cited previously:

> Your thoughts about time are *multiple and shifting*, when you *say* [i.e., express in words, whether spoken or written] that time is swift or that, by a kind of turning movement, it links the beginning again to the end, that it teaches prudence and that it brings things and carries them away again. But the Egyptian can comprehend the whole of this discourse *in one firm image* when he *paints* a winged serpent with its tail in its mouth, and so with the other images which Horus described. [86]

In the light of such propositions there is good reason to believe that the Neoplatonists enter the paragone debate squarely on the side of painting. [87] In terms of their intrinsic immediacy, pictures achieve a certain oneness and completeness that poems can only roughly approximate through the time-bound effect of ekphrasis (or more broadly, *epideixis*, sight-based descriptions of any kind). The instantly perceivable visual image of the "alatum serpentem" ("winged serpent"), or *ouroboros* (tail-eater), an age-old symbol of temporality and eternal renewal, is vastly more appropriate, intellectually and ontologically, than its prolonged and structurally splintered counterpart in words. Further, although absent from the commentaries thus far examined, the fact remains that the Neoplatonists generally regarded God Himself as a kind of plastic artist/painter. In this respect they follow not only the ancient and biblical accounts of God as artifex/artist of the universe (we are in-

---

[86] "[Q]uoniam videlicet Deus scientiam rerum habet non tamquam excogitationem de re multiplicem, sed tamquam simplicem firmamque rei formam. Excogitatio temporis apud te *multiplex est et mobilis, dicens* videlicet tempus quidem est velox, et revolutione quadam principium rursus cum fine coniungit: prudentiam docet, profert res, et aufert. Totam vero discursionem eiusmodi *una quadam firmaque figura* comprehendit Aegyptius alatum serpentem *pingens*, caudam ore praesentem: caeteraque figuris similibus, quas describit Horus": Ernst Gombrich, "*Icones Symbolicae*: The Visual Image in Neo-Platonic Thought," *Journal of the Warburg and Courtauld Institutes* 11 (1948): 172 and n. 1. The English translation appears in Krieger, *Ekphrasis*, 20. In both cases, the emphasis is mine. For more on this passage, see Gombrich, ibid., 170-73; Krieger, ibid., 20-22; Chastel, *Ficin*, 72; Horapollo, *The Hieroglyphics of Horapollo*, trans. George Boas, Bollingen Series 23 (New York: Pantheon Books, 1950), esp. 28-29.

[87] With only minor modifications in emphasis, Ernst Gombrich may be said to advance this very position in "*Icones Symbolicae*."

variably reminded of Plato's characterization of God in *Republic* 10), but also the teachings of one of the most influential forefathers of Neoplatonic thought, the legendary Egyptian sage, Hermes 'Trismegistus' ('Thrice-Great'). This mystical philosopher uses the painter analogy both to support his claims for the existence of the divine maker (just as a picture cannot be produced unless there is a painter, Hermes argues, so too all creation could not now exist without an original All-Creator) as well as to characterize God's omnipotent powers ("if it is given to one and the same painter to make heaven, gods, earth, sea, humans, things without reason and things without soul," queries the Egyptian, "is it not possible for god to make them?"). [88]

On closer inspection, however, the Neoplatonic writings betray an equal or perhaps greater mistrust of painting and the visual arts. Again, the issue is the status of the signifier. Plotinus highlights the Neoplatonists' two principal misgivings in *Enneads* 5:

> As for all the imitative arts, painting and sculpture, dancing and mime, which are in some way composed of elements from this world and use a model perceived by sense and imitate the forms and movements and transpose into their own terms the proportions which they see, it would not be reasonable to trace them back to the intelligible world except as included in the forming principle of man. (5.9.11; 5:310-11)

Notwithstanding their link to the "intelligible" (i.e., ideal or divine) universe through man's "forming principle" (i.e., his reasoning soul [89]), imitative arts like painting are typically hampered in their semantic efficacy by their materiality (here "elements") and, presumably as a consequence of that materiality, by their reliance upon

---

[88] See his discourses to Tat and to Asclepius in *Corpus Hermeticum* 5 and 14, respectively: Hermes Trismegistus, *Hermetica*, trans. and ed. Brian P. Copenhaver (Cambridge: Cambridge University Press, 1992), 19-20, 56. For more on Hermes Trismegistus and his links to Neoplatonism, see Frances Yates, *Giordano Bruno and the Hermetic Tradition* (Chicago: University of Chicago Press, 1964); John Scarborough, "Hermetic and Related Texts in Classical Antiquity," in *Hermeticism and the Renaissance*, ed. Ingrid Merkel and Allen G. Debus (Washington D.C.: Folger Books, 1988), 19-44. See below for further considerations on the influence of Hermes and Hermeticism on Neoplatonic thought.

[89] My clarifications are inspired by Stephen MacKenna's translation of this passage in Plotinus, *The Enneads* (4th ed.; London: Faber and Faber Limited, 1969), 440-41.

purely sensible reality for the objects of their mimetic operations. When painting functions mimetically, in other words, its signifiers are essentially flawed by their bond to matter ($ὕλη$), which the Neoplatonists commonly consider the lowest constituent of the sublunary world, the substance ($οὐσία$) most antithetical to the forms and God–"that which underlies figures and forms and shapes and measures and limits, decked out with an adornment which belongs to something else, having no good of its own, only a shadow in comparison with real being" (*En.* 1.8.3; 1:284-87). Indeed, as Plotinus repeatedly intones, matter is the very "substance of evil" ("$κακοῦ$ $οὐσία$"): "For this thing is not want of wealth but want of thought, want of virtue, of beauty, strength, shape, form, quality. . . . Must it not then be ugly . . . utterly vile, utterly evil?" (*En.* 2.4.16; 2:148-49). [90] Consequently, by the nature of its signs, mimetically oriented painting simultaneously contributes to and relies upon evil. As Panofsky has noted, this may well be the reason why, by Porphyry's biographical account, Plotinus was unconquerably reluctant to sit for a portrait. Dependent upon created things ($γεγονός$), and thus matter, for their subjects, portraits are fated to add to the already profuse abundance of evil in the world. [91]

On a more encouraging note, Plotinus and the Neoplatonists also understand that pictures can transcend objective reality when designed to operate heuristically (i.e., symbolically). This awareness is plain enough in the Zeus and two hieroglyph passages reproduced above. Nevertheless, even heuretic painting fares little better than poetry in encoding the *totality* of any divine truth. In this instance, however, the problem is less semiotic than metaphysical. It is a question of the ontologically elusive omnipresence of God and all His truths.

Umberto Eco offers one of the most insightful and suggestive perspectives on this metaphysical dilemma in a study of the Neoplatonic hermeneutic concept he calls either "Hermetic drift" or "Her-

---

[90] In fact, the relations between matter and evil are the focus of discussion throughout treatises 1.8 and 2.4. See also the end of *Ennead* 5.9.10, which immediately precedes the passage on painting just cited: "there is no Form of Evil; since evil here is the result of want and deprivation and failure and is a misfortune of matter and of that which becomes like matter" (5:310-11).

[91] Panofsky, *Idea*, 189-90 nn. 44, 47. A translation of Porphyry's *Life of Plotinus* is included at the beginning of MacKenna's English edition of the *Enneads* (1).

metic semiosis." [92] As its name indicates, this notion has its roots in the theoretical writings of Hermes Trismegistus, known collectively as the *Corpus Hermeticum*. Specifically, Hermetic drift is the "interpretive habit" [93] that follows from the Hermetic metaphysical principles of universal analogy and sympathy. According to these principles–which will subsequently enter and define the primary metaphysical concerns of Neoplatonists and Scholastics alike [94] –everything in the universe is related to everything else within the *discordia concors*, or *coincidentia oppositorum*, of God's original Oneness: "every item of the furniture of the world is linked to every other element (or to many) of this sublunar world and to every element (or to many) of the superior world by means of similitudes or resemblances." [95] As to the nature of Hermetic drift, then, Eco offers the following explanation:

> The main feature of Hermetic drift seems to be the uncontrolled ability to shift from meaning to meaning, from similarity to similarity from a connection to another . . . [however, it] does not assert the absence of any univocal universal and transcendental meaning. It assumes that everything can recall everything else . . . because there is a strong transcendent subject, the Neoplatonic One who (or which), being the principle of the universal contradiction, the place of the Coincidentia Oppositorum, and standing *outside of every possible determination*, . . . permits everything to connect with everything else by a *labyrinthine web of mutual referrals*. . . . [The consequence is] this world perfused with signatures, ruled . . . by the principle of universal significance . . . [and] producing a *perennial shift and deferral of any*

---

[92] See Eco's *Limits of Interpretation*, 18-20, 23-32. Properly speaking, the "drift" is a consequence or manifestation of the "semiosis." For Eco, however, the two notions are so intimately related that he shows no hesitation in using the terms interchangeably. See the citation to follow.

[93] Eco, *Limits*, 24.

[94] On the principle of universal analogy in Scholastic thought, see Eco's comments on "universal allegory" and the problems of Scholastic textual exegesis in *Art and Beauty*, 56 ff. and *Aquinas*, 141 ff. See also our discussion of Aquinas and Dante, above.

[95] Eco, *Limits*, 24. The impact of Hermes' analogical metaphysics on the Neoplatonists is, of course, substantial. See, for example, Hermetically inspired treatises on magic like Plotinus' *Ennead* 4.4.26 and 40-44, Proclus' *De sacrificio*, and Ficino's *De vita coelitus comparanda* in the *De triplici vita*. For more on this topic, see Brian Copenhaver, "Hermes Trismegistus, Proclus, and the Question of a Philosophy of Magic in the Renaissance," in *Hermeticism and the Renaissance*, 79-110.

> *possible meaning.* The meaning of a given word or of a given thing being another word or another thing, everything that has been said is in fact nothing else but an ambiguous allusion to something else. . . .
>
> Thus Hermetic semiosis transforms the whole world into a mere linguistic phenomenon but *devoids language of any communicative power.*[96]

In Hermetic Neoplatonism, therefore, linguistic signs (whether verbal or visual) encounter an insurmountable obstacle that is beyond their proper control and nature. What ultimately devoids all language of its communicative power is the inherent ineffability –perennial 'deferrability' or 'undeterminability'–of a presence which is always already absent, inextricably ensnared in the all-inclusive One's "labyrinthine web of mutual referrals."[97] By virtue of the divine Coincidentia Oppositorum, the Many that is One, any single sign must necessarily inscribe the meaning of every other. Thus semantically overloaded, every sign is doomed to short-circuit and self-efface, leaving an irremediable semantic absence.[98]

But again all is not lost for poetry and painting. For as their respect for inspirational madness and the divine frenzies clearly shows, the Neoplatonists do not confine communication to the purely rational processes of transmitting and receiving strictly determined and decipherable meanings. Neoplatonic epistemological theory also recognizes and encourages a kind of meta-rational, emotive communication. Beyond the discrete knowledge conveyed and

---

[96] Eco, *Limits*, 26-27.

[97] Regarding the ineffability of God and his infinite truths, see for example, Plotinus, *Ennead* 6 and Pico, *De Ente et Uno.*

[98] To illustrate this metaphysical predicament and the resulting semiotic conundrum, Eco evokes the well-known, Hermetically shaped arguments for the magical medicinal powers of the "orchis" (orchid) plant: "the plant orchis has the same form of human testicles; therefore not only does orchis stand for testicles but also every operation accomplished on the plant can get a result on the human body. [Thus] . . . a relationship of resemblance was established not only between the plant and the testicles but also between both and other elements of the furniture of the macro- and microcosm, so that, by means of different rhetorical relationships (such as similarity, past or present contiguity, and so on), every one of these elements could stand for and act upon every other": Eco, *Limits*, 29. This example of the Hermetic "Doctrine of Signatures" first emerges in the medical treatise of Dioscorides, a Greek botanist of the first century A.D. A survey of similar theories appears in Merle A. Reinikka, *A History of the Orchid* (Coral Gables: University of Miami Press, 1972), 3-10.

acquired through the senses and/or the intellectual faculty of reason, there is a more vague, yet infinitely more refined knowledge
that we exchange through the intuitive processes of the soul. [99]

The signs of success in this elevated mode of communication
are feelings of rapture or ravishment in the addressee. For most
Neoplatonists, these feelings–which unmistakably recall the sensations of religious ecstasy or, in a properly rhetorical vein, the impressions of sublimity and enthrallment praised and promoted by
Longinus in his literary-critical treatise of the first century A.D.,
On the Sublime–are particularly pronounced during encounters
with beauty. Indeed, Ficino holds the stimulation of rapture to
be the *sine qua non* of true beauty. As we learn from the *Commentarium in Convivium*, we know that we are in the presence of
such beauty only when we experience ravishment: "It is that
charm of virtue, or of form or sounds which calls and ravishes the
soul through thought, sight, or hearing that is most justly called
beautiful." [100]

Admittedly, unlike Longinus, who forthrightly announces that
"the object of poetry is to enthrall" (ἔκπληξις) (*Sublime* 15.2), [101]
no Neoplatonist ever openly maintains that poetry or painting
should or can achieve this rapturous mode of communication. Even
Plotinus' and Ficino's acclamations of hieroglyphs never mention
an ability to enrapture the spectator. Nevertheless, from the inclusion of poetry among the divine *furores*–as the frenzy, we recall, that
serves to "*arouse* the torpid parts" of the discordant soul–there is
reason to presume they would achieve the same effect.

However, to conclude from this that the Neoplatonists are primarily optimistic about the communicative powers of poetry and

---

[99] Cf. Gombrich, "*Icones*," 170.

[100] "Haec ipsa, seu virtutis, seu figurae, sive vocum gratia, quae animum per ra-
tionem vel visum vel auditum ad se vocat et rapit, pulchritudo rectissime dicitur":
Tatarkiewicz, *History*, 3:108 n. 2. We might compare this comment with Plotinus'
reflection on true beauty in *Ennead* 1.6.4: "But there must be those [people] who
see . . . beauty by that with which the soul sees things of this sort, and when they see
it they must be delighted and overwhelmed and excited . . . since now it is true
beauty they are grasping. These experiences must occur whenever there is contact
with any sort of beautiful thing, wonder and a shock of delight and longing and
passion and a happy excitement" (1:244-45). See also Ficino's commentary on Plotinus' passage: "It is characteristic of beauty that it allures and ravishes" ("Proprium
vero pulchritudinis est allicere simul et rapere") (ibid., 109 n. 9).

[101] Longinus, *On the Sublime*, trans. W. Hamilton Fyfe, in *Aristotle: The Poetics*
(London: G. P. Putnam's Sons, 1932), 170-71.

painting would be to strain the textual evidence. Neoplatonic aesthetic theory is simply too plagued by paradoxes to permit such an assessment. Indeed, for the same reason it is unwise to give facile credence to the critical readings that would allege the Neoplatonic philosophers prefer one form of art over another.[102] As we have seen, the Neoplatonists are loath to allow any virtue of poetry or painting to go unchecked by a counterbalancing vice. In fact, the same problem ultimately applies to all the philosophers and philosophical traditions previously inspected. Whether in the writings of any single theorist or in those of theorists of the same philosophical persuasion, every claim for the ability of poetry and/or painting to give presence to the real (whether physical or ideal) seems invariably to invite a counterclaim that undermines or squarely opposes that position.

As the paragone conflict heats up during the fifteenth and sixteenth centuries, then, there is good reason to expect a perpetuation of these paradoxes. As Renaissance poets and painters turn to these conceptual antecedents for help in propounding the superiority of their respective art forms, they are bound to reinscribe many of these inconsistencies. This is not to suggest, however, that the verbal and visual artists are always the unconscious mirrors of their paradox filled theoretical predecessors. While otherwise ensnared in the intractable ambivalences of the psychological double bind, most paragone contestants are adept at manipulating these inconsistencies to their own advantage. Although their deeper impulse to ambivalence prevents any definitive defense of one art's supremacy over another, most competing poets and painters are fully able to commandeer and exploit the theoretical ammunition that best suits their needs.

C. *The Case of Leonardo da Vinci*

Of the numerous Renaissance painters who would exemplify this ability, Leonardo da Vinci is by far the most intriguing and, for the present study, the most important. He takes the greatest advan-

---

[102] In addition to the bias for visual symbolism, and hence the visual arts, identified by Gombrich ("*Icones*"), there is the contrary and paradoxical preference for the arbitrariness of verbal signification, and thus poetry and the verbal arts, discerned by Krieger (*Ekphrasis*, 20-21).

tage of the previous theoretical paradoxes in his argument for the superiority of painting over poetry, and as the investigation of Ronsard's poetry will show, his distinctive assortment of theoretical premises may stand among the chief foils to the Pléiade leader's own positions in the paragone.

Although Leonardo's rudimentary knowledge of Latin forced him to rely on editions in his vernacular Italian and discussions with humanist contemporaries for an initiation to most of the philosophers we have pondered, there can be little doubt that he knew their ideas well. [103] Despite some claims to the contrary, his relative ignorance of the original philosophical literature scarcely impeded his discovery and understanding of the philosophical ideas themselves. [104] In fact, this less formal mode of contact may have contributed to his exceptional ability and willingness to manipulate these ideas in the way he finally does. Free from the burden of accounting for the detailed expositions of the written primary sources, Leonardo succeeds in gaining the broadest perspective on each philosopher's (and philosophical system's) principal theoretical paradoxes and the facets of those paradoxes that best serve the defense of painting.

Without a doubt Leonardo's foremost preoccupations, in the paragone passages of the *Trattato della pittura*, are the attacks on the mimetic arts mounted by Plato and the Neoplatonists. Seeking to assure that painting would ascend to the highest rank in the hierarchy of intellectual and artistic endeavors—to promote it from a mere "mechanical" art (an enterprise entailing manual labor and the mindless copying of nature) [105] to a mathematical Liberal Art of the Quadrivium, and from there to a philosophical Art of the Triv-

---

[103] On Leonardo's knowledge of Latin, his library experiences, and his association with the humanists of his time, see Martin Kemp, *Leonardo da Vinci: The Marvellous Works of Nature and Man* (Cambridge, Mass.: Harvard University Press, 1981), 91-151.

[104] François Lecercle speaks boldly of Leonardo's "éducation qui l'a protégé de toute contamination humaniste" (*Chimère*, 38). As the following pages will show, however, this humanist contamination is the very starting and ending point of his theoretical pronouncements. For more on Leonardo's debt to previous philosophers and philosophical traditions, see Anthony Blunt, *Artistic Theory in Italy 1450-1600* (Oxford: Clarendon Press, 1940), 23-38.

[105] Derived from Aristotle's concept of the applied sciences, the 'mechanical' arts receive the greatest attention in the writings of the Scholastics. For the history of this notion, see Richter, *Leonardo*, 1:16-18; and Tatarkiewicz, *History*, 1:307-14; 2:253-56.

ium, where it might join with, and ultimately surpass, poetry (which had long before earned a place within that august triad) [106]–the Florentine genius clearly understands that this goal cannot be reached without confronting their criticisms. Above all, he must counter their charge against the epistemological limitations of the painter, the notion that the pictorial artist is prevented from knowing and communicating ideal essences by the materiality of his works and a slavish dependence upon matter-based 'reality' (the 'evil' shadows of the shadows of Ideas) for objects of imitation.

To accomplish this daunting task, Leonardo mounts a multi-pronged and largely disjointed argument (due mainly to the fragmented configuration of the *Trattato* manuscripts). Its immediate purpose is to deconstruct these complaints by recalling and reshaping all of the painting-friendly commentaries at his command, including those of Plato and the Neoplatonists. The first such deconstruction focuses on redefining the locus of the ideal essences. For Plato, we recall, those essences are situated beyond the 'cave' of our common worldly experience and knowledge, in a domain accessible solely through the powers of philosophy-guided reason. Similarly, for the Neoplatonists they dwell outside of material existence, in the ineffable One that is best comprehended intuitively, through the intercessions of the soul on its return to God's original unity via the course of ever more enlightening frenzies. Hence, in both cases, the higher truths are remote from the natural and man-made entities that Leonardo and all the philosophers recognize as the principal objects of the painter's mimetic concern. For Leonardo, then, the aim is to redeem the inessential realm of the corporeal by establishing that this reality, and the painter's knowledge and representation of it, are in fact also essential, imbued or in touch with ideal presences.

In proceeding toward that end, however, he never quite takes the path we might expect. Rather than evoke any facet of Aristotle's redefinition of the real (whether out of ignorance or, what is likelier, a reasonable desire to avoid falling victim to the same paradoxes as the Stagirite [107]), he prefers to focus on painting's essential affiliation

---

[106] See above and notes 10-11. See also, Chapter Three, 213 and note 89.

[107] See above, pp. 43 ff. It is interesting to note that Leonardo likewise fails to acknowledge the related redefinition of reality offered in *Epistolae* 65 and 68 of Seneca the Younger and in the medieval commentaries on Seneca's letters by Johannes de Garlandia, Robert Grosseteste, Robert Bacon, and Dante (one of

with the sense of sight. Although this epistemologically oriented way of establishing painting's relation to the higher truths proves somewhat less direct than Aristotle's, it is also perfectly conducive to Leonardo's short- and long-range goals. At the same time it takes advantage of Plato's and the Neoplatonists' own admiration for sight to begin the process of dismantling their objections against painting, it allows for poetry, the art most intimately associated with hearing and Leonardo's most troublesome adversary, to be drawn squarely into the debate.

Trattato 19 presents one of the clearest perspectives on Leonardo's tactics and premises. The treatise appropriately begins with an affirmation of the superiority of the eye over the ear: "The eye, which is the window of the soul, is the chief organ whereby the understanding can have the most complete and magnificent view of the infinite works of nature; and the ear comes second, which acquires dignity by hearing the things the eye has seen." [108] From the start, Leonardo insists that the eye and its corresponding art form, painting, enjoy a privileged mediating position between the human faculties most intimately allied with God and the highest truths, the understanding (i.e., rational intellect) and the soul. By association, the eye and painting are likewise accorded a place in that alliance, a significant role in the communication of ideal knowledge as intermediary receiver and transmitter. Further, Leonardo invites an important (if logically dubious) inference about the metaphysical status of the natural (i.e., sublunary) world. By relating the essence-linked eye/painting with the works of nature, he implies a connection between those essences and works: a critical (albeit mediated) affinity between the supreme verities and the natural world that effectively redeems the latter much as Aristotle's metaphysical redefinition had done. Leonardo is then in a position to make his later point about mathematicians: "If you . . . mathematicians . . . had

---

Leonardo's favorite poets). See Panofsky, *Idea*, 19-25; and the relevant entries in John Edwin Sandys, *A History of Classical Scholarship*, vol. 1 (3rd ed.; Cambridge: Cambridge University Press, 1921). While it is impossible to account with certainty for this omission, it may simply be that, like Dante and his medieval predecessors, Leonardo still knew Seneca primarily for his moral and scientific theories.

[108] "L'occhio, che si dice finestra dell'anima, è la principal uia, donde il comune senso pò più copiosa et magnificamente considerare l'infinite opere di natura, et l'orecchio è 'l secondo, il quale si fa nobile per le cose raconte, le quali ha ueduto l'occhio . . ." (1:56).

never seen things with your eyes, you could report but imperfectly on them in your writing." [109] His insistence that the number philosophers depend upon sight in order to conduct their investigations does more than advance his case for promoting painting from the Quadrivium to the Trivium. It also draws attention to nature, the object of the mathematician's concerns via the eye and painting, as a bearer of numerical qualities and thus (in implied agreement with the number-privileging metaphysics of the Pythagoreans and Plato himself) ideal truths. [110]

The same passage begins to undermine the Platonic complaint against the accuracy of painted images. Whereas Plato identifies that accuracy with deception and a distancing from the ideas, Leonardo associates it with veracity and essential plenitude: "And if you, oh poet, tell a story with your pen, the painter with his brush can tell it more easily, with simpler completeness and so that it is less tedious to follow." [111] His redemption of nature and objective reality does much to move this position forward. However, they are his elaborations upon what this accuracy truly entails that finally cement the connection and bring out his most compelling and distinctive charges against poetry.

As we have learned, this accuracy is fundamentally a matter of achieving a magnificent yet simple completeness. Painting presents the infinite multiplicity of nature in a way that is at once empirically authentic and complete in its unified totality, and that is therefore easily comprehensible and engaging to the psyche and spirit (what Longinus calls 'enthralling' and the Neoplatonists, 'ravishing'). Leonardo expounds on the nature of these effects and how they are realized as *Trattato* 19 proceeds. Regarding the relative authenticity

---

[109] "[S]e uoi . . . matematici non hauestiue con l'occhio uisto le cose, male le potreste uoi rifferire per le scritture" (1:56).

[110] This relation is more explicit in *Trattato* 14, amid a reflection on the superiority of natural-sign painting over conventional-sign poetry: "Painting serves a nobler sense than poetry and represents the works of nature with more truth than the poet. The works of nature are much nobler than speech which was invented by man; *for the works of man are to the works of nature as man is to God.*" ("La pittura serve a più degno senso, che la poesia, e fa con più verità le figure delle opere di natura ch'il poeta; e sono molto più degne l'opere di natura chelle parole, che sono l'opera dell'homo, *perche tal proportione è da l'opere delli homini a' quelle della natura, qual è quella, ch'è dal homo a dio.*") (1:55: my emphasis).

[111] "[E]t se tu, poeta, figurerai una istoria, con la pittura della penna, il pittore col penello la farà di più facile sattisfatione et meno tediosa ad essere compresa" (1:56).

of poetry and painting, for example, he subsequently insists that "[alt]hough the poet is as free to invent, as the painter, his fictions do not give so great a satisfaction to men as painting, for though poetry is able to describe forms, actions, and places in words, *the painter employs the exact images of the forms and represents them as they are*." [112] For Leonardo as for the Neoplatonists, the empirical authenticity of painting is directly linked to the naturalness of visual signs. Unlike the poet, whose verbal signifiers are merely conventional and arbitrary, man-made names that "chang[e] with change of country" ("si uaria[n] in uarij paesi") (1:57), the painter uses "exact images" ("le proprie similitudini")–i.e., natural signs–"to reproduce forms as they are" ("a contrafare [113] esse forme"). [114]

This naturalistic authenticity contributes, in turn, to a more pragmatic quality of painting: its ability to produce satisfaction ("satisfatione"). A picture can fulfill certain yearnings or needs in the addressee (its spectator) that the word-bound poem cannot. But what are the precise features of this satisfaction, and which facets of the natural pictorial signs do most to make them possible? Leonardo's famous battle-scene example in the same treatise helps to answer these vital questions:

> But I shall ask no more than that a good painter should represent the fury of a battle and that the poet should describe one and that both these battles be put before the public. You will

---

[112] "[S]e 'l poeta è libero come 'l pittore nelle inuentioni, le sue fintioni non sonno di tanta satisfatione alli homini, quanto le pitture; perche, se la poesia s'estende con le parolle a figurare forme, atti e siti, *il pittore si moue con le proprie similitudini delle forme a contrafare esse forme*" (1:57: my emphasis).

[113] In the fifteenth century, the verb 'to counterfeit' still carries its neutral or positive Medieval Latin sense of 'to make in imitation' or, as in this case, 'to copy with substantial exactness'. It is not until the sixteenth century that it will begin to acquire the more negative connotations of 'to feign' or 'to falsify'. For more on this term see A. J. Greimas, *Dictionnaire de l'ancien français* (Paris: Librairie Larousse, 1968), 138; Randle Cotgrave, *A Dictionarie of the French and English Tongues, 1611* (Menston: Scolar Press Ltd., 1968); Grahame Castor, *Pléiade Poetics* (Cambridge: Cambridge University Press, 1964), 57, 123, 172-73. See also the discussion of the opening stanza of *Des peintures contenues dedans un tableau* in Chapter Two.

[114] Leonardo is more explicit about the conventionality of words and the naturalness of images in *Trattato* 14 (see note 110, above). See also *Trattato* 2: "poetry puts down her subjects in imaginary written characters, while painting puts down the identical reflections that the eye receives, as if they were real ['natural']. . . ." ("la poesia pon' le sue cose nell' immaginatione de lettere, e la pittura le da realmente fori del occhio, dal qual occhio riceve le similitudini non altrimente che s'elle fussino naturali. . . .") (52).

soon see which will draw more of the spectators and where there
will be more discussion, to which more praise will be given, and
which will satisfy the more. Undoubtedly the painting, being by
far more intelligible and beautiful, will please most. [115]

Here as elsewhere, the battle-scene example highlights crucial
premises in Leonardo's 'battle' for the supremacy of painting over
poetry. In this instance, it openly announces the dominant features
of the satisfaction at issue. For Leonardo, a battle depicted in paint
is eminently more pleasing than one described in words to the degree that it is more intelligible (i.e., informative and comprehensible) [116] and conducive to the principles of beauty. In regard to what
makes these features possible, however, it is necessary to turn to the
battle-scene remarks in *Trattato* 15. In words that strongly recall (if
not imitate and manipulate) Plotinus' and Ficino's commentaries on
the advantages of hieroglyphic images, the painter-theorist sounds
one of the most compelling and distinctive themes in all of his
paragone-related writings: the theme of pictorial simultaneity, or
synchrony:

> "If you, poet, had to represent a murderous battle you would
> have to describe the air obscured and darkened by fumes from
> frightful and deadly engines mixed with thick clouds of dust pol-
> luting the atmosphere, and the panicky flight of wretches fearful
> of horrible death. In that case the painter will be your superior,
> because your pen will be worn out before you can fully describe
> what the painter can demonstrate *forthwith* by the aid of his sci-
> ence . . . *in an instant*. . . . [E]ach figure is represented so as to
> show *completely* that part which faces the given direction. What
> long and tedious work it would be for poetry to describe all the

---

[115] "[M]a io non uoglio da questi tali altro, che uno bono pittore, che figuri 'l
furore d'una battaglia, e che 'l poeta ne scriui un' altra, e che sieno messi in pubbli-
co di compagnia. Uedrai, doue più si fermeranno li ueditori, doue più conside-
reranno, doue si darà più laude, et quale satisfarà meglio. certo la pittura *di gran
longa più uttile et bella* più piacerà" (1:57: my emphasis).

[116] We agree with Richter in imputing to "uttile" a properly intellectual signification not immediately apparent in its more common modern meaning of 'useful'.
This reading is not only consistent with the use of the term throughout the history
of Western aesthetics (as in Plato's and Horace's insistence on the moral and intellectual 'utility' of art in the *Republic* and the *Ars Poetica*, respectively), but it also
agrees with Leonardo's other comments about the intelligibility of painting (see the
excerpt from *Trattato* 20 reproduced in Chapter 2). See also our discussion of
Aquinas, above (p. 55 and n. 55); and Barasch, *Theories*, 136.

movements of the fighters in such a battle and the actions of their limbs and their ornaments. This is accomplished with *great directness and truth* in painting." [117]

The synchronous ontology of the visual sign is among the chief advantages of painting over poetry. By being directly and entirely present to the eye in an instant, the visual image enjoys not only a certain completeness, but also a privileged veracity and intelligibility, even in the case of the pictorial recreation of a multi-faceted battle. In poetry, on the other hand, such qualities are invariably absent. Like Ficino, Leonardo finds verbal diachrony a threat to the communication of ideas. The temporal sequentiality of words imposes a delay on the representational process that the reader-addressee can only find tedious and confusing.

The quality of simultaneousness also abets the true and satisfying imitation of beauty. Although this benefit is never fully identified in the present passage, it receives full attention in *Trattato* 21. Here Leonardo shifts his concern from battles to portraits so as to inject more felicitously the Pythagorean and (Neo-)Platonic aesthetic concepts of harmony and proportion and, ultimately, in order to introduce notions reminiscent of the Longinian enthrallment and the Neoplatonic rapture:

> And from painting which serves the eye, the noblest sense, arises *harmony of proportions*; just as many different voices joined together and singing *simultaneously* produce a harmonious proportion which gives such satisfaction to the sense of hearing that listeners remain *spellbound with admiration as if half alive*. But the effect of the beautiful proportion of an angelic face in painting is much greater, for these proportions produce a *harmonious concord* which reaches the eye *simultaneously*, just as (a chord in) music affects the ear; and if this beautiful harmony be

---

[117] "Se tu, poeta figurerai la sanguinosa battaglia, si sta con la oscura e tenebrosa aria, mediante il fumo delle spauenteuoli et mortali macchine, miste con la spessa poluere intorbidatrice dell' aria, e la paurosa fuga delli miseri spauentati dalla horribile morte. In questo caso il pittore ti supera, perche la tua penna fia consumata, inanzi che tu descriua a' pieno quel, che *immediate* il pittore ti rapresenta con la sua scientia . . . *in un istante*. . . . [I]n ciascun corpo è *l'integrità* di quella parte, che per un solo aspetto puo dimostrarsi, il che longa et tediosissima cosa sarebbe alla poesia a ridire tutti li mouimenti delli operatori di tal guerra, e le parti delle membra, e lor' ornamenti, delle quali cose la pittura finita con *gran' breuità e uerità*" (1:53: my emphasis).

shown to the lover of her whose beauties are portrayed, he will without doubt remain *spellbound in admiration and in a joy without parallel and superior to all other sensations.*[118]

However paradoxical the musical analogy might seem given its possible poetic connotations and Leonardo's paragone with the musician's art in other treatises,[119] it permits a convenient connection between painting and the Pythagorean, Platonic, and Neoplatonic concepts of ideal beauty, whose common model is the proportioned and all-unifying *harmony* of the celestial spheres. As Leonardo carefully points out, painting can generate just such a harmony, and hence just such a perfect beauty, precisely because it presents itself to the senses "simultaneously" ("in uno medesimo tempo"). Like a chord in music, a picture is able to conjoin a multitude of diverse elements in proportions that render a beautiful "harmonious concord" ("armonico concento"). Accordingly, like that beautiful concinnity, painting can also excite a certain ravishment in the soul. By virtue of its inherent all-at-onceness, it can spellbind to cause a kind of ecstatic half-death (or here, half-life). For Leonardo, this effect is especially apparent in the case of the painted portrait. Because of its synchronous ontology, such a picture can reproduce an angelic face in all of its proportioned and harmoniously unified beauty and, in so doing, enthrall and enrapture the most discriminating viewer in an unparalleled admiration and joy ("istupenda ammiratione e gaudio").

---

[118] "[M]a della pittura, perche serue al' occhio, senso più nobile, che l'orecchio, obbietto della poesia, ne risulta *una proportione armonicha*, cioè, che si come di molte uarie uoci insieme aggionte *ad un medesimo tempo*, ne risulta una proportione armonicha, la quale contenta tanto il senso dello audito, che li auditori restano *con stupente ammiratione, quasi semiuiui*. ma molto più farà le proportionali bellezze d'un angelico uiso, posto in pittura, della quale proportionalità ne risulta un' *armonico concento*, il quale serue al' occhio *in uno medesimo tempo*, che si faccia dalla musica all' orecchio, e se tale armonia delle bellezze sarà mostrata allo amante di qualla, da chi tale bellezze sono imitate, sanza dubbio esso resterà *con istupenda ammiratione e gaudio incomparabile e superiore a tutti l'altri sensi*" (1:59-60: my emphasis).

[119] See Richter, *Leonardo*, 69-81. Despite this analogy, Leonardo is always careful to avoid a full identification of painting and music. Their differences are more clearly drawn in *Trattato* 23: "But the harmony of music is less noble that the harmony which appeals to the eye, because sound dies as soon as it is born, and its death is as swift as its birth, and this cannot happen with the sense of sight." ("le proportionalità detta armonia . . . di diverse uoci . . . è men degno, che quello dell'occhio, perche tanto, quanto ne nasce, tanto ne more, et è si veloce nel morire, come nel nascere. il che intervenire non pò nel senso del vedere.") (1:61).

By contrast, a poem about the same angelic face can capture none of that satisfying beauty. Its diachronous signs prevent the representation of more than one facial feature at a time. That poem can never render the whole, and thus never recreate the essential proportions and harmonious concinnity of true angelic beauty: "a poem which aims at the representation of perfect beauty has to describe separately each particular part that makes up the harmony of a picture; . . . [it is as] if a face were to be revealed bit by bit with the part previously shown covered up, so that we are prevented by our forgetfulness from composing any harmony of proportions. . . ." [120]

Thus, by cleverly manipulating the salient paradoxes of some of the most enduring aesthetic commentaries of his theoretical antecedents, Leonardo manages to overcome virtually all of the major complaints against the painter and his art (if only, it is true, within the confines of the problematic logic of the *Trattato*). Indeed, he can even deconstruct the most famous of all theoretical pronouncements on the pictorial arts, the chiasmic aphorism that Plutarch attributes to the sixth- or fifth-century B.C. poet, Simonides of Ceos: painting is mute poetry; poetry a speaking picture.[121] Although this proverbial declaration is in fact one of the original rallying cries for inter-art parity and the vogue of literary pictorialism more typically identified with the (pseudo-)Horatian principle of ut pictura poesis, Leonardo reads 'muteness' as a poet's codeword for 'dumbness', a lack of communicative ability, and thus Simonides' overall assertion as a thinly veiled claim for the preeminence of poetry, which can 'speak' (communicate). [122] From his position on the primacy of the eye and the arsenal of premises that serve to support that proposition, Leonardo finally counters by reminding the conceited poets that "if you call painting dumb poetry, the painter may

---

[120] "[D]ella poesia, la qual s'abbia à stendere alla figuratione d'una perfetta bellezza con la figuratione particulare di ciaschuna parte, della quale si compone in pittura la predetta armonia, . . . come se uolessimo mostrare un' uolto à parte à parte, sempre ricoprendo quelle, che prima si mostrano, delle quali dimostrationi l'obliuione non lascia comporre alcuna proportionalità d'armonia . . ." (1:60).

[121] *Moralia* 346f (in the essay, *Bellone an Pace Clariores Fuerint Athenienses*, or simply, *De Gloria Atheniensium*). For the original Greek, see Plutarch, *Moralia* 4, trans. Frank Cole Babbitt (Cambridge: Harvard University Press, 1936), 500.

[122] This interpretation was fairly common among the poets and painters of Leonardo's day. See, for example, Francesco d'Hollanda's protests against the poets in his second *Dialogo* (Richter, *Leonardo*, 1:56 n. 23.2).

call poetry *blind* painting" ("se tu dimanderai la pittura mutta poesia, anchora il pittore potra dire la poesia *orba* pittura") (*Tr.* 19; 1:56: my emphasis).

In the end, then, Leonardo's painter is able to do virtually anything. Besides imitating the 'reality' of the material world, he can portray every sort of abstract truth and idea. Just as the legendary Greek master, Apelles, could figure diverse customs and morals in his allegorical portrait of Calumny ("si pò dimostrare molti morali costumi, come fece Apelle con la sua calunnia": *Tr.* 19; 1:58) at the end of the fourth century B.C., so too Leonardo's painter can depict whatever he has "first in his mind and then in his hands" ("prima nella mente, e poi nelle mani": *Tr.* 13; 1:54) at the end of the fifteenth century A.D. In fact, as we learn from *Trattato* 13, so great are the painter's powers to depict "whatever exists in the universe, in essence, in appearance, in the imagination" ("ciò, ch'è nel' uniuerso per essentia, presentia o' immaginatione": 1:54) that the Florentine would make him a veritable god: "If the painter wishes to see beauties that charm him . . . he can be lord and God thereof; . . . if he wants from high mountain tops to unfold a great plain extending down to the sea's horizon, he is lord to do so. . . ." [123]

※ ※ ※

Pierre de Ronsard's approach to the contest between poetry and painting bears important similarities to that of Leonardo da Vinci one half century earlier. Of course, it is unlikely Ronsard could have laid hands on Leonardo's original commentaries since, although written between 1489 and 1518, [124] the *Trattato* notes were never formally published before 1651, and since after Leonardo's death in 1519, the manuscripts were guarded like relics ("come per reliquie") [125] by his disciple and inheritor, Francesco Melzi, at the latter's Vaprio villa near Milan. [126] Nevertheless, their enthusiasm for

---

[123] "Sel pittore vol vedere bellezze, che lo innamorino . . . ei n'è signore et dio . . . se vole delle alte sime de' monti scoprire gran campagne, et se vole dopo quelle uedere l'orizzonte del mare, egli ne signore . . ." (1:54).

[124] Blunt, *Theory*, 23.

[125] Giorgio Vasari, *Le Vite de' più eccellenti pittori, scultori ed architettori*, ed. Gaetano Milanesi, 9 vols. (rpt. 1906; Florence: G. C. Sansoni, 1981), 4:35.

[126] The manuscripts became far more accessible after Melzi's death in 1570, though again it is doubtful Ronsard had the opportunity to see them or (as we shall see) ever needed to do so. See Richter, *Leonardo*, 1:5-11.

the paragone is very much the same. Both painter and poet are equally caught up in the fiery revival of this perennial competition for presence. While indebted to the treasure of ekphrastic literature that precedes him, in other words, Ronsard is in no way that literature's idle caretaker. When the Pléiade laureate describes or refers to a painting in his poetry, he engages the central issues of the paragone debate with the same persistent passion as Leonardo. In addition, both contestants are deeply inspired by the philosophers and aesthetic commentators that precede them. Although neither man's paragone-related writings actually name these antecedents, their influence is unmistakable. This is not to imply that the Florentine painter and the French laureate merely parrot what was said in the past. Like the Leonardo we have just examined, Ronsard takes a highly original approach in presenting his position in the debate. And as with Leonardo's approach, that of Ronsard derives its efficacy from the manipulation of the paradoxes plaguing the theoretical substructure. More than borrow shrewdly from the conducive metaphysical, epistemological, semiotic, and aesthetic principles of the past, it takes inspiration for new theoretical directions from their very inconsistencies.

For all of their similarities, though, Ronsard and Leonardo take sharply opposing sides in the inter-art contest. Despite their common theoretical foundation, the poet and the painter move first to exalt their own respective art forms. As our examination of the poems on narrative painting will show, Ronsard sets out primarily to advocate the power of poetry. In fact it will also reveal that Ronsard's most immediate conceptual foils in that pursuit often resemble the notions and arguments Leonardo puts forward. Again, this in no way means that Ronsard ever enjoyed direct access to Leonardo's manuscripts. Nor is it likely he would have needed such contact. The thoughts they contain had almost certainly perfused French artistic culture long before Ronsard's day, since at least the time Leonardo gained the patronage of Louis XII in French-controlled Milan between 1506-1513, and later, the support and friendship of François I, at whose invitation the Florentine moved to Amboise in 1516 [127] (hence for about half the span of years Leonardo devoted to his original *Trattato* notes).

---

[127] Jean Adhémar, *Le Dessin français au XVIe siècle* (Luzon: Mermod, 1954), 99.

Beyond that most obvious difference, however, the poet is also more deeply affected by a sense of ambivalence in this rivalry. Unlike Leonardo, who pursues his glorification of painting with a distinct singleness of mind, Ronsard experiences moments of hesitation. This hesitation becomes especially apparent when it comes to painted portraiture. There the laureate betrays an admiration for the possibilities of painting that signals an inability to escape the effects of the paragone's concomitant double bind: the conflictual desire to be both different from and like one's artistic rival. The signs, sources, and consequences of Ronsard's complex role in the paragone are the focal points of the chapters that follow.

CHAPTER TWO

THE POEMS ON NARRATIVE PAINTING

When the King had seen this model [for a palace door at Fontainebleau] . . . I uncovered the other model . . . it figured a fountain shaped in a perfect square, with handsome steps all around.... In the middle of the fountain I set a pedestal, projecting somewhat above the margin of the basin, and upon this a nude male figure. . . . In his right hand he raised a broken lance on high; his left hand rested on a scimitar; he was poised upon the left foot, the right being supported by a helmet of the richest imaginable workmanship. At each of the four angles of the fountain a figure was sitting, raised above the level of the base, and accompanied by many beautiful and appropriate emblems.

The King began by asking me what I meant to represent by the fine fancy I had embodied in this design, saying that he had understood the door without explanation, but that he could not take the conception of my fountain, although it seemed to him most beautiful; at the same time, he knew well that I was not like those foolish folk who turn out something with a kind of grace, but put no intention into their performances. (Benvenuto Cellini, *Vita,* 2.22)[1]

---

[1] "Veduto il re questo modello . . . gli scopersi l'altro modello . . . nel quale avevo fatto una fontana in forma d'un quadro prefetto.... In mezzo a detta fontana avevo fatto un sodo, il quale si dimostrava un poco più alto che 'l ditto vaso della fontana: sopra questo sodo avevo fatto . . . una figura ignuda.... Questa teneva una lancia rotta nella man destra elevata in alto, e la sinistra teneva in sul manico d'una sua storta fatta di bellissima forma: posava in sul piè manco, e il ritto teneva in su un cimiere tanto riccamente lavorato, quanto immaginar si possa: e in su e' quattro canti della fontana avevo fatto, in su ciascuno, una figura a sedere elevata, con molte sue vaghe imprese per ciascuna. Cominciommi a dimandare il re che io gli dicessi che bella fantasia era quella che io avevo fatta; dicendomi che tutto quello che

In one of the early critical commentaries on Pierre de Ronsard's poetry about painting, Jean Plattard maintained that, like all the major French writers of his day, the Pléiade laureate had the highest regard for the historical, mythological, and biblical paintings produced at Fontainebleau by the hands and workshops of imported Italian masters such as Giovanni Battista Rosso and Francesco Primaticcio (fig. 3). By Plattard's estimation, Ronsard would even prefer this story, or 'narrative', type of painting[2] to the genre of pictorial portraiture that grew increasingly more popular during the second third of the century following the extraordinary accomplishments of royal and court portrait painters like François Clouet and Corneille de Lyon. According to this critic, Ronsard and his poet contemporaries "donn[ent] naturellement à ces peintures historiques et mythologiques la préférence sur les portraits."[3]

The appeal, Plattard claimed, is two-fold. On the one hand, such early modern narrative painting displays a distinctive frankness in the treatment of the naked body, or what the critic euphemistically called a "hardiesse et . . . liberté de l'imagination." Unlike the French portraits of the period, in which Plattard found only an "expression toujours modeste et chaste," the story paintings regularly make the most of "la fougue, la volupté, la sensualité," attributes that best define the essence of the human (especially human female) form. On the other hand, such pictures are also endowed with "l'ampleur de la conception." This vaguely defined property subsumes two complementary characteristics. In one sense, story paintings typically feature a multiplicity of subject matters—a variety of figures and, often, a number of different episodes. Portraits, by contrast, would make a conscious reduction of all such variety ("une élimination presque systématique des accessoires et du décor") and exhibit a near obsessive attention to petty physiognomic detail ("une application minutieuse concentrée uniquement sur la physionomie du modèle"). In another sense, story pictures

io avevo fatto alla porta, sanza dimandarmi di nulla lui l'aveva inteso, ma che questo della fonte, se bene gli pareva bellissimo, nulla non intendeva; e ben sapeva che io non avevo fatto come gli altri sciocchi, che, se bene e' facevano cose con qualche poco di grazia, le facevano senza significato nissuno." Benvenuto Cellini, *Vita*, ed. Ettore Camesasca (Milan: Rizzoli, 1954), 279-80; *The Life of Benvenuto Cellini*, trans. John Addington Symonds, 2nd ed. (New York: Charles Scribner's Sons, 1920), 299-300.

[2] See the Introduction.
[3] Plattard, "Les Arts," 491.

FIG. 3: Il Rosso Fiorentino, *Galerie François I* (1528-40), Fontainebleau (Réunion des Musées Nationaux)

can accomplish a special semantic transcendence. Beyond portraiture, where Plattard (citing Joachim du Bellay's *Discours au roy sur
la Poésie*) detected an ability only to represent "'après le vif un naturel visage'," the purely material "caractère de l'original" perceivable to the outer eye, narrative painting can imitate both physical
matter and abstractions. It can depict events, sentiments, and ideas
understandable to the inner eye and proper to the highest order of
universal realities. [4]

Plattard was undeniably correct when he asserted that Ronsard
considers these virtues as "caractéristiques du génie de la poésie et
des arts en général." [5] Sensual frankness and conceptual magnitude,
in both senses, are explicit and implicit goals throughout his poetry.
Nevertheless, it is far from certain that the poet's esteem for these
qualities truly translates into a high regard for narrative painting.
On the contrary, there is strong evidence to suggest that Ronsard
denies all but the most superficial virtues to this art form. While acknowledging the affinity of story painting for visual variety and a
certain sensual accuracy (particularly as concerns its true-to-life
mimesis of the physical world), the Pléiade laureate conveys serious
misgivings about its ideational capabilities. As if to transpose and
build upon François I's perplexed reaction to Benvenuto Cellini's
maquette for the Fontainebleau fountain (as observed by the visit-
ing Florentine sculptor in the spring of 1542), Ronsard discerns and
decries the conceptual conundrums produced by the iconographically overloaded narrative picture. In word and example he is loath
to allow that such artworks can give presence to the celestial and
super-celestial realities. However skillfully the story picture may be
rendered, it, like Cellini's beautiful allegorical fountain, is doomed
to semantic multiplicity and obscurity as its physically fragmented
visual subject matters resist combination into meaningful conceptual harmonies. [6] Thus the very essence of the picture impedes it from
disentangling the Neoplatonists' "labyrinthine web of mutual refer-

---

[4] Plattard, "Les Arts," 490-92.
[5] Plattard, "Les Arts," 492.
[6] Although Cellini reports that the king subsequently announced, "'Verily I
have found a man here after my own heart'" ("'Veramente io ho trovato uno uomo
sicondo il cuor mio'") (*Life*, Symonds, 300; *Vita*, Camesasca, 280-81), in fact this
appreciation is not expressed before the sculptor has provided a lengthy verbal explanation of his proposed masterpiece.

rals," from successfully taming the shifting and deferring of all possible meanings in the perennial drift of Hermetic semiosis.

I. PAINTING IN THE 'DRIFT'

A. *A son Luc*

Ronsard's earliest words on narrative painting appear amid the Horatianesque tribute to the divinity of the poetic enterprise in *A son Luc*, the oldest known ode of his career, presumed to date from 1541-1543.[7] Following a revealing remark about the special affective qualities of portraits (to which we shall return in the next chapter), Ronsard takes up the case of story paintings, recognizable by the reference to the landscape (in verse 99).[8] Here the poet raises many of the key issues on which he will focus time and again throughout his paragone-related commentaries:

> C'est un celeste present
> Transmis çà bas où nous sommes,
> Qui regne encore à present
> Pour lever en haut les hommes:
> Car ainsi que Dieu a fait
> De rien le monde parfait,

---

[7] 2:155-56 n. 2. Unless otherwise indicated, Paul Laumonier is my authority for all chronological identifications of Ronsard's odes. Specific dates are taken from his notes to the *Œuvres complètes* or from his monumental study, *Ronsard poète lyrique* (Geneva: Slatkine, 1972) (henceforth *RPL*).

[8] It is true, of course, that atmospheric and terrestrial elements had served as important symbolic adjuncts of character and mood in portraiture since at least the Quattrocento; and by the mid-sixteenth century, landscape painting was in fact emerging as a pictorial genre in its own right. At the same time, however, the landscape likewise represented a distinctive feature of early modern mythological and historical painting (not to mention the religious art, which effectively constitutes a synthesis of both). The works of Charles Dorigny, Noël Jallier, Jean Cousin the Elder, and, later, Nicolò dell'Abate provide the best examples of the use of landscape in the narrative painting of the first half of the sixteenth century. See the relevant entries in Sylvie Béguin, et al., *L'Ecole de Fontainebleau* (Paris: Musées Nationaux, 1972); Louis Joxe, et al., *Fontainebleau*, 2 vols. (Ottawa: National Gallery of Canada, 1973); Anthony Blunt, *Art and Architecture in France 1500-1700* (4th ed.; New York: Penguin Books, 1982). For more on the history of landscape painting as a genre in Renaissance France, see Lucile M. Golson, "Landscape Prints and Landscapists of the School of Fontainebleau," *Gazette des Beaux-Arts*, 73 (1969): 95-110.

Il veut qu'en petite espace
Le paintre ingenieus face
(Alors qu'il est agité)
Sans avoir nulle matiere
L'aer, la mer, la terre entiere,
Instrument de deité.

(2:160-61, vv. 89-100)

In isolation, this stanza reads like an unqualified acclamation of the narrative painter and his works. Reminiscent of the commonplace Neoplatonic parallel between plastic artists and the Divine *Artifex*,[9] it seems to suggest that little would distinguish the accomplishments of the painter from those of the Almighty at the creation. When sufficiently endowed with wit and inspiration, the maker of story pictures enjoys a God-like ability to form an entire world *ex nihilo*. What is more, like the Neoplatonists' hieroglyph engraver and Leonardo da Vinci's portrait painter, Ronsard's painter of stories would appear to cause a kind of uplifting rapture. The opening reference to "un celeste present . . . *Pour lever en haut les hommes*" might possibly be taken as a tribute to the artist's ability to transport the spectating public to a higher plane of consciousness.

Such impressions of commendation quickly fade, however, when the story-painting passage is reconsidered in the context of *A son Luc* as a whole. Notwithstanding the assertion that the narrative painter attains a measure of creative prominence through the Gods' good graces, there is no question that Ronsard reserves his strongest praise for the poet. Beyond enjoying the most intimate and active relation with the Divine, the maker of verses stands alone in his ability to communicate the intellectual and spiritual rewards of that relation:

La poësie est un feu consumant
Par grand ardeur l'esprit de son amant,
    Esprit que jamais ne laisse
    En repos tant elle presse.
Voila pourquoi le *ministre des dieus*
Vit sans grands biens, d'autant qu'il aime mieus
    Abonder d'inventions
    Que de grands possessions.
Mais Dieu juste qui dispense

---

[9] See Chastel, *Ficin*, 59-70.

Tout en tous, les fait chanter
Le futur en recompense
Pour le monde épovanter.
Ce sont les seuls interpretes
Des vrais Dieus que les poëtes

. . . .

Certes je suis glorieus
D'estre ainsi *ami des Dieus*,
Lesquels m'ont fait recevoir
Le meilleur de leur sçavoir
Pour me paistre, & m'en nourrir. . . .

                    (2:158-62, vv. 41-54, 113-17: my emphasis)

The poet is the unique beneficiary of two extraordinary privileges. On the one hand, he is the exclusive mortal "ami des Dieus," the sole human being permitted to enjoy the friendship and confidence of the Gods. As such, the poet is the only living creature allowed to acquire "Le meilleur de leur sçavoir," full knowledge of the divine plan–from the physical workings of the sensible world to the metaphysical and moral principles that give meaning to all existence.

The second privilege complements the first. In *A son Luc*, as throughout Ronsard's poetry, the poet is also a *vates*. Following Plato and such notable literary models as Homer, Pindar, Horace, and Ovid, Ronsard presents the verbal artist as the exclusive recipient of the prophetic fury, as the only true "ministre" and "interprete" of the Gods. In this capacity, he is able to translate and transmit the mysteries of the divine *sçavoir* into a language that is both filled with meaning and *meaningful*. While often veiling those mysteries under a "fabuleux manteau" in order to confound and silence the uninitiated and unworthy readers and critics,[10] his idiom is otherwise intellectually and spiritually comprehensible to all who are prepared to accept its truth.

The intelligibility of this language is more explicitly acknowledged in Ronsard's famous treatise on poetry, the 1565 *Abbregé de l'Art poëtique françois*. Borrowing boldly from Aristotle's theory of invention in the *Poetics* (1460b 2)[11] and Horace's warnings against

---

[10] See below. On the image of the "fabuleux manteau," see the *Hymne de l'Automne* (12:50, vv. 77-86) and the *Hymne de l'Hyver* (12:71-72, vv. 71-78).

[11] Ronsard's familiarity with Aristotle's concept of invention is examined in Silver, *Evolution*, 2:335-37 and Castor, *Poetics*, 53-62. See also, Jürgen V. Stackelberg, "Ronsard und Aristoteles," *Bibliothèque d'Humanisme et Renaissance*, 25 (1963): 349-61.

'grotesquerie' at the beginning of the *Epistola ad Pisones* (vv. 1-13),[12] Ronsard promotes the poet's duty to respect "la belle disposition," a suitable (though not necessarily linearly logical) ordering, as a precondition for fulfilling his higher obligation to make his "inventions," the divine *sçavoir* to which he is privy, understandable to everyone:

> le but . . . du Poëte est d'imiter, inventer, & representer les choses qui sont, qui peuvent estre, ou que les anciens ont estimé comme veritables: & ne fault point douter, qu'apres avoir bien & hautement inventé, que la belle disposition de vers ne s'ensuyve, d'autant que la disposition suit l'invention mere de toutes choses, comme l'ombre faict le corps. Quand je te dy que tu inventes choses belles & grandes, je n'entends toutesfois ces inventions fantasticques & melencoliques qui ne se rapportent non plus l'une à l'autre . . . sans ordre ny liayson: mais tes inventions, desquelles je ne te puis donner reigle pour estre spirituelles, seront bien ordonnées & disposées: & bien qu'elles semblent passer celles du vulgaire, *elles seront toutesfois telles qu'elles pourront estre facilement conceues & entendues d'un chascun.* (14:13, ll. 176-95: my emphasis)[13]

And so the poet not only *ought to* make his inventions meaningful, but he *cannot do otherwise* when those inventions are the fruits of his intercourse with the Divine, the 'spiritual' kind of knowledge for which there are no rules. Comprehensibility is as much the inseparable "ombre" of that "corps" of knowledge as is the "belle disposition" that makes it possible.[14]

During an earlier period, the idea of intelligibility appears, with a poetic formulation, in the 1550 ode *A Joachim du Bellai angevin*:

---

[12] For an overview of the Horatian concept of the grotesque in early modern French literature, see Glyn P. Norton, "The Horatian Grotesque in Renaissance France: The Genesis of a Poetic Formula," *Romanic Review*, 65 (1974): 157-74.

[13] On Ronsard's "aspiration à l'ordre" in general, his quest for a poetic, social, and metaphysical stability throughout the odes, see François Rouget, *L'Apothéose d'Orphée: l'esthétique de l'ode en France au XVIe siècle, de Sébillet à Scaliger (1548-1561)* (Geneva: Droz, 1994), esp. 117-58.

[14] On Ronsard's paradoxical notion of the poet as a beneficiary of divine *fureur* who must nevertheless refine his craft through conscious practice, and the many avatars of this notion throughout his career, see Olivier Pot, *Inspiration et Mélancolie: L'épistémologie poétique dans les Amours de Ronsard, Etudes Ronsardiennes IV* (Geneva: Droz, 1990).

Comblés de segrés divers,
Ils chantent par l'univers
D'une vois où dieu abonde,
Et l'ardeur de leur faconde
Sert d'oracles, & sont faits
Les ministres plus parfaits
De la deité parfonde.

(1:145, vv. 18-24)

While attacking the odious critic who fails to recognize God's prophets in poets like himself and his good friend and Pléiade associate, Joachim du Bellay ("Celui qui ne nous honore / Comme profettes des dieus . . .": 1:144, vv. 1-2), Ronsard singles out ardent eloquence ("faconde")–i.e., sweet and meaningful delivery [15]–as evidence of the divine ministrations of all such poets.

The same notions about poets and poetry are inscribed, expressly and tacitly, in *A son Luc*. In addition, however, this ode alludes to a properly emotive mode of communication that recalls the meta-rational epistemology of the Neoplatonists and, if still as yet only coincidentally, the rhetorical aesthetics of enthrallment of Longinus (whose treatise on sublimity is unavailable before Francesco Robortello undertakes its first modern printing in 1554). [16] Ronsard identifies–or what is perhaps more accurate, during the early stages of his career, *intuits*–a poetic discourse beyond the confines of positivistic reasoning. In exercising their gift of prophesy, poets are able to frighten their worthy addressees into a kind of astonishment or rapture: "Dieu...les fait chanter / Le futur... / Pour le monde *epouvanter*" [17] (vv. 49-52, my emphasis). By the grace of God, the *vates* can reach not only the mind, but also the soul, the source of humanity's purest knowledge of the divine truths. [18]

---

[15] Cotgrave defines "faconde" as "Eloquence, redie utterance, gracefull speaking, sweet deliverie." That this term should also connote meaningfulness (or illumination), however, is apparent in Ronsard's praise of Jean Dorat's *guiding* "faconde" in his 1550 ode to his former college principal and master: "Certes ma chanson sucrée / Qui les grands Princes recrée / Te pourra bien derider, / Apres ta peine publique / *Où ta faconde s'aplique / Pour la jeunesse guider*" (*A Jan D'Orat*, 1:127, vv. 15-20: emphasis added).

[16] See John Edwin Sandys, *Classical Scholarship*, 1:288-92 and 2:141; and Silver, *Evolution*, 2:335-36 n. 103.

[17] Beyond the sense of "to fright" or "fill with horror or terror," Cotgrave allows that "espoventer" may also mean to "astonish by feare."

[18] See also the poet's transcendental impact on the listening/reading audience

By contrast, *A son Luc* pays a tempered, even ironic, tribute to the narrative painter. In the first place, the artist's rapport with the Gods is an essentially subservient one. As we learn from the suspended apposition in verse 100, the narrative painter is never more than an "*Instrument de deité.*" He remains a mere *tool* of the deity, with all that that implies, in the context of the paragone, about his inability to escape manual labor and the stigma of plying an art form that is merely mechanical. [19] In the second place, unlike the poet, who enjoys a communion with the highest orders of truth, the narrative painter is reduced to knowledge of a visible material world which, by Platonic and Neoplatonic standards, is but a shadow of the divine idea whence it derives. However demiurgic he might appear when creating a world from nothing, the artist is restricted to depicting sensible elemental things: "L'aer, la mer, la terre entiere." Further, as Ronsard insists in verse 95, the very center of the narrative-painting stanza, this depiction is circumscribed within a "petite espace." Unlike the poet, whose ability to represent truth is fettered only by the censorship of public ignorance (as we learn in the ode *A Joachim du Bellai angevin* and throughout Ronsard's repeated complaints against the "monstre Ignorance"), [20] the narrative painter is bound to scale down the limited knowledge at his disposal by the naturalness of his visual signs, as well as the sensory quality of his medium and the diminutive nature of the canvas, panel, or wall surface on which he works. [21]

---

announced in Calliope's request to Jupiter on behalf of all "Chantres divins" in the 1552 *Ode à Michel de l'Hospital*: "Donne nous encor la puissance / D'arracher les ames dehors / Le salle bourbier de leurs corps, / Pour les rejoindre à leur naissance." (3:139, vv. 361-64). We shall return to this special quality in the next chapter.

[19] The idea of man as the "instrument" of God is hardly new. The Scholastics and Neoplatonists made this claim about all of nature: "Natura enim divinitatis est instrumentum." See Marsilio Ficino, *Opera Omnia*, "In Timaeum Commentarium" (rpt. 1576: Turin: Bottega d'Erasmo, 1959, 1983). Cf. also, the Neoplatonic reflections of the "Sage" in Marguerite de Navarre's *Comédie de Mont-de-Marsan* (sc. 3, vv. 294-299): in *Théâtre Profane*, ed. V. L. Saulnier (Geneva: Droz, 1963), 287. Clearly Ronsard has adapted this cosmological notion to his own aesthetic ends in the present instance.

[20] See the discussion of *La Lyre* below. For more on this theme see Silver, *Evolution*, 2:42-45.

[21] Brian Barron interprets this phrase to mean simply "microcosme" ("'Ut Pictura Poesis'," 130). I, on the other hand, see an ironic side to this designation that is absent from the traditional Renaissance understanding of 'microcosm' as the reflection of God's infinite plenitude in the finite beings and objects of this world. On the history of this idea from the earliest Neoplatonists to Boethius, Nicholas of

Finally, then, it is clear we must also revise our initial reading of the uplifting "celeste present" at the start of the problematic narrative-painting stanza. It is not that the painter possesses a heavenly gift that allows him to "lever en haut" other men; rather the painter is raised above other men by possessing this extraordinary gift. Like the poet, who is "glorieus / D'estre . . . ami des Dieus," the narrative painter is the beneficiary of a divine privilege that promotes him beyond the common ranks of humanity. Yet where the poet's "present" includes a prophetic skill that, in turn, allows him to "epouvanter" the human soul, the artist's endowment stops at physical mimesis, and thus at a level of representation that only further cements corporeal bonds. Reminding men of all things earthly (air, sea, and land) is the painter's foremost objective and limitation.

B. *Des peintures contenues dedans un tableau*[22]

The assaults on narrative painting both continue and widen in *Des peintures contenues dedans un tableau* of the 1550 *Second Livre des Odes*. The importance of this 102-verse ekphrastic poem as a gauge of Ronsard's position toward the major issues of the paragone cannot be overstated. In fact, it represents the poet's sole attempt to describe a narrative picture in the form of a painting. While other such descriptions more closely follow the traditional examples of literary pictorialism by evoking stories embroidered, engraved, or etched upon baskets, cloaks, and other ontologically autonomous objects,[23] *Des peintures* stands alone in considering a narrative design in paint on a two-dimensional surface. It therefore constitutes Ronsard's most clearly focused commentary on such art-

---

Cusa, and Lefèvre d'Etaples, see Jean Seznec, *The Survival of the Pagan Gods*, trans. Barbara F. Sessions (1953 rpt.: Princeton: Princeton University Press, 1972), 49; Alexandre Koyré, *From the Closed World to the Infinite Universe* (New York: Harper & Row, 1958), 5-27; Jasper Hopkins, *Nicholas of Cusa's Metaphysics of Contradiction* (Minneapolis: Banning, 1983), 97-112. As we shall see in Chapter Three, Ronsard reverses himself on this quality in the case of portraiture.

[22] The ensuing analysis of *Des peintures contenues dedans un tableau* amends and elaborates the arguments and conclusions first advanced in my article, "The Arts in Conflict in Ronsard's *Des peintures contenues dedans un tableau*," *Romance Quarterly* 39 (1992): 411-24.

[23] The poems of this more traditional sort are the focus of the second half of the present examination.

works.[24] Further and more significantly, this ode introduces Ronsard's most damaging and enduring complaint against narrative painting. Defying one of the mainstays in Neoplatonic and Leonardian claims for the supremacy of the visual arts, the Pléiade laureate underscores the incomprehensibility of painted stories and, ultimately, the inability of painters to tame the Hermetic drift, to fill the communicative void of their 'natural' visual language with the presence of complete and unified ideas.

If this shortcoming is never attacked explicitly, it is otherwise implicitly impugned in the two features of the poem that have attracted unanimous concern among modern-day commentators: its apparent incoherence and obscurity. At issue, for example, is the relatedness (or rather unrelatedness) of the five distinct subjects that comprise the ninety-six verses of the *tableau* in question–its three mythological episodes: the making of Jupiter's thunderbolt at Vulcan's forge (vv. 7-30), Jupiter's storm (vv. 31-48), and Juno's seduction of Jupiter (vv. 49-66); and its two 'historical' scenes: Charles V's 1535 armada assault against Tunis (vv. 67-90) and the imaginary entrance into Paris of a triumphant Henri II with the Holy Roman Emperor as his pale and frightened captive (vv. 91-102). Similarly problematic is the language and style with which these scenes are presented. Throughout his description the poet adopts a concision and dryness of expression that perpetually subverts any sense of narrative wholeness. This is not to say that *Des peintures* has no narrative center. As Philip Ford has discovered on analyzing the many intertextual allusions of the ode to Homer's *Iliad* (18 and 23), Virgil's *Aeneid* (8) and *Georgics* (1, 3, and 4) and Heraclitus' commentaries on the Homeric allegories, the *tableau*

---

[24] As regards the ontological status of the "tableau" in question, however, there is considerable critical disagreement. Laumonier presumes that the painting in question actually existed, that Ronsard was describing a real narrative picture "de visu" (*RPL*, 389). François Lecercle likewise assumes that "un tableau précis" serves as Ronsard's model (*Chimère*, 22). Terence Cave, on the other hand, is more cautious. While acknowledging that the thematically composite type of tableau presented here bears an undeniable resemblance to the frescoes of the Galerie François Premier at Fontainebleau, this critic concludes that Ronsard's references to painting apply in only "a loose, metaphorical sense" ("Ronsard's Mythological Universe," in *Ronsard the Poet*, ed. Terence Cave, 159-208 [London: Methuen & Co., 1973], 164, 171). To my mind, it is ultimately impossible to say whether this picture existed in reality or only in the poetic language of the poet. Nor is it necessary to make such a determination since the essential point is that the *tableau* should bring to mind the kind of narrative paintings in vogue in Ronsard's day.

may actually be read "as an allegory representing the struggle over the years between French monarchs and the Holy Roman Emperor, with divine providence acting as the controlling force." [25] Nevertheless, the work continues to resist our reading. Despite Ford's discerning conclusion, the signifiers (language and style) of the poem are no less at odds with its signified (the political-historical meaning).

In truth, however, this signified is precisely as elusive as it ought to be, for the thematic discontinuity and semantic opacity of the ode are in fact the signifiers of a concomitant preoccupation of *Des peintures*: the fundamental disunity and incomprehensibility of narrative painting. Undoubtedly these troubling characteristics bear some significant relation to Ronsard's early affection for Horace's and Pindar's aesthetic of "copieuse diversité"–the style of thematic and formal complexity that the poet overtly applauds in his *Au Lecteur* to the 1550 edition of the *Quatre premiers livres des Odes*. [26] And surely they conform to Ronsard's pledge, likewise stated in the 1550 *Au Lecteur*, to obey the age-old aesthetic precept requiring that all art "ressemble la nature, laquelle ne fut estimée belle des anciens, que pour estre *inconstante, & variable* en ses perfections" (1:47: my emphasis). [27] Beyond such explanations, it is equally certain that these features should pertain to the narrative genre of painting immediately at issue in *Des peintures*. Moreover, on closer examination, this incoherence and obscurity soon emerge as the very reasons why story pictures are inherently inferior to poetry in Ronsard's hierarchy of the arts. Far from being the objects of praise

---

[25] Philip Ford, "Ronsard the Painter," esp. 42. See also his *Ronsard's "Hymnes*," 37.

[26] "Je ne fai point de doute que ma Poësie tant varie ne semble facheuse aus oreilles de nos rimeurs, & principalement des courtizans, qui n'admirent qu'un petit sonnet petrarquizé, ou quelque mignardise d'amour qui continue tousjours en son propos: pour le moins, je m'assure qu'ils ne me sçauroient accuser, sans condamner premierement Pindare auteur de telle copieuse diversité, & oultre que c'est la sauce, à laquelle on doit gouster l'Ode" (1:47, ll. 91-100). This explanation is eloquently advanced by Terence Cave in *RP*, 164-66. A summary of this theory and others–including those of Brian Barron, Philip Ford, and Margaret McGowan–appears in my "Arts in Conflict," 412-13. For a recent discussion of Ronsard's recourse to copia and diversity as a stylistic commonplace of the ode genre in which he so often indulged, see Rouget, *L'Apothéose d'Orphée*, esp. 159-79.

[27] The origins of this precept are addressed in our discussion of the aesthetics of Plato, Aristotle, and the Neoplatonists in Chapter 1. See also, Castor, *Poetics*, 57.

or desire, such qualities are to be overcome in favor of unity and clarity, among the most important virtues of poems in the laureate's paragone-related aesthetics.[28]

* * *

Signs of this preoccupation and how it will develop are present from the outset, in the very titles of the ode: both the original 1550 formulation, *Des peintures contenues dedans un tableau*, and the final version, first employed in 1555, *Les peintures d'un Païsage*. From the form of the articles alone, for example, it is evident that Ronsard will focus on the opposition between the ideas of multiplicity (indicated by the plurals "Des"[29] and "Les") and unity (suggested by the singular "un"). Furthermore, since the plurals modify the word "peintures" in each version, it is clear that the notion of plurality should pertain to painting and, especially, to narrative painting (the specific object of consideration in the ode). For the complement of the unity idea, on the other hand, it is necessary to understand the reference, in the later title, to the "Païsage." Although this term already denotes landscape painting by the middle of the sixteenth century,[30] its capitalization here[31] invites a metaphorical reading more in keeping with Ronsard's use of the word (uncapitalized) at the opening of his 1560 *Elegie à Louis des Masures*:

---

[28] Although I entirely concur with Margaret McGowan when she observes that *Des peintures* purposefully "lays bare Ronsard's preoccupations with painting," I would disagree with her dismissal of this poem as a work in which the poet simply "got too close to paint" and therefore "failed to control [its] overall structure" (*Ideal Forms*, 83-88). As the analysis to follow shall demonstrate, this failure is in truth Ronsard's great success, the very essence of his strategy to discredit the value of narrative painting and to affirm the preeminence of poetry.

[29] Whether it is a matter of the indefinite article 'des' (some) or, what is likelier, the contraction of 'de' and 'les' (in the sense of 'on the'), the idea of plurality is the same.

[30] Cf. n. 8 above, and Edmond Huguet, *Dictionnaire de la langue française du seizième siècle*, 8 vols. (Paris: Didier, 1925-66), 5:693.

[31] Beginning in 1555, the capitalization in question is in fact consistent with all printings of the title in its proper position at the start of the poem. It also coincides with Laumonier's transcription in his note on editions (1:259). On the other hand, quite the reverse is true in the tables of contents for the editions and printings of 1555, 1560, 1567, 1571, 1573, and 1578. For unknown reasons the editors and publishers prefer to employ a lower-case "p" in those locations.

> Comme celui qui voit du haut d'une fenestre
> Alentour de ses yeux un *païsage* champestre,
> . . . .
> Celuy qui list les vers que j'ay portraicts ici
> Regarde d'un trait d'oeil meinte diverse chose
> Qui bonne & mauvaise entre en mon papier enclose.
>
> (10:362-63, vv. 1-14: my emphasis)

To the degree the viewer of the "païsage champestre" is like the reader of the "papier," or poem, then the landscape becomes a metaphor for the poem and, by extension, for poetry in general. The "Païsage" of *Des peintures* inscribes the same idea. Although we must wait for the verses that follow to discover how this is so, the latter 'Landscape' is likewise a metaphor for the poem and poetry, and it is this poem/poetry that finally assumes the property of unity signalled by the article "un."

What is more, the titles anticipate not only an antithesis between these terms and ideas, but also a synthesis of them. The linking phrases "contenues dedans" ("contained within") and "*d*'un" (whether read as "in" or "of" [i.e., belonging to]) create the expectation that the unity/poetry will subsume–and eventually supplant– the multiplicity/narrative painting. It seems, in other words, that the poem will bring oneness to the multiplicity of the narrative picture it describes, that poetry will tame the incoherence and obscurity of painting.

The precise origins of narrative painting's failings and poetry's compensatory success may be found in the philosophical and aesthetic conception of unity that emerges from the interstices of the opening stanza, the only more or less explicit, authorial reflection on the "tableau" as a whole:

> Tableau, que l'éternelle gloire
> D'un Apelle avouroit pour sien,
> Ou de quelque autre dont l'histoire
> Celebre le nom ancien,
> Tant la couleur heureusement parfaite
> A la Nature en son mort contrefaite.
>
> (1:259-60, vv. 1-6)

The paradoxical twist of verse 6 is especially revealing. Here we learn that despite the hyperbolic salute to the perfection of the tableau in the first five lines–a perfection that even the legendary painters of Antiquity like Apelle would envy–, the "Nature" at issue has been "en son mort contrefaite." This entire six-syllable hemistich seems at odds with the notions of joy, perfection, and immortality that pervade the rest of the stanza. But what does this phrase truly mean, and how does it relate to the term "Nature," whose capitalization (like that of "Païsage") suggests a metaphorical or abstract significance?

The solution turns on the senses of "son," at the syllabic center of the verse, and "contrefaite" (the feminized past participle of the verb *contrefaire*), at its end. A topic of some debate in the past, the first word is most simply and effectively understood to be the masculine noun meaning 'sound'. As such, the locution "en son mort" would signify 'in dead sound', or in a more colloquial English, 'in dead silence'.[32] This interpretation concurs with Ronsard's intense concern for the 'silence' of his narrative tableau later in the ode (as we shall witness), as well as with the negative connotation of Simonides' "muteness" comment on painting, which the poet evokes numerous times in other paragone poems (as we shall also see). Accordingly, the phrase under consideration may be assumed to recall the very notion to which Leonardo da Vinci takes such fierce exception in the *Trattato della pittura*: the idea that the natural signs employed by the pictorial arts rob them of the 'voice', or language, necessary to express anything beyond superficial materiality.[33]

---

[32] Heretofore, most critics have assumed that "mort" is the noun in this expression. Following Edmond Huguet's definition of "le mort" as the "Etat" or "aspect d'une personne morte" (*Dictionnaire*, 5:340), Charles Guérin, for example, has taken "en son mort" to mean "sur son image inanimée" (*Les Odes de Ronsard*, [Paris: Cèdre, 1952], 385). In another instance, L. Mellerio has suggested that this locution should be read as "en son état d'immobilité" (*Lexique de Ronsard* [Paris: Plon, 1895], 154). Brian Barron offers a third perspective. He regards Ronsard's use of the phrase as either a reprise of the Horatian *exegi monumentum* theme or an attack by Ronsard on the silence and immobility that characterize poetic description, the feature of poetry that conflicts with the vitality and movement of the opposite poetic impulse toward narration ("'Ut Pictura poesis'," 260). My "Conflict" (414-15) advances yet another possible interpretation, one which I hereby withdraw in favor of the present reading.

[33] The only other instance of this phrase in Ronsard's poetry is consistent with this interpretation. It appears in the 1555 didactic poem *A mes Dames*. While reflecting on the education of Henri II's three young daughters, and, above all, on the importance of cultivating the powers of the mind at least as devotedly as the beauty of the body, the poet evokes the analogy of a painting as the first in a series of warnings against ignoring this wisdom: "Peu de tans la beauté dure, / Et le sang qui des

The meaning of *contrefaire* follows directly from our understanding of "son." Of course, this verb often denotes simply 'to imitate', both in the common parlance of the century and in numerous other instances throughout Ronsard's poetry.[34] In the present case, however, it is the equally prevalent, pejorative connotation that dominates. By association with the negative phrase "en son mort," *contrefaire* takes on the sense of 'to make a deceptive and inadequate copy'.[35] It thereby acquires a distinctly Platonic and Neoplatonic relevance, and more importantly, it signals that all of the poem's comments on painting reflect something of Plato's and the Neoplatonists' fundamental misgivings about the ideational 'absence' of the mimetic arts.

To apply these interpretations to the meaning of verse 6 as a whole, it is suddenly apparent that the narrative painting does decisive violence to the "Nature" it would presumably reproduce. By virtue of the utterly dead silence of the *peintures* that comprise it, the tableau is limited to the imitation of visible physical *n*ature (uncapitalized), which is but the deceptive and inadequate copy of ideal *N*ature (capitalized), the absolute and immutable forms and truths that shape, yet always transcend, the physical world according to Plato and the Neoplatonists.

Rois sort, / Si de l'esprit on n'a cure: / *Autant vaut quelque peinture / Qui n'est vive qu'en son mort*" (7:78, vv. 71-75: my emphasis). Especially revealing is the opposition between "esprit"–which, in the context of the poem as a whole, can only be understood as the immortal, essential quality of mind (cf. vv. 76-85)–and "beauté"–one's perishable and, hence, inessential, physical attributes. Since the poet likens a woman whose only virtue is her beauty to a painting that is alive only "in dead silence," it follows that this "silence," or voicelessness, should pertain to the inessential qualities of a person or thing–that which belongs to the realm of superficial visible matter and which is 'silent' (voiceless) with respect to the meanings of the higher realities.

[34] Cotgrave translates "contrefaire" as "to counterfeit, imitate, resemble, faine." Other instances of the non-pejorative mimetic sense may be found in Ronsard's *Au Lecteur* for the 1550 *Odes* (1:44, l. 27) and his ode *A Michel de l'Hospital* (3:137, v. 322).

[35] Cf. Grahame Castor's remarks on the difference between "feindre" and "contrefaire" in Pléiade poetic theory (*Poetics*, 57, 123), and Claude-Gilbert Dubois' notion of mimesis as "multiplication [that] is the very negation of the ideal model" ("Problems of 'Representation'," 462). In Ronsard's own poetic works, the 1555 *Meslanges* offers three clear examples of the negative use of "contrefaire": in the *Ode prise d'Anacreon*: "Et tu veus contrefaire encore le jeune homme" (6:198, v. 4); the *Ode à sa Maistresse*: "Contrefais-tu la nonnain" (6:219, v. 17); and the *Epigramme à Julien*: "Tu veux avecques ton bel art / Du bon sophiste contrefaire" (6:244, vv. 9-10).

As paradoxical as it might seem, Ronsard's insistence on the perfection of the picture's color in verse 5 lends important support to this reading. Rather than betray a belief in the conceptual plenitude of the tableau, this remark underscores the inviolable link between the narrative picture and physicality. Indeed, not only does the poet ascribe an inherent chromatic dimension to the realm of physical nature, but like all the major theorists of painting and aesthetics since Plato,[36] he also considers color, and so physical nature too, as an inextricable element of the painter's art. The last connections are driven home at the start of sonnet XLII of the 1578 *Premier livre des sonets pour Helene*. Amid a praise of the particular values of physical love that raises a favorite theme replayed throughout his poetry,[37] Ronsard draws an instructive analogy between the importance of his beloved Hélène's corporal virtues and that of the colors in paintings: "En choisissant l'esprit vous estes mal-apprise, / Qui refusez *le corps, à mon gré le meilleur . . . / Vous aimez les tableaux qui n'ont point de couleur. / Aimer l'esprit, Madame, est aimer la sottise*" (17:230, vv. 1-8: my emphasis). Hence an amorous relationship maintained on a purely spiritual or intellectual level–i.e. without physicality–is, Ronsard insists, as worthless as paintings deprived of their own 'physicality', their essential property of color.[38]

---

[36] See the discussions of Plato, Aristotle, Theodulf of Orleans, and Aquinas in Chapter One. Leonardo also includes color ("colore") among the ten ornaments of nature ("dieci ornamenti della natura") to which the painter has unique access (*Tr.* 20; 1:59). In Ronsard's own day, Lodovico Dolce reaffirms the same connection, making color one of the three essential parts of painting: "The whole sum of painting is, in my opinion, divided into three parts: invention, design and coloring" ("Tutta la somma della Pittura a mio giudicio è divisa in tre parti: Inventione, Disegno, e Colorito") (*Dolce's 'Aretino' and Venetian Art Theory of the Cinquecento*, ed. and trans. Mark W. Roskill [New York: New York University Press, 1968], 117 [see also 151-57]). Finally, among Ronsard's peers, Louis Le Caron acknowledges this fundamental relation in his fourth *Dialogue*: "Aucuns escrivent la fable estre en la poësie, ce que la couleur en la peinture, laquelle a plus de force que la ligne, pour faire regarder l'image bien tirée. . . ." (*Dialogues*, eds. Joan A. Buhlmann and Donald Gilman [Geneva: Droz, 1986], 270).

[37] See André Gendre, *Ronsard poète de la conquête amoureuse* (Neuchâtel: Baconnière, 1970), esp. 17, 41-58. See also the summative reflections in our concluding chapter.

[38] The same point arises at the opening of Ronsard's poetic lament to Marie Stuart, in the 1564 *Elegie sur le depart de la Royne d'Ecosse*: "Comme un beau pré despouillé de ses fleurs, / *Comme un tableau privé de ses couleurs, / . . . / Ainsi perdra la France soucieuse / Ses ornemens, en perdant la beauté / Qui fut sa fleur, sa couleur, sa clarté*" (12:193-94, vv. 1-10; my emphasis). We remark, in particular, the

To return to the idea of unity and the origins of the correlative strengths and weaknesses of poetry and painting, two primary conclusions may at last be drawn. First, this unity relates, in an essential way, to ideal Nature. From the association, in the titles, between the idea of multiplicity and painting, and the connection, in the opening stanza, between painting and physical nature, it is now clear that multiplicity and painting are conceptually joined to physical nature: multiplicity-painting-physical nature. By analogy, then, we may infer that ideal Nature, as the antithesis of physical nature (in Platonic and Neoplatonic metaphysics), is fundamentally linked to unity: unity-ideal Nature. The second conclusion follows readily from the first. Given the affinity, likewise connoted in the titles, between unity and poetry, we may finally presume that the origin of poetry's special ability to tame the multiplicity of narrative painting is its privileged relation with ideal Nature: unity-poetry-ideal Nature. The power of poetry to produce unity, in other words, derives from its special ability to express abstract, transcendent meanings and truths. As for the origin of painting's multiplicity (i.e., incoherence and resultant incomprehensibility), on the other hand, it will ultimately reside in the restriction of that art form to the imitation of physical nature.

* * *

In a certain respect, then, the titles and opening sextet of *Des peintures* may be said to advance the primary thesis that painting is inferior to poetry on the Platonic and (especially) Neoplatonic grounds that the former, epitomized by narrative painting, is incapable of overcoming its own multiplicity, and thus the semantic superabundance of the Hermetic drift, due to its inescapable affiliation with natural signs and physical matter. By contrast, the art of

---

connection between color—as much the *sine qua non* of painting as the other analogues for Queen Marie constitute the distinguishing features of their related places and objects—and the notion of physicality, metaphorically raised in the term "ornemens." Of course, it is also necessary to distinguish this usage from Ronsard's conception of "color" in regard to his poetry and the beauties of nature. In the last case, color evokes two related ideas: multiplicity and fertile vitality—i.e., life itself (cf., the 1559 *Suyte de l'hymne de tres-illustre Prince Charles cardinal de Lorraine* [9:145-53, esp. 145, vv. 1-7]). Clearly, this quality takes on a substantially different meaning in the poet's paragone poems.

poetry, exemplified by the ekphrasis of the ode itself, both can and does unify (as certified by the very presence of this message and the political-historical meaning identified by Philip Ford). It can and does subdue the endless semiosic deferral thanks to the capacity for abstraction that derives from the freer, non-natural (arbitrary) signs of verbal language. Yet what actually becomes of these ideas throughout the remainder of the poem? How are they embedded in the ninety-six verses devoted to the tableau itself? The answer bears again upon the discontinuous style that characterizes the ode and obfuscates its meanings. It is apparent that the discontinuity of the poetic "tableau" has been carefully cultivated in order to recreate the disjointedness of a real narrative painting and, consequently, in order to translate into words the semantic deficiency of that visual art form.

This objective defines the precise nature and specific effects of the two stylistic features most responsible for the discontinuity in question. First, there is Ronsard's obvious silence about the relatedness of the five *peintures* of the poem. Such reticence is highly unusual for Ronsard. Even in those poems where his debt to the stylistic diffuseness of Horace and Pindar is most conspicuous, the poet typically takes great care to insure detection of the unifying, thematic framework–whether through subtle allusion or overt commentary.[39] This exceptional silence is evident from the beginning of the tableau description, in stanza 2:

> Où la grand bande renfrongnée
> Des Cyclopes laborieus,
> Est à la forge embesongnée,
> Qui d'un effort industrieus
> Haste un tonnerre, armure pour la destre
> De ce grand Dieu, à le ruer adestre.
>
> (vv. 7-12)

---

[39] Cf. the 1552 ode *A Michel de l'Hospital* (3:118-63), the paradigm of Ronsard's aesthetic of "copieuse diversité" and doctrine of "poetic fury." However complex this poem may be, the laureate never lets us forget that the central story (relating the mythological origins of the Muses and their divine powers) is above all an allegory intended to praise his friend and advocate, Michel de l'Hospital, and, by extension, to attack his detractors at court (especially Mellin de Saint-Gelais). See Strophe 1 (vv. 1-12), Antistrophe 15 (vv. 489-500), and Strophes 20-24 (vv. 647-816). For analyses of this work, see Henri Chamard, *Histoire de la Pléiade*, 4 vols. (Paris: Henri Didier, 1939-40), 1:364 ff.; D. B. Wilson, *Ronsard Poet of Nature* (Manchester: University Press, 1961), 30-32; Cave, *Cornucopian Text*, 230-33.

The opening relative pronoun "Où" is deceiving. While its link to the first word of the ode, "Tableau," raises the expectation that stanza 2 will continue the authorial commentary begun in stanza 1 and that, perhaps, the poet will broach the political-historical message of the poem, in truth no such continuity arises. As the focus shifts instantly to the images themselves all allusions to the central significance of the picture disappear. The poet offers nothing to contextualize the episodes that follow, and so, nothing to help the reader understand their unifying meaning.

Although this silence persists throughout the poem, it is nowhere more striking than in the abruptness of the concluding stanza. The ode simply ceases as the poet completes his account of the fifth painting, the king's triumphant entry into Paris:

> Paris tient ses portes decloses
> Recevant son Roi belliqueur,
> Une grande nue de roses
> Pleut à l'entour du chef vainqueur.
> Les feus de joie ici & là s'alument,
> Et jusque au ciel les autels des Dieus fument.
>
> (vv. 97-102)

Once again Ronsard eschews all commentary, direct or indirect, that could help to establish the thematic unity underlying the five episodes of the tableau.

Contributing to the impression of authorial reticence are the phrases employed to conjoin the five *peintures*. Rather than use the customary markers of narrative emplotment, terms that might indicate something about the causal or temporal relations between the various episodes, Ronsard opens each succeeding description with an allusion to some kind of spatial orientation. Moreover, the spatial cues employed are, in the end, nearly meaningless. However precise expressions like "Un peu plus haut" (v. 31) and "Au meilleu de" (v. 73) might first appear, they never fulfill their referential promise. Missing is such essential information as the relative size of the various scenes and their orientation with respect to any of the standard, pictorial points of reference: top, bottom, left side, right side, and center.[40] The result is a sense of spatial randomness and

---

[40] The same point may be made for the other connecting spatial expressions: "entre" (v. 37), "A cousté gauche" (v. 49), "deçà & là" (v. 61), "Pres de" (v. 85) and "Tout au bas" (v. 91).

the fundamental paradox that the tableau in question is virtually impossible to visualize. [41]

As to the literary inspiration for this silence, Ronsard unquestionably owes thanks to the ekphrasis of Achilles' shield in the *Iliad* (a debt plainly signaled by the inclusion of the Vulcan-forge *peinture* at the opening of the ode). Homer's spatial directions are just as referentially empty, and his overall pictorial object is likewise both impossible to envision and resistant to interpretation. [42] Admittedly, Virgil's episode on Aeneas' shield in *Aeneid* 8 (ll. 626-730) is a more important model for specific scenes in Ronsard's *tableau* (especially for the 'historical' images of Ronsard's last two *peintures*, where Ford identifies significant resemblances to the description of Octavian's battle with and victory over Mark Anthony and Cleopatra). [43] However, in contrast to Homer, and thus to Ronsard, Virgil never conceals the prophetic meaning of the pictures he has represented. Notwithstanding his elliptical style and generous use of spatial connectives, the Latin author provides abundant clues about the underlying symbolism of his shield's iconography. [44]

For the philosophical dimension of this feature, on the other hand, Ronsard is undoubtedly indebted to Simonides of Ceos' *pictura poesis muta* idea. In essence, this silence is the demonstration to accompany the poet's opening claim that the "Tableau" is "en son mort"–the verbal equivalent of the muteness imputed to all the pictorial (and plastic) arts. In addition, by the sense of discontinuity and confusion to which it gives rise, Ronsard's reticence becomes the palpable manifestation of the limited expressivity of narrative painting, and thus the proof of its impotence to resist the tow of the semiosic drift. The second source of semantic incoherence reinforces this philosophical significance. It is a matter of Ronsard's em-

---

[41] See also Cave, "Mythological Universe," 164; and Ford, "Painter," 32.

[42] See, especially, the analyses of Homer's description of Achilles' shield by Murray Krieger, *Ekphrasis*, 17-18; and James Heffernan, *Museum of Words*, 10-22.

[43] Ford, "Painter," 39-41. These resemblances are in fact one of the principal premises in Ford's final political-historical interpretation of the ode.

[44] See, for example, *Aeneid* 8.626-29: "There the story of Italy and the triumphs of Rome had the lord of Fire fashioned, not unversed in prophecy, or unknowing of the age to come; there, every generation of the stock to spring from Ascanius, and the wars they fought one by one" ("Illic res Italas Romanorumque triumphos / haud vatum ignarus venturique inscius aevi / fecerat Ignipotens, illic genus omne futurae / stirpis ab Ascanio pugnataque in ordine bella"): *Virgil*, trans. H. Rushton Fairclough, 2 (Cambridge: Harvard University Press, 1954), 102-103.

phasis on the idea of present time throughout the ode. Like the silence, this feature–evident in the extraordinarily high number of present-tense verbs and present-progressive constructions (not to mention present participles used adjectivally) [45]–may be said to undermine any sense of emplotment, both within and between the various episodes. Much as the connecting terms substitute an illusion of spatiality for the idea of causality, the poet's emphasis on present time creates an impression of simultaneity that relentlessly subverts the possible chronology of the events recounted. There is more. With the apostrophes to the reader/spectator ("Vous") and the other more or less explicit references to the receptor sprinkled throughout the poem, [46] Ronsard injects a sense of 'nowness' into this simultaneity. As a result, the events seem to take place both all at once and at the same moment in which the reader of the poem (the spectator of the painting) experiences them.

This sense of immediacy reaches a kind of climax midway through the present-tense description of the third *peinture*: Juno's amorous seduction of Jupiter. In verses 55-60, hence at the organic (if not properly numerical) center of the poem, Ronsard introduces a parenthetic digression, likewise in the present tense, about a picture on the richly decorated "baudrier," or warrior's girdle, that the queen of the Gods has borrowed from Venus (presumably in the hope that its aphrodisiac powers will help rekindle the original amatory ardor of her husband, Jupiter):

> (Là, les amours sont portraits d'ordre,
> Celui qui donte les oiseaus,
> Et celui qui vient ardre & mordre
> Le cueur des Dauphins sous les eaus.
> Leandre, proie à l'amour inhumaine,
> Pendu aus flots noue où l'amour le meine.)
>
> (vv. 55-60)

---

[45] A careful inspection uncovers fifty-eight examples of the present tense (including passive forms) and twenty-four present-progressive constructions as compared to only three instances of the past tense.

[46] See, for example, the reference to "on" in verse 74. This receptor is likewise inscribed in every analogy that is drawn: e.g., "Comme un etang" (v. 30); "En forme de lances errans" (v. 44); "Egalle aus chans" (v. 48); "Comme grandes forests" (v. 74). For more on the function of analogies as signals of the receptor-narratee, see Gerald Prince, "Introduction à l'étude du narrataire," *Poétique* 14 (1973): 178-96, esp. 185.

There can be little doubt that the three "amours" described in this passage–which Ford traces to Homer and the manifestations of Eros on Aphrodite's *cestos* in *Iliad* 14.214-17: spiritual love, impatient desire, and maddening lust [47]–relate directly to the seduction theme of the third *peinture*. They may even symbolize the nuances of love at work in Juno's own heart and mind. Nevertheless, why are these images introduced as components of a miniature picture within this painting? In this regard, Ronsard surely owes nothing to his two primary literary models. Never do Homer and Virgil refer to a tableau within the scenes on Achilles' or Aeneas' shield. For this reason, the likeliest source of inspiration would be the narrative pictures produced before and during the composition of *Des peintures*, in the late 1540s. [48] Such *mise-en-abîme* effects were widely available for public consideration at the time. In the Cathedral to Saint Mamas at Langres, for instance, Ronsard and his contemporaries might well have admired the iconographically ornate temple friezes that complete the scenery *all' antica* in the hagiographic tapestry designed by Jean Cousin the Elder, *St. Mamas Giving Himself up to the Tribunal of the Governor of Cappadocia* (1543-44) (fig. 4). [49] What is more, such pictorial layering was clearly among the favorite effects employed by the renowned school of Italian and French painters assembled at Fontainebleau. [50] Il Rosso's acclaimed Galerie François I (1528-40) is rife with examples. When considered as pictorial 'units' in their own right, the fourteen bays that fill out this extraordinary artistic program are each a grand picture that accommodates a panoply of other pictures–from the image-charged friezes, cartouches, roundels, and stucco reliefs to the narrative fresco at the center of the whole. In many cases, the component pic-

[47] Ford, "Painter," 37-38.

[48] Based upon the events described in the final stanza, Laumonier assigns the composition of the ode to June 1549, when Henri II made his official royal entrance into Paris (*RPL*, 41).

[49] St. Mamas was a Caesarean shepherd of the third century A.D. celebrated for his humble lifestyle and extraordinary rapport with wild beasts. For more on the story of this Orphic figure, see Herbert Thurston and Donald Attwater, *Butler's Lives of the Saints*, 3 vols. (New York: Kennedy, 1956), 3:339-40. In fact, the present tapestry is one of three, each depicting a different moment in the Saint's life, that were produced for the Cathedral at Langres. See the commentaries on these artworks in Béguin, *L'Ecole de Fontainebleau*, 346-47.

[50] For more on the history of the Fontainebleau school, see Jean-Jacques Lévêque, *L'Ecole de Fontainebleau* (Neuchâtel: Editions Ides et Calendes, 1984); and Béguin, *L'Ecole de Fontainebleau*; Blunt, *Art and Architecture*, 104-31.

FIG. 4: Jean Cousin the Elder, *St. Mamas Giving Himself up to the Tribunal of the Governor of Cappadocia* (1543-44), Louvre, Paris
(Réunion des Musées Nationaux)

tures are themselves the contexts for still more pictorial decorations. Such is the situation, for example, in the so-called *Danae* compartment, where the central fresco includes three additional pictures (two of which adorn the column pedestals while the third occupies a niche in the palace wall) (fig. 5), and in the *Unity of State* bay, whose fresco contains a number of background reliefs (or perhaps statues) of human figures, and where the right panel accommodates a boat with an elaborately engraved bow (fig. 6: panel not shown).[51]

In a sense, then, the *baudrier* stanza is the best signal yet of the relevance of contemporary narrative painting to the meaning and design of *Des peintures*. Still problematic, however, is the curious manner in which this stanza has been included. Why does Ronsard place it at the center of the ode, one of the most privileged spots in the structure of any (pre-modernist) literary work, while simultaneously marking it off in parentheses? Insofar as the poet normally reserves this punctuation for purely subordinate, explanatory, and personal digressions,[52] such a position would seem, on the surface, wholly inappropriate. It is true that, by evoking the "Dauphins sous les eaus" (v. 58), the passage anticipates the more naturalistic breed of porpoises, the "Dauphins aus dos courbés," that "nouent, / . . . follatrent & jouent" (vv. 71-72) in the first of the historical scenes that follow (vv. 67-90). Thus, on one level, these lines are particularly well located to prepare the transition from the mythological beginning of the ode (*peintures* 1-3) to its historical ending (*peintures* 4-5). From a logical point of view, however, such an important structural function would again seem to preclude the use of parentheses.

[51] On the history of the Galerie François I and strategies for reading individual bays as well as the overall program, see especially Erwin Panofsky and Dora Panofsky, "Iconography," 113-90; Panofsky and Panofsky, "La Galerie François Ier au château de Fontainebleau," *Revue de l'Art* 16-17 (1972); and W. McAllister Johnson, "Once More the Galerie François Ier at Fontainebleau," *Gazette des Beaux-Arts* 103 (1984): 127-44. Regarding the iconography of the *Danae* bay, see "Galerie," 132-33; and Henri Zerner, "Le système décoratif de la Galerie François Ier à Fontainebleau," in *Actes du Colloque International sur l'Art de Fontainebleau*, ed. André Chastel (Paris: Editions du Centre National de la Recherche Scientifique, 1975), 31-34. For readings of the *Unity of State* compartment, see Panofsky and Panofsky, "Iconography," 127-31; and "Galerie," 137-38. On 'Fontainebleau' as a school of art, see Lévêque, *L'Ecole de Fontainebleau*.

[52] Compare, among many other poems, the ode *A Jouachim du Bellai Angevin* (1:108-21, vv. 85, 106, 190), the ode *A Bouju Angevin* (1:121-25, vv. 5-6), and the *Palinodie à Denise* (1:252-57, v. 50).

FIG. 5: Il Rosso Fiorentino, *Danae*, *Galerie François I*, Fontainebleau
(Réunion des Musées Nationaux)

FIG. 6: Il Rosso Fiorentino, *The Unity of State*, *Galerie François I*,
Fontainebleau (Réunion des Musées Nationaux)

The solution to this dilemma rests eventually with the contribution the *baudrier* sextet makes to the quality of simultaneity developed throughout the ode. For by including a description, in the present tense, of a miniature picture within the description, also in the present tense, of a painting that is but a component of the present-tense description of the tableau as a whole, Ronsard succeeds in reinforcing the impression that all parts of the poem exist synchronously. Hence, in the same complex gesture the poet once more manages to imitate in words a property inherent to every work of visual art: the ability of a painting to deliver its multiple elements to the viewer in the same instant. Yet insofar as that simultaneity plays such an important part in the overall discontinuity and incomprehensibility of the ode/tableau, Ronsard is above all able to underscore the acute communicative inadequacies of narrative painting. By enclosing this passage in parentheses while paradoxically placing it at the center of the ode, the laureate effectively spotlights the subversive impact of visual synchrony on the ability of narrative painting to restrain and convey the transcendent meanings caught in the perpetual Hermetic drift.

With this remarkably powerful maneuver Ronsard leaves no room to doubt that the paragone plays a thematic role in the poem at least as important as the historical-allegorical message he advances. By insisting on the disadvantages of pictorial simultaneity, he directly confronts the paragone theorists who praise this very quality as one of painting's most commendable assets. In fact, Ronsard's principal unnamed foil may again be Leonardo da Vinci. Not only do the poet and the painter focus on precisely the same issues, but they manifest an equivalent measure of zeal in advancing their respective causes. In *Trattato* 22, for example, Leonardo is equally concerned with the connection between all-at-onceness and comprehensibility, and although his conclusion is the antithesis of Ronsard's, the sharpness of his remarks cannot but recall the pointedness in the laureate's paradoxical treatment of the *baudrier* passage:

> Now look what difference there is between listening for a long time to a tale about something which gives pleasure to the eye and actually seeing it all at once as works of nature are seen. Moreover, the works of poets are read at long intervals; they are often not understood and require many explanations, and

commentators very rarely know what was in the poet's mind. . . .
But the work of the painter is immediately understood by its
beholders.[53]

* * *

It is clear that *Des peintures* does far more than allegorize the
struggle between Henri II and Charles V and the role played by
the Gods in insuring a French victory. As evidenced by the title, the
opening stanza, and the principal features responsible for its apparent obscurity, the ode also levies an incisive attack upon the expressive weaknesses of painting–especially narrative painting–as well as
upon some of the most eminent theoretical defenses of the pictorial
arts in Western culture.

Still unresolved, though, is how the ode has demonstrated the
other thesis raised in the title and initial sextet, the converse proposition that would place the superior ability to imitate ideal Nature
in the pen of the poet. The explanation is surprisingly simple. Despite its discontinuous design, the poem succeeds in giving a comprehensible presence to two major notions: its historical-allegorical
message and, now, its idea about the semantic supremacy of poetry
over painting. Of course, the inscription of this last position raises
yet another fundamental question. Why is the ode understandable
at all? If it is true that a narrative painting is "en son mort contrefaite" with respect to ideal Nature, how is it that *Des peintures* can
coherently express any metaphysical thoughts after the effort Ronsard puts into imitating the two most essential properties of the
pictorial arts, their muteness and visual simultaneity? The answer
relates ultimately to the nature of poetry itself. More precisely, it pertains to the intrinsic conceptuality and temporality of poetry's medium of conventional and diachronic verbal language. For in the end
the ideas raised in this ode are too complex to be confined to the
naturalness or instantaneity of the visual signs of painting. They are

---

[53] "Hor uedi, che differentia è dal udire raccontare una cosa, che dà piacere al
occhio con lunghezza di tempo, o uederla con quella prestezza, che si uedono le
cose naturali. et anchora che le cose de' poeti sieno con longho interuallo di tempo
lette, spesse sono le uolte, che le non sonno intese e bisogna farli sopra diuersi co-
menti, de' quali rarissime uolte tali comentatori intendono, qual'fusse la mente del
poeta. . . . Ma l'opera del pittore immediate è compresa dalli suoi risguardatori"
(1:60).

the products of an intellection that exceeds anything sensually perceptible and an evolution that depends upon the succession through time of one word to the next or, in the present case, of the first *peinture* to the fifth, the mythological debut to the historical end. Contrary to Leonardo's protests in *Trattato* 22 (and elsewhere), it is the very non-naturalness and non-synchronousness of verbal language that allows the poet to subdue the flow of the infinite drift.[54]

II. POETRY AGAINST THE 'FLOW'

Although Ronsard never expounds on the sources for his distinctive characterization of the poet's manifold advantages over the painter, he assuredly shares an important intellectual kinship with the major contributors to the inter-art paragone who preceded him. What surprises, however, is the seeming ease with which he switches from one philosophical system of thought to another in advancing his position. To call Ronsard opportunistic in this regard is no exaggeration. Throughout his criticisms of painting, he relies heavily upon Plato and the Neoplatonists. Their basic opposition between corrupt material reality and an ideal Nature that is ever-shifting and inherently ineffable is key to his degradation of the matter-oriented and synchronous pictorial arts. Similarly, in his bid for the supremacy of poetry, Ronsard depends strongly on the Platonic and Neoplatonic concepts of poetic madness and the poet's divine ministry as the *vates* of God's supreme truths. Yet, in order to take the

---

[54] In discussing the patterns of *imbrication* that emerge in *Des peintures*, Ford has recently made the point that "while it is true that readers of poetry have a series of lines of verse imposed upon them as they read through a poem from beginning to end, it is not necessarily true that this order should be the one that their minds will retain when they think about the poem and attempt to make sense of it." He has further affirmed that "the activity of the spectator and of the reader are not so dissimilar, once linear presentation in a poem breaks down, as is the case here": *Ronsard's "Hymnes,"* 38, and n. 24. While there is no denying that the patterns he discerns are real, and that, in practice, the spectator's and reader's activities bear many fundamental similarities, it is also true, as we have shown, that the emergence of the overarching allegorical-historical meaning of the ode depends primarily on the poet's linear presentation of the five scenes, and that, for Ronsard as for Leonardo da Vinci and the principal adversaries in the inter-art rivalries of the Renaissance, the *theoretical* emphasis was always on the *differences* between seeing and reading.

next required step and promote his art's *semantic* plenitude, the laureate can no longer abide these same theoretical paradigms: their underlying conception of the semiosic drift denies the communicative efficacy of all languages, visual and verbal. It is then that the poet proves as paradoxical as his antecedents, abandoning Plato and the Neoplatonists for a fundamentally Aristotelian and Scholastic mode of thinking. Like the Stagirite, Aquinas and, most of all, Dante, Ronsard articulates a faith in the power of poetry to seize and transmit every level of meaning–physical, rational, and spiritual. Not only is the verbal language of poetry intrinsically diachronic, and thus able to represent reality 'in action' (the true object of art for Aristotle), but as Aquinas would concede, it is a manifestation of the 'Word', the semiotic inscription of God Himself, and hence an ally of the mind and spirit. Furthermore, as Dante steadfastly insists, poetry has the power to make these material, intellectual, and divine truths intelligible. As *A son Luc* and *Des peinture* effectively reaffirm, it can transmit those truths meaningfully to the worthy addressee-reader and thereby tame the superabundant meanings (or drift) of the Word-God.

Poetry assumes the same extraordinary privileges in Ronsard's more traditional ekphraseis of narrative paintings, those which, like the pictorial (re-)creations of Homer and Virgil, come embedded within larger poetic narratives and evoke the pictorial embellishments on three-dimensional objects presumed to exist independently of those decorations. Four such ekphraseis stand out in Ronsard's *oeuvre*. The first three describe the complex iconographical renderings on a guitar, a flower basket, and a cloak. They are introduced, respectively, in three odes published with *Des peintures* in the 1550 *Quatre premiers livres des Odes*: *A sa guiterre*, *La defloration de Lede*, and *Le ravissement de Cephale*. Written before the "tableau" poem by several years or months (from as early as 1543-45 in the case of *A sa guiterre*, to 1546 for *La defloration*, and the beginning months of 1549 for *Le ravissement*),[55] these mythology-rich poetic stories relating or reflecting the pleasures and pains of the poet's quest for his beloved's affections are likewise the testing grounds for the thoughts on poetry and narrative painting that Ronsard subsequently distills in *Des peintures*. In contrast, the

---

[55] Theories on the probable dates of composition are presented by Laumonier, *RPL*, 44, 54-56; and Guérin, *Odes*, 378.

fourth ekphrasis appears in a strongly autobiographical piece composed and published some twenty years after the previous odes: the
1569 elegy *A Monsieur de Belot*, or simply *La Lyre*, of the *Sixiesme
livre des Poëmes*. This work, which features the lengthy verbal representation of a superbly engraved *lyre à archet* putatively offered to
the poet by his benefactor, Jean Dutreuilh de Belot, affords tangible
evidence that Ronsard's previous paragone concerns endure well
into the middle of his career.

A. *Of Guitars, Baskets, Cloaks, and Lyres*

The signs of a confidence in the artistic supremacy of poetry are
apparent from Ronsard's first fully developed ekphrasis, the description of the guitar's exquisite "fust" (or wooden body) in quatrains 6-11 of the ode *A sa guiterre*. Well before that segment, however, stanzas 1-3 of the poem are found to forecast that conviction
in the praise lavished on the "guiterre" for being the source of a
music that is identical to poetry itself:

> Ma Guiterre je te chante,
> Par qui seule je deçoi,
> Je deçoi, je ron, j'enchante,
> Les amours que je reçoi.
>
> Nulle chose tant soit douce
> Ne te sçauroit egaler,
> Toi qui mes ennuis repousse
> Si tost qu'ils t'oient parler.
>
> Au son de ton armonie
> Je refréchi ma chaleur
> Ardente en flamme infinie,
> Naissant' d'infini malheur. . . .
> (1:229, vv. 1-12)

This opening tribute to the capacity of the instrument's music to
soothe the sufferings of love, to cool the eternal flames of the "infini
malheur," distinctly recalls the reflections on poetry proper (and especially lyric poetry) expressed in the chief classical models for
these lines. In his eleventh *Idyll*, "The Cyclops," for instance, The-

ocritus likewise considers the effects of music in remedying the wounds of love. For the Greek poet, however, that music is explicitly the "medicine" of the poetic Muses (the "Pierian Maids"): "It seems there's no medicine for love, . . . but only the Pierian Maids. . . . Thus did Polyphemus tend his love-sickness with music, and got more comfort thereout than he could have had for any gold" (vv. 1-4 and 80-81).[56] Similarly, at the start of his 1560 poem, *Le Cyclope amoureux*, another imitation of the same *Idyll*, Ronsard leaves little doubt that all such curative music is the 'song of the nine sisters', the poetry of the Muses: "Contre le mal d'amour qui tous les maux excede, / On ne sçauroit trouver plus suffisant remede / Que celuy des neuf soeurs, qui sçavent enchanter / Venus & son enfant quand on sçait bien chanter" (10:275, vv. 1-4). Ronsard makes the same connection between music and poetry in *A sa guiterre*. When he extols the instrument in the earlier ode, he does so not for the visual beauty of its painted decorations—not, in other words, out of an admiration for what the art of narrative painting is able to produce—but rather for its value as a source of poetry.

This general praise for poetry becomes a specific acclaim for the semantic superiority of poetry over painting immediately before the actual ekphrasis, in the prefatory remarks of quatrains 4-5:

> Plus cherement je te garde
> Que je ne garde mes yeus,
> Desquels ton fust je regarde
> Peint desus en mile lieus.
>
> Où le nom de ma Déesse
> En maint amoureus lien,
> En maints laz & neuds se laisse
> Joindre en chiffre avec le mien.
>   (1:230, vv. 13-20)

As in *Des peintures*, Ronsard opposes the oneness of poetry (implied in the singular term "fust," the body of the guitar/poetry) with the plurality ("en mile lieus") of narrative painting. Moreover, he again forces the conclusion that this inherent tendency toward multiplicity presents the narrative painter with an intractable prob-

---

[56] Theocritus, *The Greek Bucolic Poets*, ed. and trans. J. M. Edmonds (Cambridge: Harvard University Press, 1970), 140-41, 146-47. See also the other two sources for this passage: Horace's *Odes* 1:32 and Ovid's *Sorrows* 4:10.

lem of signification. By the careful selection of the preposition "desus" (otherwise highlighted by its location at the caesura of verse 16 and by its rhyme with "fust" and the adverb of intensity, "Plus," which never quite loses its alternative quantitative significance), Ronsard reaffirms not only that the painting in question is superficial in the spatial sense–i.e., that it relates solely to the visible, outward materiality of the guitar's wooden body–but also that its orderless multiplicity renders it superficial in the ideational sense–i.e., that it lacks referential depth.

Poetry, on the other hand, would be able to make up for this shortcoming. For Ronsard, a poem can improve the painter's work of art by turning the visual desultoriness of pictorial images into an understandable, harmonious whole. This idea develops metaphorically in stanza 5, as the guitar/poetry becomes the site where the multiple "laz," or fine threads, that comprise the graphic inscription of the beloved's name converge with the signature of the poet-lover. At the same time these threads foreshadow the "mile rets," or thousand nets, evoked during the blason description of the beloved's hair in the penultimate stanza of the ode ("Chanton donc sa chevelure, / De laquelle Amour vainqueur, / Noua mile rets à l'heure / Qu'il m'encordela le cueur . . ." [1:233, vv. 81-84]), they also anticipate the linear elements of the narrative pictures on the "fust." But these elements are more than simply formal. Insofar as lines are a (or even *the*) primary source of pictorial design (*disegno*), or conceptual content, for virtually all aesthetic theorists since Aristotle,[57] the threads/lines of Ronsard's "guiterre" likewise connote the ideational qualities of those pictures. With the affirmation that the guitar is the locus of their conjunction, then, this stanza portends the ability of poetry to unify (and presumably to clarify) the entangled conceptual multiplicity of the painted images.

The ensuing six-stanza ekphrasis of the three-part narrative painting not only fulfills this prediction, but, like the verbal pictures

---

[57] As noted in Chapter One, Aristotle equates pictorial line with plot, the unifying conceptual element of drama. See also, Aquinas: *ST* 1a-2ae 49 a 2 and 1; and especially, Leonardo da Vinci, *Tr.* frag. 102 (cited in Tatarkiewicz, *History*, 3:138 n. 10). It should also be noted that Renaissance theorists often fold the quality of line into the fundamental aesthetic concepts of form, proportion, grace, and beauty (see Barasch, *Theories*, 219-24). Of course the importance of line to the overall beauty and affective impact of painting is frequently called into question as theorists like Lodovico Dolce take up the cause of the Venetian colorists.

of *Des peintures*, it also reveals the sources of the poet's special powers. On examining the description of the first two painted scenes (quatrains 6-8), for example, we are immediately struck by the particular figures represented and their singular rapport with the world that surrounds them:

> Où le dieu qui lave & baigne
> Dans le Loir son poil doré,
> Du luc aus Muses enseigne
> Dont elles m'ont honnoré.
>
> Son laurier preste l'oreille,
> Si qu'au premier vent qui vient,
> De ressifler s'appareille
> Ce que par cueur il retient.
>
> Ici, les forests compaignes
> Attire à lui, & les vens,
> Orphée, qui les campaignes
> Ombrage de bois suivens.
>
> (1:230-31, vv. 21-32)

Despite their potentially wide range of symbolic meanings, the two mythological personages in question, Phebus-Apollo [58] and Orpheus, have in this instance assumed the one role they share in common: that of the archetypal *lyric* poet. As a result, they and the ekphrastic passages in which they appear illustrate and reaffirm what the preceding verses have already implied: narrative painting is dependent upon the lyre/guitar and poetry for its ontological and semantic existence. Indeed, in an unmistakable biasing of the otherwise (theoretically) egalitarian ut pictura poesis topos, quatrains 6-8 would also emphasize that the similarities between poetry and painting commence with the painter's reliance upon the poet for much or all of his subject matter. [59]

---

[58] This reference becomes clearer when, in 1555, Ronsard replaces the original verse 21 with "Où le beau *Phebus* qui baigne" (my emphasis).

[59] In this fashion, Ronsard departs from the position advanced by most major art theorists since Antiquity. For the latter, neither the poet nor the painter has the upper hand in this regard. In terms of their subject matters, verbal artists depend as much on visual artists as the reverse, their influence is reciprocal and equal. Cf. the poet-artist comparisons in the next chapter and the discussion of Benedetto Varchi's *Lezzione* in Lecercle, *Chimère*, 25-30.

More importantly, though, the poet figures evoked would point the way to the origins of poetry's referential supremacy over painting. Especially revealing are the implications of Ronsard's decision to disregard all but one aspect of the complex Apollo and Orpheus myths: the idea (most likely borrowed from Virgil and Horace) that these divine poets are masters over all the forces of nature. Just as Phebus-Apollo moves the "laurier" to "preste[r] l'oreille" and to "ressifler" the lute's divine tunes, so too Orpheus employs his magical song to "Attire[r] à lui" the "forests" and "vens."[60] Taken in relation to Ronsard's earlier intimations about poetry, and in the broader context of his artistic reflections in *A son Luc* and *Des peintures*, this focus instantly recalls the unparalleled access of the poet to both *n*ature and Nature, to the physical world and the metaphysical powers that shape and move it. Above all, it also calls to mind his message about the poet's unique ability to turn incomprehensible multiplicity into intelligible unity, to rescue (narrative) painting from the flow.

To understand how this ability operates, however, we must proceed to quatrains 9-11. Here Ronsard details the third (and last) painted scene on the guitar, the kidnapping of Ganymede by Jupiter from the forest-cloaked slopes of Mount Ida:

> Là, est Ide la branchue,
> Où l'oiseau de Juppiter
> Dedans sa griffe crochue
> Vient Ganymede empieter.
>
> Ganymede delectable,
> Chasserot delicieus,
> Qui ores sert à la table
> D'eschançon là haut aus cieus.
>
> Ses chiens apres l'aigle aboient,
> Et ses gouverneurs aussi,
> En vain étonnés le voient
> Par l'air emporter ainsi.
>
> (1:231, vv. 33-44)

---

[60] See Virgil, *Eclogue* 6, vv. 82-83, in the first case, and Horace, *Odes* 1.12, vv. 7-12, in the second.

On the surface, this representation seems to preclude the possibility that the instrument's iconography might follow any coherent program of meaning. The subject matter appears to herald an abrupt departure from the thematic context prepared earlier. Unlike Phebus-Apollo and Orpheus, Ganymede is hardly among the customary figures for the poet. Notwithstanding the Neoplatonic tradition likening the Phrygian youth and his abduction to the enraptured mind in the course of its ascent to God's ideal love,[61] and hence the potential for Ganymede to be identified metaphorically with the poet as lover (in terms of his transcendent experience before the divine beauty of his beloved), in truth such identifications are noticeably rare.[62] It is also significant that, in contrast to the poet personages of the first two pictures, who exhibit a definite mastery over n/Nature, Ganymede has no such command. On the contrary, as his capture by Jupiter's eagle forcefully symbolizes, n/Nature has complete dominion over him. Why, then, has Ronsard included the scene? Is it simply another symptom of what Terence Cave calls the poet's "love of surface ornament, of changing patterns and textures," the product, in other words, of his fondness for the *copia* aesthetic of the period?[63] Perhaps, but why does Ronsard grant it the added distinctions of being the longest of the guitar's painted scenes (equal in verses to the preceding two pictures) and of occu-

---

[61] Consider, for example, Christoforo Landino's commentary on Dante's evocation of this myth in *Purgatorio* 9.19-27: "Sia adunque Ganimede l'humana mente, la qual Gioue, cioè, il sommo Iddio ama. Siano i suoi compagni le altre potentie dell'anima, come è la uegetatiua, & sensitiua. Apposta adunque Gioue, che essa sia nella selua, cioè, remota dalle cose mortali, & con l'aquila già detta l'innalza al cielo" (*Dante con l'espositione di Christoforo Landino, et di Alessandro Vellutello* [Venice: Appresso Giouambattista, Marchio Seba & Fratelli, 1564], 195). For more on the Neoplatonic interpretations of Ganymede, see Panofsky, *Iconology*, 213-18 and James M. Saslow, *Ganymede in the Renaissance: Homosexuality in Art and Society* (New Haven: Yale University Press, 1986), 2.

[62] Perhaps the closest identification of this sort is the one advanced by the fourteenth-century theologian, Petrus Berchorius, in his *Ovidius Moralizatus*. According to Berchorius, Ganymede symbolized St. John the Evangelist and the eagle, his Muse-like divine inspiration (Panofsky, *Iconology*, 213). Primarily, however, Ganymede served as a metaphor for either male beauty (cf. Theocritus' *Idyll* 20 and the translation of that text by Baïf, *Eclogue* XII, "Le Pastoureau") or homosexuality (e.g., Du Bellay, *Regrets*, Sonnet 103). By contrast, comparisons between the poet and the Jupiter-eagle in other rape myths are relatively common (e.g., Scève, *Délie* 120). For more on the literary and artistic uses of the Ganymede myth during the Renaissance, see Guy Demerson, *La Mythologie classique dans l'oeuvre lyrique de la "Pléiade"* (Geneva: Droz, 1972), and Saslow, *Ganymede*, ibid.

[63] Cave, "Mythological Universe," 165.

pying the prominent center point of this twenty-two-stanza, eighty-eight-verse ode?

An explanation is once more suggested by the thematic context prepared in stanzas 4 and 5 and our readings of *A son Luc* and *Des peintures*. In short, the Ganymede picture seems to be included precisely because it does disrupt the iconographic program on the guitar. What is more, it appears that the special emphasis it receives is designed specifically to stress the propensity for disorder and incomprehensibility of narrative painting and, conversely, the power of poetry to reorder that confusion into a meaningful whole.

Once again the stylistic features that serve to accentuate this sense of incoherence strongly support this understanding. As in *Des peintures*, Ronsard resorts to a series of relationally ambiguous spatial connectives ("Où," "Ici" and "Là") and present-tense verbs ("lave," "enseigne," "preste," "vient," "s'appareille," "retient," "Attire," "est," "Vient," "sert," "aboient," and "voient"). [64] At the same time both effects intensify the sense of narrative discontinuity in the ode, they also draw attention to the qualities of randomness and simultaneity that undermine the expressive potential of real narrative paintings.

Further corroboration for this reading resides in the fact that the Apollo, Orpheus, and Ganymede scenes actually do correlate, and that, in the end, only the lexical coincidences and thematic connections provided by the poet make this correlation possible. At the lexical level, for example, the three pictures are united not only by the present-tense verbs noted previously (albeit, paradoxically, for their opposite effect upon the potential sense of chronology among the images), but also by the recurrence, in each case, of words evoking trees and forests ("laurier," "forests," "bois," and "branchue") and wind and air ("vent," "siffler," "vents," and "air").

To discern the thematic connections, on the other hand, we are obliged to go beyond the painting ekphrasis. Our attention must turn to all that precedes and follows the *fust* description–to what might be called the 'poem part' of the ode, where the author's voice

---

[64] The obvious exception to the present-tense verbs is the *passé composé* that Ronsard employs in verse 24: "Dont elles m'ont honnoré." Virtually a parenthetic aside, however, this case does little to disrupt the immediacy of the surrounding description. On the contrary, its very difference hightens the sense of nowness of the other verbs.

is typically easiest to distinguish. Two coherent interpretations are the result. The first may be inferred from the pair of stanzas (12-13) that immediately follows the guitar episode:

> Tu es des dames pensives
> L'instrument approprié,
> Et aus jeunesses lascives
> Consacré & dedié.
>
> Leurs amours, c'est ton office,
> Non pas les assaus cruels,
> Et le joieus exercice
> De soupirs continuels.
>
> (1:231-32, vv. 45-52)

From this perspective the decorations on the body of the instrument may be said to represent pictorially the two facets of love most properly suited to the guitar's music/lyric poetry: pensive melancholy love (the sentiment of the "dames pensives") and lascivious passion (the lusts of the "jeunesses lascives"). In keeping with the grievous experiences of love traditionally associated with Apollo and Orpheus,[65] the initial two scenes may be taken as alluding to the first kind of sentiment (that from which the poet seeks relief at the opening of the poem), whereas the forceful abduction of Ganymede by Jupiter featured in the third picture would signify a purely carnal affection (like the one threatened by the poet-lover in *La defloration de Lede*, and elsewhere).[66]

Another meaning is suggested by quatrains 14-18. As in the principal source for these stanzas, the opening lines of Virgil's sixth *Eclogue*, the issue is the kind of poetry that should accompany the poet's guitar.

> Encores qu'au tens d'Horace,
> Les armes de tous costés
> Sonnassent par la menasse
> Des Cantabres indontés,

---

[65] See, for example, Ovid's account of Apollo's first experience of love for the elusive Daphne (*Metamorphoses* 1.452-567) and his story of Orpheus' tragic love for Eurydice (*Metamorphoses* 10.1-105).

[66] Brian Barron draws essentially the same conclusion in his dissertation: "la guitare est un instrument doublement utile, consacré à la fois aux 'dames pensives' et aux 'jeunesses lascives'" ("Ut pictura poesis," 226).

Et que le Romain empire
Foullé des Parthes fust tant,
Si n'a il point sur sa Lire
Belonne acordé pourtant.

Mais bien Venus la riante,
Ou son fils plein de rigueur,
Lalage, ou Clöe fuiante
Davant avecques son cueur.

Quand sur toi je chanteroie
D'Hector les combas divers,
Et ce qui fut fait à Troie
Par les Grecs en dix ivers,

Cela ne peut satisfaire
A l'amour qui tant me mord:
Que peut Hector pour moi faire,
Que peut Ajax qui est mort?

(1:232-33, vv. 53-72)

On the one hand, there is the poetry of "Bellone," the goddess of war: a reference to epic poetry, whose main purpose is to celebrate the military accomplishments (the "combas divers") of legendary political rulers, past (Hector and Ajax) as well as contemporary. On the other hand, there is the poetry of "Venus la riante": an allusion to lyric, the songs through which the poet expresses his most intimate feelings toward his lady, and which the last two stanzas lead us to believe he favors for its cathartic ability to relieve the sorrows of love.

Perhaps, then, the scenes on the guitar would serve as a pictorial rendering of this opposition along with a premonitory glimpse of Ronsard's preference for lyric. [67] In that case, the Apollo and Orpheus paintings represent the lyric poet in his favorite role as servant to Venus, while the Ganymede picture symbolize the dissatisfaction which the poet of love experiences when forced to restrict his song to the political glories of his monarch.

Whichever reading we prefer, or even if we embrace the two solutions simultaneously (since, in truth, both interpretations are le-

---

[67] André Gendre comes to a similar conclusion in his study of Ronsard and the *conquête amoureuse* (cf. esp. 53-57).

gitimate and compatible), the fact remains that the guitar's three-part tableau can gain unifying meaning only in the context of the poem as a whole. Thus, like *Des peintures*, *A sa guiterre* underscores the fundamental opposition between the confusing plurality of narrative pictures and the unifying meaning of poems, between painting 'in the drift' and poetry 'against the flow'.

* * *

Poetry is again the unique source of meaning for the multifarious narrative paintings featured in *La defloration de Lede*, *Le ravissement de Cephale,* and *La Lyre*. In the first poem, for example, the multiple pastoral and mythological pictures on Leda's "panier" described in octets 10-15 (vv. 73-116) appear to achieve little referential connection. Qualities of color and material seem the only noteworthy links among the painted images of a golden Aurora and a horse-driven sun, a skulking wolf and an inattentive shepherd, quarreling Satyrs and head-butting rams. Indeed, no description rings truer than the poet's first allusion to the flower basket as "Paint *de diverses couleurs*, / Et paint *de diverse sorte*" (2:71, vv. 71-72: my emphasis).

In the context of the ode as a whole, however, the same concoction regroups meaningfully around the ode's center-most themes of suffering and violent conquest in response to Cassandre's refusal to requite the poet's love. The Aurora and sun images of octets 10-12 suddenly stand out as the pictographic equivalents of the eternity and intensity of the poet's amorous torments:

> D'un bout du panier s'ouvroit
> Entre cent nuës dorées,
> Une Aurore qui couvroit
> Le ciel de fleurs colorées:
> Ses cheveus vagoient errans
> Soufflés du vent des narines
> Des prochains chevaus tirans
> Le souleil des eaus marines.
> . . . .
> Ce soleil tumbant au soir
> Dedans l'onde voisine entre,
> A chef bas se laissant cheoir
> Jusqu'au fond de ce grand ventre.
>
> (2:72-73, vv. 73-96)

These pictures plainly recall the love-torn poet's affirmation from eight stanzas earlier: "Et le souleil ne peut voir / Soit quand le jour il apporte, / Ou quand il se couche au soir / Une autre douleur plus forte" (2:68, vv. 13-16). Hence the basket's visual periphrases of the dawn-till-dusk solar journey would serve as iconographic reminders that at no time during its travels would the sun witness a greater suffering than the poet's.

Likewise, the ensuing three scenes of impending or actual violent confrontation clearly rework the story of Jupiter's rape of Leda, which soon takes over as the ode's narrative preoccupation when the anguished poet threatens to follow the lustful Swan's example should Cassandre continue her cruel rejections. The shepherd and sheep of octet 13 are as much the doubles for Leda as the wolf of the same stanza is the loupine counterpart of the cygnaline king of the Gods:

> Sur le sourci d'un rocher
> Un pasteur le loup regarde,
> Qui se haste d'aprocher
> Du couard peuple qu'il garde:
> Mais de cela ne lui chaut,
> Tant un limas lui agrée,
> Qui lentement monte en haut
> D'un lis, au bas de la prée.
>
> (2.73, vv. 97-104)

Just as the wolf hastens to approach his prey, Jupiter is "époinçonné / De telle amoureuse rage" and "Impatient du desir" for Leda (vv. 25-36); and like the carefree shepherd who takes an all-absorbing interest in watching a snail ascend a lily,[68] the unsuspecting Leda is both intensely "studieuse des fleurs" of the fields where she plays (vv. 65-70) and "apprivois[é]" (i.e., transfixed or tamed) by the "gaie façon" and "chançon" of the Swan-Jupiter (vv. 153-56).[69]

---

[68] My translation of "limas" differs from that of Doris Delacourcelle who, like Laumonier (cf. Chant Pastoral, 9:85, n. 5), prefers the idea of "limaçon," or slug (Le Sentiment de l'art dans la "Bergerie" de Remy Belleau [Oxford: Blackwell, 1945], 78). I agree instead with the theory advanced by Hélène Naïs, according to whom "limas, limace et limaçon désignent . . . habituellement notre escargot" (Les Animaux dans la poésie française de la Renaissance [Paris: Didier, 1961], 195).

[69] It is also relevant that snails and other such mollusks were commonly a symbol of bad luck in the Renaissance. Witness, for example, Ronsard's remarks on the

Further, the fighting satyrs and rams that 'conclude' the decorations in octets 14-15 become the obvious pictorial counterparts to the poetic account of the violent conclusion to Jupiter's deceitful seduction:

> Un Satire tout follet
> En folatrant prend, & tire
> La panetiere, & le lait
> D'un autre follet Satire.
> L'un court apres tout ireus,
> L'autre defend sa despouille,
> Le laict se verse sur eus
> Qui sein, & menton leur souille.
>
> Deus beliers qui se hurtoient
> Le haut de leurs testes dures,
> Portréts aus deus borts estoient
> Pour la fin de ces paintures.
>
> (2:73-74, vv. 105-16)

The images of grabbing, pulling, chasing, defending, and head butting unmistakably foreshadow the squeezing, constraining, struggling, pinching, and biting of the actual rape episode recounted seven stanzas later:

> Il va ses ergots dressant
> Sur les bras d'elle qu'il serre,
> Et de son ventre pressant
> Contraint la rebelle à terre.
> Sous l'oiseau se debat fort,
> Le pince, & le mord, si est-ce
> Qu'au milieu de tel effort
> Ell'sent ravir sa jeunesse.
>
> (2:76-77, vv. 169-76)

Despite the color discrepancy, the milk that "se verse" and "souille" in the satyr scene also anticipates the blood that spatters and sullies

---

inauspicious prophetic significance of the "Limas" (and the turtle) in his 1569 poem, *Le Chat*: "Autant en est de la tarde Tortuë, / Et du Limas qui plus tard se remuë, / . . . / *L'homme qui voit, songeant, ces animaux, / Peut bien penser que longs seront ses maux* . . . " (15:46, vv. 155-62: my emphasis). Thus, on another level, the picture of the shepherd and the snail would foreshadow Leda's ill-fated fascination for the Swan in the verses that follow.

during Jupiter's savage attack: "Le cinabre çà & là / Coulora la ver-gogneuse" (2:77, vv. 177-78).[70]

The semantic determinacy of the narrative pictures embroi-dered on Neptune's "manteau," described in the first of the three "poses" comprising *Le ravissement de Cephale* (octets 4-10, vv. 25-76), is equally dependent on poetry. Although the images of a storm-racked sea (vv. 29-56), panic-stricken mariners (vv. 31-32), and a compassionate Neptune who summons his great power to rescue the pale mortals and quell the furious waves and winds (vv. 57-72) maintain a topical coherence missing from Ronsard's other narrative-painting ekphraseis, their primary meanings are delimited solely as the poem unfolds. Only when the sweet-voiced Nereid, Naïs, recalls the ode's title by retelling the myth of Aurora and Cephalus in the twenty-one stanzas of the second "pose" (octets 11-31) does the psychological subtext of the tempest and sailors come into focus:

> Desarmée est leur navire
> Du haut jusqu'au fondement,
> Cà & là le vent la vire
> Serve à son commandement,
>
> . . . .
> La mer pleine d'inconstance
> Bruit d'une bouillante eau,
> Et toute dépite tance
> Les flancs du vaincu bateau.
>   (2:135, vv. 33-44)

The sensations of the crew whose ship is buffeted wildly upon the storm-tossed sea clearly coincide with the tumultuous 'undulations' that plague Aurora's mind and heart in the absence of her beloved Cephalus:

---

[70] The preceding conclusions differ sharply from the commentaries on *La deflo-ration* by Terence Cave, for whom none of the basket's motifs "is overtly related to the others or to the story of Leda" (*RP*, 164), and from those of Brian Barron, who finds the basket's pictures especially disconcerting for having "une dimension em-blématique plutôt obscure" ("Ut pictura poesis," 302). They do however concur with the remarks by Margaret McGowan, for whom "the basket . . . carried scenes prophetic of the maiden's wooing by Jupiter" (*Ideal Forms*, 186-90), and by Françoise Joukovsky, who clearly understands that "ces ekphrasis [sic] sont en rap-port étroit avec la composition du poème" (*Bel objet*, 131).

Et bien que de loin absente
De l'absent Cephale soit,
Comme s'elle étoit presente
En son esprit l'aperçoit:
Ores pronte en ceci pance,
Et ores pance en cela,
Sa trop constante inconstance
Ondoie deçà & là.[71]

(2:142, vv. 177-84)

And it is apparent that the narrative pictures should serve an orac-
ular function exclusively in relation to the third and final "pose,"
where the grand priestess Themis makes her prophecy to Neptune's
daughter, the sea goddess Thetis, who is about to marry the mortal
Argonaut Peleus (octets 33-36). The storm image presages the war
at Troy; and the embroidered Neptune, who "[s]e montre seul gou-
verneur" of the "humide monde" (2:136, vv. 70-71), prefigures the
one who "donnera matiere / Aux Poëtes de chanter" (2:146, vv.
267-68)–i.e., Achilles, the son to whom the union of Thetis and
Peleus will give life, and who, like the king of the sea, will wield his
great might to settle the human melee at Ilium.[72]

By the end of the poem, then, the ekphrasis of Neptune's cloak
assumes another significance as well. Like Ronsard's other poet-
icized commentaries on narrative painting, it inscribes a concern
about the unequal abilities of poets and painters to overcome the
Hermetic drift. Indeed it casts that disparity in the most palpable
metaphorical terms. While the hapless sailors could easily represent
the painters at the mercy of the infinite deferral of meanings, Neptune could denote the poet empowered to 'rescue' those artists by
restraining the semiosic flow.[73]

---

[71] Other textual echoes are also apparent. Among these is the compelling connection between the sailors' physiological reaction to their predicament–rendered
"Palles" (v. 31) and "bléme" (v. 59) by the ocean's perils–and Aurora's response
upon first seeing Cephalus and hearing his doleful plaint before the lifeless form of
his wife, Procris: "Mal seine [she] perd sa couleur" (v. 138). There is also the parallel between the fire and flames of love that torture Aurora in every facet of her
being (vv. 148, 158, and 163) and the "flammes" of lightening that fill the stormy
sky represented on Neptune's manteau (vv. 37-38).

[72] "Et apres avoir de Troie / Le fort rampart abatu, / Ilion sera la proie / Des
Grecs, & de sa vertu" (2:147, vv. 285-88).

[73] The last identification is supported by the parallel that arises between Neptune and Naïs. In much the same manner as the first convenes his "troupes" and

Although composed and published two decades after the previous pieces, *La Lyre* reenacts the same fundamental relationship. As before, the narrative painting portrayed upon an object–here the "ventre" of Ronsard's extraordinary "lyre à archet" (vv. 301-456)–assumes its proper meaning only in respect to the poem that describes it. And as in *Des peintures*, *A sa guiterre*, and *La defloration*, that meaning also unifies a disparate collection of scenes. Only, in this instance the powers of poetry are noticeably more imposing, for that collection is substantially grander than the others. Besides occupying 156 verses in all (hence sixty verses more than the tableau of *Des peintures*), [74] the ekphrasis in *La Lyre* contains at least nine distinct mythological tales, or "fictions d'arguments fabuleux" (v. 299):

- (1) Apollo singing at the banquet of the gods (vv. 301-06);
- (2) Pallas (Peace) and Neptune (War) vying for the prerogative to protect Athens (vv. 307-26);
- (3) Marsyas suffering punishment for his unsuccessful hubristic challenge to Apollo and his music (vv. 327-34);
- (4) Apollo and Neptune competing to construct the walls of Troy (vv. 335-50);
- (5) Apollo serving as cattleherd for Admete and singing to his love-fired bovine charge (vv. 351-72);
- (6) the three Graces following Venus and Cupid (vv. 373-80);
- (7) Bacchus holding an overflowing cornucopia and intervening between the Pallas and Neptune of scene 2 (vv. 381-414);
- (8) Mercury catching a turtle and fashioning it into an incomparably melodious lyre (vv. 415-40);
- (9) Mercury offering this instrument to an angry Apollo as recompense for the theft of the latter's cattle (vv. 441-48).

Especially valuable to the referential unity of these stories is the imposing presence of autobiography and poetic theory in the work. As many critics have noted, *La Lyre* is fundamentally about the

---

issues his "lois," the second (who stands as an even more obvious poet figure) rallies the sleeping Nereids at the very beginning of the ode and "de sa parolle / Feit . . . resonner l'air" (vv. 77-78) as she begins the tale of Aurora and Cephalus that will supplant the picture description.

[74] In this count, I ignore the six prefatory verses (vv. 295-300) relating the overall material composition of the instrument and the fabulousness of its ornamentation.

"Gaulois Apollon," both Ronsard's own career and the vocation of poetry in general.[75] The autobiographical dimension is evident from the outset, with the reference, in the original title (*A Monsieur de Belot*), to Jean Dutreuilh de Belot, the "maître des requêtes" for Charles IX who became one of the poet's most generous patrons after their propitious meeting, we are later reminded, "aux bords de la Garonne" in 1565.[76] In addition, there are the many unmistakable allusions to the stages of Ronsard's artistic development: from his ambitious prolific youth to the period of cynicism and creative sterility brought about, during the 1550s and early 1560s, by his clash with "la sotte & maligne Ignorance" (15:28, v. 286), his detractors at court, in the Church, and among the Reformers.[77] In fact, the role of this poem as a milestone in Ronsard's recovery from that depression is a principal theme throughout the first third of the work:

> Belot, parcelle, ains le tout de ma vie,
> Quand je te vy je n'avois plus envie
> De voir la Muse, ou danser à son bal,
> Ou m'abreuver en l'eau que le cheval
> D'un coup de pied fit sourçoyer de terre.
> . . . .
> Mais aussi tost qu'aux bords de la Garonne
> Je te connu d'Esprit & d'Ame bonne,
> Courtois, honneste, hospital, liberal,
> Toutes vertus ayant en general:
> Soudain au coeur il me prist une envie
> De te chanter. . . .
>   (15:15-23, vv. 1-154)

From the outset, then, the autobiographical relevance of *La Lyre* is fully evident: Belot and the lyre in question (purportedly a "pre-

---

[75] See Cave, *Cornucopian Text*, 256-68, and "Ronsard's mythological universe," 190-93; McGowan, *Ideal Forms*, 114-18; Barron, "Ut pictura poesis," 329-35; Silver, *IER* 1:297 and 2:174, 414; Isidore Silver, *Ronsard and the Hellenic Renaissance in France II: Ronsard and the Grecian Lyre*, 3 vols. (Geneva: Droz, 1981-87), 2:106; Laumonier, *RPL*, 224, n. 2. As the following pages will reveal, the present reading of *La Lyre* is deeply indebted to all of these analyses, as both models and foils.

[76] See Laumonier's editorial comment, 15:15, n. 1. In fact, Belot's name is mentioned six different times in the course of the poem.

[77] See, especially, vv. 1-58, 141-48, 281-94 and 457-68.

sent" from his patron) have restored a voice to our laureate's long-silenced poetic heart.

This first preoccupation includes an important reflection on poetic theory as well. *La Lyre* has rightly been compared to Ronsard's best recognized versified meditation on his art, the 1552 ode *A Michel de l'Hospital*.[78] Like that earlier piece, *La Lyre* expounds at length on the nature of the *furor poeticus* and the status of the *poeta vates*:

> Car, comme dit ce grand Platon, ce sage,
> Quatre fureurs brulent nostre courage,
> Bacchus, Amour, les Muses, Apollon,
> Qui dans nos coeurs laissent un aiguillon
> Comme freslons, & d'une ardeur segrette
> Font soudain l'homme & poëte & prophette.[79]
>
> (2:18, vv. 53-58)

The poet thereby makes another case for the divine foundations of his profession. While boldly citing Plato as his authority, Ronsard reaffirms the poet's unique affiliation with the four furies–Bacchus, Love, the Muses, and Apollo–and reemphasizes his resulting prophetic gift to divine the truths beyond the reach of worldly appearances.

The framework of these complementary foci is indispensable to the semantic fulfillment of the pictorial decorations on the lyre. Despite indications of this meaning in the repetition of Apollo among the images, a unifying significance only truly comes to light when the multifarious pictures are associated with the poem's "Gaulois Apollon." Then it is clear that the assorted confrontations between Marsyas and Apollo (scene 3), Neptune and Apollo (sc. 4) and Mercury and Apollo (scs. 8-9) are diverse reformulations of the same quarrel between Ronsard and the *maligne Ignorance*, and further, that this *Ignorance* should also include those whose art resists this unifying identification, the narrative painters themselves. Similarly, it then becomes apparent that the image of Apollo herding cattle for Admete, "pour luy complaire" (15:32, v. 353) (sc. 5),

---

[78] McGowan, *Ideal Forms*, 116-17.

[79] In fact, this reflection on poetic theory is considerably longer (vv. 41-140). We may compare this with Jupiter's response to the Muses' request for the gift of poetry in *A Michel de l'Hospital* (vv. 375-510).

should recall Ronsard's obliging service to Belot, and that the scenes of Venus with her entourage (sc. 6) and Bacchus with his cornucopia (sc. 7), situated at the midpoint of the description, should symbolize the renewal of poetic fertility that follows the support of such truly worthy patrons.

It is finally possible to seize the full meaning of the singing Apollo at the start of the ekphrasis (sc. 1), the episode of the "vieille discorde" between Neptune and Pallas (sc. 2), and above all, the surprising return to that *discorde* in the cornucopian Bacchus picture (sc. 7):

> Entre la Guerre & la Paix est ce Dieu,
> Ny l'un ny l'autre, & s'il tient le millieu
> De tous les deux, ensemble pour la lance,
> Ensemble propre à conduire une danse.
>
> (15:35, vv. 411-14)

The description of an intervention by Bacchus ("ce Dieu") between the quarreling Neptune ("Guerre") and Pallas ("Paix") of scene 2 is far more than an attempt at verbo-visual verisimilitude, a hint at circularity designed to recreate in words the curvature of Ronsard's "lyre *courbe*" (15:29, v. 292) and the roundness of Mercury's original turtle-shell lyre (evoked in scenes 8-9). It is also a metanarrative commentary on the ability of poetry to restore semantic order and stability to the semiosis. In this case, however, the Hermetic drift becomes a combat of the "lance" between competing meanings, symbolized by the age-old mythological rivalry between Neptune and Pallas. [80] And in this instance, the role of the poet is given at once to Bacchus (praised elsewhere, we recall, as the "fureur" of poetry) and to the Apollo of scene 1, who "accorde / Frapant son Luc, cette vieille discorde" (15:29, vv. 305-06). For both poet figures, the task is the same: they bring together ("ensemble"), or reconcile ("accorde[nt]"), those competing meanings so they might at

---

[80] It is interesting to compare Ronsard's picture with the engraving by Antonio Fantuzzi of a similar scene attributed to Il Rosso that appears in the *Elisha Whittelsey Collection* of the Metropolitan Museum of Art in New York. Where the poet gives the role of intercessor to another poet figure, the painter grants it to the quintessential *artifex*, Jupiter, who sits among the goddesses in a cloud suspended above the conflict.

last "conduire une danse," i.e., effect the harmony and order required for intelligibility.[81]

* * *

In a very real sense all of these ekphraseis achieve precisely what any part of a good poem ought to accomplish: they acquire their fullest measure of meaning in the context of the poem as a whole. They therefore demonstrate not only Ronsard's principle of "inventions . . . bien ordonnées & disposées," introduced among his reflections on poetic disposition in the 1565 *Abbregé*,[82] but also the theory of the true poet that he presents in the 1587 (posthumous) *Preface sur la Franciade*.[83] Following a censure of grotesquerie reminiscent of his earlier pronouncements on the topic, and a biting rebuke to the "versificateurs," the mediocre poets who "se contentent de faire des vers sans ornement, sans grace et sans art,"[84] Ronsard contrasts the "Historiographes" with the "Poëte bien advisé," the epitome of the genuine poet in the *Franciade* and throughout his poetic oeuvre. Whereas the historians present their subject matters in a manner that strictly obeys the dictates of linear logic ("poursuivent de fil en esguille . . . leur subject entrepris du premier commencement jusques à la fin"), the true poet does precisely as Ronsard has done in the ekphrastic poems just studied:

> le Poëte bien advisé, plein de laborieuse industrie, commence son oeuvre par le milieu de l'argument, quelquefois par la fin: puis il deduit, file & poursuit si bien son argument par le particulier accident & evenement de la matiere qu'il s'est proposé d'escrire, tantost par personnages parlans les uns aus autres, tantost par songes, propheties & *peintures inserees* contre le dos d'une muraille & des harnois, & principalement des boucliers, . . .

---

[81] The association between dance and harmony appears earlier, in the image of the astral "dançe ordonnée" that determines our destiny and the meaning of our lives at the end of the 1555 *Hymne des Astres* (8:160-61, vv. 252-54). For more on the place of danse in Ronsard's poetry, see McGowan, *Ideal Forms*, esp. 209-41, and Joukovsky, *Bel Objet*, 152-56. On Bacchus as a figure for the poet (indeed for Ronsard himself), see the *Hinne de Bacus* of the 1555 *Meslanges* (6:176-90, esp. vv. 168 ff).

[82] See above, pp. 92-93.

[83] Although the *Preface* stages the figure of the heroic poet in particular, Ronsard's theory may apply more broadly to all true poets.

[84] See also the 1561 *Elegie* to Jacques Grevin (14:193-99, esp. vv. 65 ff).

tellement que *le dernier acte de l'ouvrage se cole, se lie & s'enchesne si bien & si à propos l'un dedans l'autre, que la fin se rapporte dextrement & artificiellement au premier poinct de l'argument.* Telles façons d'escrire, & tel art plus divin que humain est particulier aux Poëtes. . . . (16:336-37: my emphasis)

On a certain level, then, Ronsard's narrative-picture poems have little direct bearing on the relations between poetry and painting. Functioning to highlight the differences between the good poet and the bad, and between poetry and history, they engage problems of a purely poetic and literary import.

To conclude that this is the only level of concern, however, would entail a serious misjudgment of the evidence. As Ronsard's preoccupation with the Hermetic drift clearly shows, these poems are equally attentive to the principal philosophical issues pondered by the Platonic, Neoplatonic, and Scholastic theorists of the paragone throughout the centuries. Indeed, on inspecting the last three poems one more time, we would discover thoughts on several additional controversies of fierce interest to the inter-art contest competitors.

In *La defloration de Lede*, for instance, Ronsard takes particular exception to the idea that painting is inherently more durable than poetry. This objection is subtly folded into the striking authorial aside that completes the episode, immediately after the ekphrasis segment, relating how Leda fills her 'diversely painted' basket with the multifarious flowers of the field:

> Tel panier en ses mains meit
> Lede qui sa troppe excelle,
> Le jour qu'un oiseau la feit
> Femme en lieu d'une pucelle.
> . . . .
> A l'envi sont ja cueillis
> Les vers tresors de la plaine,
> Les bascinets, & les lis,
> La rose, & la marjolaine:
> Quand la vierge dist ainsi
> *(Jettant sa charge odorante*
> *Et la rouge fueille aussi*
> *De l'immortel Amaranthe.)*
> (2:74-75, vv. 117-36: my emphasis)

Leda's abandonment of her basket and its colorful and odorous flo-
ral contents is highly significant. On the one hand, it symbolizes the
future 'deflowering' of Leda by the Swan-Jupiter. Ronsard promotes this meaning on four separate occasions: in the title of the
ode (*La 'defloration' de Lede*), in the opening verses of the present
flower-gathering episode ("Le jour qu'un oiseau la feit / Femme en
lieu d'une pucelle"), in the basket's painting of satyrs fighting over
milk and a "panetiere," which foreshadows Leda's subsequent
struggle with her divine violator, as well as in the young victim's
lament to heaven as she realizes what the deceitful Swan is doing:
"O ciel qui mes cris entens, / . . . mon beau printens / Est *depouillé
de sa rose*" (2:77, vv. 189-92: my emphasis).

On the other hand, the same event also inscribes a denial of the
natural-sign aesthetic and the indestructibility of the pictorial arts.
This message is figured in the emphatic rejection of the flower
whose very name, "Amaranthe" (from the Greek αμαραντος, "un-
fading"), signifies "immortel." Beyond the sexual connotations it
acquires in respect to the rape theme, the amaranth also symbolizes
painting. This additional identification follows both from the association of that flower with its basket container, which likewise assumes the identity of a painting as its pictorial decorations over-
whelm its exterior surface (including, the poet insists, the "voie
courbe & torte" of the "anse," where the painted horse-driven sun
"Come au ciel . . . fait son tour" [2:72, vv. 81-84]), and from its explicit affiliation with color (synecdochically encoded in the chromatic qualifier, "rouge"), long considered a defining property of the
painter's materials and the physical nature that supplies his object
of representation.[85] Hence, through various and circuitous connections, the putative immortality of the flower would evoke the per-
durability of painting, and the final desertion of the first would
symbolize the peremptory renunciation of the second.[86]

---

[85] See above, p. 103 and n. 36. In fact, all of the flowers in Leda's basket may
be said to evoke painting since they too are distinguished principally by their color
(vv. 121-28).

[86] This reading is also supported by the end of the poem. There Leda agrees to
Jupiter's request for corporal submission following his offer to immortalize her as
"La belle seur de Neptune" and the time-honored mother of the "Futurs ornemens
du monde" (Castor, Pollux, and Helen) (2:78-79, vv. 213-32). If the abandonment
episode were merely a metaphor for the sexual deflowering, the present rejection of
the amaranth would contradict Leda's later consent to Jupiter's wish: "A ces mots
ell' se consent. . . ." (v. 229). Other meanings of Leda's consent are explored below.

By raising the immortality issue, Ronsard inevitably engages one of the most popular literary topics of all time: the *exegi monumentum* topos. And he will return to this theme in a variety of contexts and ways in numerous poems to come.[87] In the present instance, however, that engagement seems more coincidental than deliberate. In its purest formulation, which Horace provides in the thirtieth and final ode of his *Carminum liber 3*, the *exegi monumentum* topos would advance that monuments in words endure the ravages of time better than monuments in bronze and stone:

> Exegi monumentum aere perennius
> regalique situ pyramidum altius,
> quod non imber edax, non Aquilo impotens
> possit diruere aut innumerabilis
> annorum series et fuga temporum.

> (I have finished a monument more lasting than bronze and loftier than the Pyramids' royal pile, one that no wasting rain, no furious north wind can destroy, or the countless chain of years and the ages' fight.)[88]

By contrast, Ronsard suppresses all but the vaguest reflection on the permanence of poetry in *La defloration de Lede*. While it is possible to infer that Jupiter's pledge, at the end of the ode, to make Leda the mother of Helen, "La beauté au ciel choisie" (2:79, v. 226), implies a promise of immortality in the eternal fame that her daughter will acquire through the songs of Homer's 'immortal' *Iliad*, the textual preparation for that conclusion is rather weak. Further, unlike Horace, Ronsard takes a distinctive interest in the pictorial arts. His rejection of durability applies specifically to painting, not to sculpture or architecture.

Thus, in the present ode, as in so many poetic comments on the durability of painting to follow, Ronsard would appear to be more profoundly preoccupied by the pro-painting discourses of the paragone theorists. By their sheer boldness on the topic, for example, the remarks of Leonardo da Vinci might represent the perfect

---

[87] See the discussion of this theme in relation to the poetry on painted portraits in the chapter that follows.

[88] *Horace: The Odes and Epodes*, trans. C. E. Bennett (Cambridge: Harvard University Press, 1964), 278-79.

foil to Ronsard's position. This boldness is especially evident in *Trattato* 19:

> If you were to say that poetry is more lasting, I say the works of a coppersmith are more lasting still, for time preserves them longer than your works or ours; nevertheless they display little imagination. And a picture can be made more enduring by painting upon copper in enamel colours. We by our art may be called the grandchildren of God. [89]

While concluding that painting is inherently more durable than poetry by the very sturdiness of the materials upon which pictures are often rendered, Leonardo further suggests that painters are therefore virtual demigods, the "grandchildren of God" ("nipoti à dio").

In *Le ravissement de Cephale*, Ronsard broaches still other heated contest topics: the inveterate belief that sight is the highest of our sensual faculties, and the concomitant notion that visible phenomena enjoy a certain ontological advantage over other kinds of reality. The merit of both ideas suffers serious erosion in the course of the second *pose*, Ronsard's word- and hearing-biased representation of Naïs' Cephalus story (which is itself a digression within the poet's overarching *verbal account* of the preparations for Thetis' wedding to Peleus). In truth, this bias first shows forth before the Nereid ever begins that narration. It surfaces at the end of the Neptune scene, as the entire image- and sight-centered ekphrasis of the cloak draws to a close:

---

[89] "[S]e uoi dicesti, la poesia è più eterna, per questo dirò essere più eterne l'opere dun calderaio. chel tempo più le conserva che le vostre o' nostre opere, niente dimeno è di poca fantasia; e la pittura si può, depingendo sopra rame con colori di vetro, farla molto più eterna. noi per arte possiamo esser detti nipoti à dio" (*Tr* 19; 1:58). Leonardo returns to the durability of painting in *Trattato* 31b, an essay on music: "With Painting the images of Gods are made. . . . Lovers come to it for portraits of those they love, and by its means beauty is preserved which otherwise Nature and Time would destroy; by it we preserve the likenesses of our famous men" ("Con questa si fa i simulacri alli dij . . . ; con questa si dà copia alli amanti della causa de' loro amori, con questa si riserua le bellezze, le quali il tempo e la natura fa fugitive, con questa noi riserviamo le similitudini degli huomini famosi . . .") (Richter, 1:78). On the deification of the painter, cf. Alberti, *Della pittura*, ¶ 26: "Therefore, painting contains within itself this virtue that any master painter who sees his works adored will feel himself considered another god" ("Adunque in sé tiene queste lode la pittura, che qual sia pittore maestro vedrà le sue opere essere adorate, e sentirà sé quasi giudicato un altro iddio") (Spencer, 64; Grayson, 46). We shall return to Leonardo's appropriation of the *exegi monumentum* topos in the next chapter.

> Elles finoient de portraire
> De verd, de rouge, & vermeil,
> L'arc qui s'enflamme au contraire
> Des sagettes du souleil,
> Quand Naïs de sa parolle
> Feit ainsi resonner l'air:
> Avec sa vois douce & molle
> Le sucre sembloit couller.
>
> (2:136-37, vv. 73-80)

Unlike the uncommented conclusion to the pictorial representation of *Des peintures*, the embroidery ekphrasis of *Le ravissement* is explicitly displaced by poetry: rather than lapse into a void of silence, the present visual recreation gives way to a plenitude of "parolle" when Naïs convokes her sisters, in a "vois douce & molle," to listen to her tale of Aurora's ill-fated "amour aveuglé."

As Naïs' narration progresses, this preference for *parole* soon registers a more direct assault on sight and visual experience. To start, the target is the standing of ocular realities in general. In an appeal to the classic body-mind dichotomy, a clear contrast is drawn between the superficial and contingent domain of the visible physical world and the infinitely deep and essential realm of thought and spirit: both of which, we are never allowed to forget, the *parole* of Naïs and Ronsard can recreate with equal facility.

This distinction and the expressive flexibility of words receive marked attention in the report of Aurora's initial encounter with Cephalus. As the beautiful youth sounds an anguishing "plainte mal saine" over the body of his wife, Procris, who has succumbed to the wound inflicted by her husband's miscast hunting "Javelot," the goddess of the dawn suddenly experiences "Un feu d'amour aveuglé" so profound that her complexion alternately "perd sa couleur" and "Au pourpre . . . [s']allume" and her body temperature grows "ores chaude, ores glacée" (2:140-41, vv. 137-68). It is true, of course, that Aurora's adoration is merely tentative prior to her visual contact with Cephalus. In this regard, Ronsard's account coincides with the most familiar classical and Petrarchan versions of the *innamoramento*. Nevertheless, it is equally true that this love is *blind* ("aveuglé"). Moreover, the *need* for it (personified earlier in the ode as "Le fils de Venus" [2:137, v. 89]) is present well before the ocular encounter. In a departure from the standard enamorment topos, the true locus of Aurora's amorous turmoil, and the starting point of the visible physiological reactions that ensue, is ultimately the pre-visual mind and soul.

Later in the narration, the focus turns specifically to the weaknesses of the eye and sight. As the relation of Aurora's suffering continues, aesthetic theorists from Plato to Leonardo are put on notice when the poet moves to emphasize the comparative vulnerability of the eyes. Not only are those organs a prey to the lure of sleep, but they (and sleep too) are defenseless against the stinging emotions of the heart:

> Si tost par la nuit venue
> Les cieus ne sont obscurcis,
> Qu'el' se couche à terre nue
> Sans abaisser les sourcis,
> Car l'amour qui l'eguillonne
> Ne soufre que le dormir
> *En proie à ses yeus* se donne:
> Elle ne fait que gemir.
>
> (2:141-42, vv. 169-76: my emphasis)

What is more, the corporeal eyes have only a limited range of operation: a lover and a beloved can actually be "absent" from one another's physical sight. Mind and spirit, on the other hand, suffer no such limitations. Especially in the matter of love's desires and pains, the "esprit" supplies a presence all its own:

> Et bien que de loin absente
> De l'absent Cephale soit,
> Comme s'elle étoit presente
> *En son esprit l'aperçoit*:
> Ores pronte en ceci pance,
> Et ores pance en cela,
> Sa trop constante inconstance
> Ondoie deçà & là.
>
> (2:142, vv. 177-84: my emphasis)

Where physical sight can no longer operate, a truer kind of seeing takes over: a spiritual 'sight' that is at least as moving as anything the corporeal eye can achieve. [90]

---

[90] Of course, Ronsard is also operating within a time-worn tradition in making this point. As Laumonier notes, the present verses are directly inspired by Virgil, *Aeneid* 4.80-83: "Illum absens absentem auditque videtque" (2:142, n. 2).

Lastly, the value of pictorial images in particular comes under fire. When Aurora finally dares to speak to her beloved, who persists in grieving for his dead wife, the first words from her lips are those we might now expect from Ronsard as the critic of painting:

> Pourquoi pers tu de ton age
> Le printens à lamenter
> Une froide & morte image
> Qui ne peut te contenter?
>
> (2:144, vv. 221-24)

Within the boundaries of Aurora's fictional experiences and Naïs' story about them, the "froide & morte image" would denote the cold, dead cadaver of Cephalus' Procris. In the context of *Le ravissement* as a whole, the "image" in question would likewise allude to the iconography on Neptune's cloak, and to painting in general. Hence the qualifiers "froide & morte," and the accompanying notion of discontentment, would pertain to the idea that pictorial signs are unsatisfactory for their inability to tame the Hermetic drift. But as we have learned from our examination of *Des peintures*, the qualifier "mort/e" might further denote the reason for that inability: the fact that pictorial images are "en *son* mort," without sound and *parole*. Moreover, reconsidered in the light of the complaints against painting in *La defloration de Lede*, the same reference to death might evoke the relative perishability of painting. In that case, the discontentment would follow as a response to the susceptibility of pictorial images to suffer the ravages of time.

The sense that this remark could be another rejection of the durability of pictures is reinforced in the next stanza. While contrasting Procris' human mortality with her own immortality, Aurora raises the possibility of sharing that quality with Cephalus in the hope of enticing him to switch his amorous allegiance:

> Elle à la mort fut sugette,
> Non pas moi le sang des Dieus,
> Non pas moi Nimphe qui jette
> Les premiers raions aus cieus:
> Reçoi moi donques, Cephale,
> Et ta basse qualité,
> D'un étroit lien égalle
> A mon immortalité.
>
> (2:144, vv. 225-32)

Classical mythology often makes immortality a reward for mortals who willingly comply with the carnal desires of the gods. Though rarely is a promise of that privilege made explicitly, and certainly it is never done in the source texts for the Aurora-Cephalus story: Ovid's *Metamorphoses* 7 and *Amores* 1.13, Hesiod's *Theogony,* and Euripides' *Hippolytus.* This passage is more intimately linked to Ronsard's own poetic rhetoric of amorous conquest. Indeed, Aurora's experiences of unrequited love and her *carpe-diem*-like reproach to Cephalus for wasting his youth in the preceding stanza ("Pourquoi pers tu de ton age") make her a virtual double for the Ronsardian poet-lover. What is more, the pictorial implications of her previous comment on the *image* prepare her to be a poet-painting critic like the narrator of the Leda story in *La defloration.* And like that other critic, she mediates a paragone-related message on the durability of painted artworks. In this instance, however, the message is more than a condemnation of pictorial perishability. In agreement with the traditional *exegi monumentum* topos, it is also a bid for the dual permanence of poetry: the immortality of words, and the power of those words to render their subjects (Aurora) and objects (Cephalus) immortal.

Another issue of deep interest to Ronsard and the paragone theorists is the relative 'reality' of exteriors and interiors, the comparative truth merit of matter and form. This topic, which ultimately subsumes or intersects all of the controversies previously considered, provides one of the chief conceptual foci for what may be called the theme of the *habit*-versus-*coeur*, in the case of *La defloration de Lede*, or the *dehors*-versus-*dedans*, in *La Lyre.* At the same time this theme imparts its more traditional religious and philosophical moral to look beyond initial appearances when judging the worth of a person or thing, it also makes an art-theoretical statement about the various ways in which the visual (*habit/dehors*) is inferior to the verbal (*coeur/dedans*). For that reason it invariably confronts the painting-friendly metaphysics and aesthetics of Aristotle and Dante. In their views, we recall, substance and form are fundamentally coextensive. Outer matter and its various art-produced simulacra are (or can be) accurate and intelligible reflections of inner essence. Similarly, and perhaps more deliberately, this theme contradicts the theory of physiognomics adopted by Renaissance painters from medieval treatises on the subject, such as Michael Scot's *Liber phisionomiae.* Simply formulated, this principle maintains that any feature or gesture of the countenance or body can manifest the deepest secrets of the mind and soul. For Leonardo da Vinci, physiognomics supplies the speculative basis not only for his famous sketch, *A Group of Five Grotesque Heads* (fig. 7), but also for his memorable counsel to the painter in the essay, "How to Keep in Mind the Form of a Face" ("Del modo del tenere a mète la forma d'ù uolto"). On the premise that every human sentiment, thought, and virtue corresponds to a particular physical characteristic, the Florentine advises the artist to practice rendering the twenty-one types of noses: the ten in profile (straight, bulbous, concave, etc.) and the eleven in full face (thick or thin in the middle or tip, with nostrils wide or narrow, etc.).[91]

In *La defloration*, this theme comes into focus on three occasions, all (as we might expect) in the context of the Leda story proper. It first appears as a seemingly neutral narrative detail, in the account of Jupiter's metamorphosis. Seized by an "amoureuse rage" for the naive mortal maiden, the king of the gods *hides* his true inner identity and burning desire *beneath the shape* of a swan whose feathers are whiter than the milk curds deposited on a "jonchée," or rush-stem cheese filter: "Et sa deité cachée / Sous un plumage plus blanc / Que le laict sus la jonchée" (2:69-70, vv. 38-40). As a consequence of this dissimulation, of course, the maiden is subsequently tricked and 'deflowered'. The disdainful complaint that follows the resulting assault accommodates the second evocation of the theme. This time, however, a sense of hierarchy infiltrates the outer-inner antithesis as Leda explicitly denounces Jupiter's "habit" for deceptively masking the genuine nature of his evil "cueur":

> D'où es tu trompeur vollant,
> D'où viens tu, qui as l'audace
> D'aller ainsi violant
> Les filles de noble race?

---

[91] See Richter, *Leonardo*, 1:338-39, cit. 572. Leonardo makes a more explicit allusion to his theory of physiognomics in a revealing reflection on portraiture in *Trattato* 109: "the signs of faces show in part the nature of the men, their vices and their complexions" (Kemp, *Leonardo*, 158). For more on this theory (inspired partly by Michael Scot's *Liber phisionomiae*, of which Leonardo is known to have owned a copy), see Kemp, ibid.; and Richter, *Leonardo*, 1:28 and 2:238, § 1141-43. As Richter further notes, Lomazzo was another proponent of this view (Richter, ibid., 1:29).

FIG. 7: Leonardo da Vinci, *A Group of Five Grotesque Heads*, Windsor, Royal Library (RL 12495: The Royal Collection ©: Her Majesty Queen Elisabeth II)

Je cuidoi ton cueur, helas,
Semblable à l'habit qu'il porte,
Mais (hé pauvrette) tu l'as
A mon dam d'une autre sorte.
(2:77, vv. 181-88)

This doleful lament raises several important ideas. In one respect, it clearly privileges *cueur* over *habit*. The inner is the locus of reality and truth (however diabolical), which we all (like Leda) ideally seek to know; the outer is the domain of distortion and falsehood, which frustrates us (and Leda) in that search. On another level, it acknowledges two modes of signification. The one most acutely in evidence resembles the Hermetic semiosic model. It involves a corrupt class of signs that, by accident or design, always defer the truth. These signs are exemplified by the milk-white plumage of the swan's exterior which signals a purity that impedes knowledge of the real evil in Jupiter's heart. On the other hand, it assumes the existence of an ideal, univocal kind of signification, one in which the signs are always perfectly appropriate to their meanings, and where those meanings actually *are* the truth.[92] For Leda, the latter signs are the sort that Jupiter, or anyone, ought to employ to assure an accurate representation and communication of reality.

With the third manifestation of this theme, the aesthetic ramifications of these antithetical modes of signification are introduced. The context is Jupiter's full confession to Leda, who awaits the corporal (exterior) death that will faithfully reflect the spiritual (interior) death she has suffered through the Swan's defiling audacity:

Vierge, dit il, je ne suis
Ce qu'à me voir il te semble,
Plus grande chose je puis
Qu'un cigne à qui je resemble.
Je suis le maistre des cieus,
Je suis celui qui deserre
Le tonnerre audacieus
Sur les durs flancs de la terre.

La contraignante douleur
Du tien plus chaut qui m'allume,

_____

[92] For more on this quasi-Cratylistic concept of language, see Krieger, *Ekphrasis*, 72-73; and Screech, *Rabelais*, 377 ff.

M'a fait prendre la couleur
De cette non mienne plume. . . .

(2:78, vv. 201-12)

Like Leda, Jupiter prefers inner-being (*coeur-être*) and ideal signification over false outer-seeming (*habit-res/sembler*) and Hermetic
semiosis. However much his amorous suffering may have constrained him to assume the "non mienne plume," he would rather
have gained the maiden's favors as the "maistre des cieus," in his
own true skin (just as the poet-narrator, at the beginning of the ode,
would rather the obdurate Cassandre love him as he is, and not as
he threatens to become should treachery afford the only means to
ply her affections). But in this case, the deceitful exterior and the
faulty signification are more openly affiliated with painting and
painting's dependence on sight and the realm of visible nature. As
elsewhere, these connections are suggested by a few select terms.
The "couleur" simultaneously recalls the milk-white plumage that
precipitates the final deception and the "diverses couleurs" that
distinguish Leda's basket and every painter's palate and canvas.
Likewise the "voir" evokes at once the unique ocular encounter
that misleads Leda alone as well as all sight-based experience,
which necessarily exposes every seeing individual to the perils of
external appearance.

Conversely, the authentic interior and ideal signification are associated with words and oral/aural modes of communication. After
all, only the verbal signs actually set the deceptive visual record
straight. The revelation of true being beneath the semblances and
resemblances occurs solely through the intervention of Jupiter's *parole*: "Vierge, *dit* il, je ne *suis*. . . ." It is due to this truth-bearing
power of words that, at the end of the ode, the pure-hearted Leda
finally concedes to satisfy the deity's desires: "*A ces mots* ell' se consent / . . . / Et ja de peu à peu sent / Haute élever sa ceinture"
(2:79, vv. 229-32: my emphasis).

These notions reappear with even greater emphasis in the *dehors-dedans* theme of *La Lyre*. This theme arises in a revival of one
of the most prominent outer-inner examples of Western literature,
Plato's analogy between Socrates and the strange Silenus busts in
the *Symposium* (215)–or to be more precise, the reformulation of
that comparison in Erasmus' *Sileni Alcibiadis* adage (3.1.1) and, es-

pecially, Rabelais' prologue to the *Gargantua*.[93] In a 131-verse tribute to his patron Jean Belot, Ronsard likens this superior individual, whose imperfect physical appearance belies his inner intellectual and spiritual beauty, to a Silenus-like apothecary jar, whose fantastic and often repulsive exterior ornamentation misrepresents or contradicts the aromatic oils and curative medicines within:

> Ta face semble & tes yeux solitaires
> A ces vaisseaux de noz Apoticaires,
> Qui par dessus rudement sont portraits
> D'hommes, de Dieux à plaisir contrefaits,
> . . . .
> Et toutefois leurs caissettes sont pleines
> D'Ambre, Civette & de Musq odorant,
> Manne, Rubarbe, Aloës secourant
> L'estomac foible: et neantmoins il semble
> Voyant à l'oeil ces Images ensemble,
> Que le dedans soit semblable au dehors.
>
> (15:24-25, vv. 181-95)

The message about painting in these verses is basically the same as in *La defloration de Lede*. Naturally motivated visual signs ("ces Images") are often false; sight ("Voyant à l'oeil . . . ") is the faculty by which that falseness reaches the intellect to cause misunderstanding. What does change, however, is the apparent veracity of the complaint. By raising it in association with such an easily recognizable and time-honored apothegm, Ronsard effectively imbues his attack with the totality of that apothegm's legitimacy.

This validity will likewise accrue to Ronsard's concomitant claims about *parole* and poetry. Again as in *La defloration*, verbal language is unique for its potential to reveal the truths of the inner (the marvelous and beautiful *dedans* of the "Silenus" Belot), and the poet is exceptional for his ability to turn that potential into a reality. Both privileges receive particular recognition at the formal center of the original 1569 version of the ode. Following a conspicuous strategic shift in Belot analogues (whereby an animate and speech-capable Socrates supersedes the inanimate and speech-inca-

---

[93] In the *Gargantua* prologue, for example, Rabelais not only presents a similar apothecary jar example, but he also mentions three of the same perfume oils that Ronsard will recall.

pable jar), Ronsard proceeds to praise, in words, the generosity of soul that his patron displays, also in words:

> Car dans ton vase abondant tu receles
> Dix mille odeurs estranges & nouvelles,
> Si qu'*en parlant* tu donnes assez foy
> Combien ton ame est genereuse en toy,
> *Par la vertu de ta langue* qui pousse
> Un hameçon aux coeurs, tant elle est douce.
>
> (15:27, vv. 253-58: my emphasis)[94]

Thus words and poetry once more prevail over visual images and the arts of the eye. Poets and poets-at-heart like Belot can give a presence to the essential inner that painters, as artists of the outer, can never do.

And their expressive preeminence does not stop there. Poets can also immortalize that inner. Ronsard in fact presents this message twice. At the outset of the Belot encomium, it shapes the description of his epiphanic first meeting with his exceptional benefactor:

> Soudain au coeur il me prist une envie
> De te chanter, afin qu'apres ta vie
> Le peuple sceust que tes Graces ont eu
> Un chantre tel, amy de ta vertu,
> Pour ne souffrir que tant de vertus tiennes
> Cheussent là bas aux rives Stygiennes. . . .
>
> (15:23, vv. 153-58: my emphasis)

In this instance, the poet succeeds in rendering that presence permanent by registering Belot's "Graces" upon the eternal collective memory. Later, in the verses that close the ekphrastic segment and the poem as a whole, a similar lesson drives Ronsard's reflection on

---

[94] In the same passage, Ronsard insists that this verbal prowess gives vivid testimony to Belot's vast erudition: "Car quand tu veux refraischir la memoire / Des plus sçavants . . . / Ou quand tu veux *parler* des Republiques, / . . . / Ou quand tu veux *parler* de la Justice, / . . . / Et *discourir* des Astres & des Dieux, / Ou à propos de quelque autre science: / Lors de ta *voix* distille l'Eloquence, / Un vray Socrate, & ton *docte parler* / Fait le doux miel de tes levres couler, / Montrant au jour la vertu qui t'enflame, / Ayant caché au plus profond de l'ame / Je ne sçay quoy de rare & precieux / *Qui n'aparoist du premier coup aux yeux*" (15:26-27, vv. 233-52).

the immortality he has conferred upon Belot by creating the *Sixiesme livre des Poëmes* ("ce livre"), produced while playing his patron's magical lyre ("elle") as the agent of the Muses:

> Ce que j'ay peu sus elle fredonner,
> Petit fredon, je l'ay voulu donner
> A l'Amitié, le tesmoing de ce livre,
> Non aux faveurs, present qui te doibt suivre
> Outre Pluton, si des Muses l'effort
> Force apres nous les efforts de la Mort.
>
> (15:38, vv. 463-68)

The poet would overcome "les efforts de la Mort" by virtue of his privileged relation with the immortal Muses and by his sheer magnanimity, his willingness to offer Belot "ce livre" not for the "faveurs" he might earn, but as a gift of "Amitié" (we note the capitalization), the kind of selfless spiritual friendship that transcends all physical and temporal constraints.

With a pair of well-placed remarks, then, Ronsard not only manages to fold the *dehors-dedans* discussion and the subsequent lyre ekphrasis into another reprise of the *exegi monumentum* topos, but he also reemphasizes the superiority of poetry to painting in the most hotly contested regards. In addition to providing meanings that are coherent and understandable (i.e., rescued from the Hermetic drift), poetry can represent the highest kinds of ideas (meanings that correspond to the abstract essences of the inner), and do so in a manner that withstands the destructive effects of time ("les efforts de la Mort").

B. *A Temple for All Time*

Without a doubt, the concept of time remains a focus throughout Ronsard's commentaries on the relations between poetry and narrative painting. In *Des peintures contenues dedans un tableau*, the advantages of verbal diachrony over visual synchrony are a principal interest; in the *exegi monumentum* pieces, the differences in poetic and pictorial (im)permanence are a central concern. However, the only work to underscore the *relatedness* of these advantages and differences is the *Temple de Messeigneurs Le Connestable, et des*

Chastillons.[95] This heroic historical poem of the 1555 *Hymnes*[96] focuses on an imaginary temple filled with engraved, sculpted, and
painted narrative pictures depicting the feats and distinctions of the
renowned commander ("Connestable") of François I and Henri II,
Anne de Montmorency, and four of his military and ecclesiastical
kinsmen of the Coligny-Châtillon family: his brother, the *maréchal
de France* Gaspard de Coligny, and three nephews–the admiral Gaspard II de Coligny, the *colonel général* François de Coligny, and the
cardinal of Châtillon, Odet de Coligny, Ronsard's patron and the
dedicatee of the present poem and the collection in which it appears. Here alone the measure of immortality and immortalizability
of poetry and painting is specifically associated with the particular
temporal qualities of each art form. Moreover, only in the *Temple*
does Ronsard extend these considerations to relate the durability
question to the status of each artist's rapport with the Divine and
the differing aptitudes of words and images to dispel the confusion
of the semiosic drift. Hence, for the sheer number of paragone issues that converge in its 258 alexandrine verses, this hymn marks an
important climax in Ronsard's poetic contribution to the inter-art
contest.[97]

Like all the works previously considered, the *Temple de Messeigneurs* accords the highest favor to the poet and poetry. And as
before (in *Des peintures*, especially), this bias shows forth from the
outset. The prefatory pledge to Ronsard's "Mecenas," Odet de Co-

---

[95] The bases for the analysis that follows were first explored in my article,
"Mannerist Conflict and the *Paragone* in Ronsard's *Temple de Messeigneurs*," *L'Esprit Créateur* 33 (1993): 9-19.

[96] A useful typology of the various pieces in the first collection of *Hymnes* is
presented by Henri Chamard, *Histoire de la Pléiade* (Paris: Henri Didier, 1939),
175-207. For more recent discussions of the *Hymnes* as a collection and the hymn
as a genre, see Madeleine Lazard, ed., *Autour des 'Hymnes' de Ronsard* (Paris: Librairie Honoré Champion, 1984) (esp. Michel Dassonville, "Eléments pour une
définition de l'Hymne ronsardien," 1-32); and Georg Roellenbleck, "Les *Hymnes*
de 1555-1556: Questions de genre," in *Ronsard en son IVe Centenaire: L'art de
poésie*, eds. Yvonne Bellenger, et al., *Etudes Ronsardiennes* 2 (Geneva: Librairie
Droz, 1989), 23-27.

[97] From the start, then, it is clear that the analysis to follow differs substantially
from the commentaries on the *Temple* by McGowan, for whom this hymn is primarily a heroic poem that explores the classical models for praising princes (*Ideal
Forms*, 128-33); and by Joukovsky, who regards this work as another Pléiade profession of optimism about the aesthetic and cultural value of pagan Antiquity (*Bel
objet*, 21-23; and *La Gloire dans la poésie française et néolatine du XVIe siècle*
[Geneva: Librairie Droz, 1969], 338-41).

ligny, affords a singularly comprehensive panorama of the numerous themes to follow:

> Je veux, mon Mecenas, te bastir, à l'exemple
> Des Romains & des Grecz, la merveille d'un Temple,
> Sur la rive où le Loing, trainant sa petite eau,
> Baigne de ses repliz les piedz de ton chasteau.
> Là, d'un voeu solennel au meillieu d'une prée,
> Je veux fonder les jeux d'une feste sacrée,
> Chommable tous les ans, & pendre le laurier,
> Digne prix de celui qui sera le premier
> Publié le vainqueur (comme au lustre Olympique)
> Soit de lutte, ou de course, ou de lance, ou de pique.
>
> (8:72-73, vv. 1-10)

The series of Olympic-style athletic tournaments evoke not only the multiple military and political confrontations of Montmorency and his relatives, but also conflicts in general and the inter-art contest of the paragone in particular. The judicious coordination of the terms "laurier" and "premier" at the rhymes of verses 7 and 8 even leads us to expect a paragone favoring the victory of poetry. At the same time the laurel stands as the customary sign of supreme military and civic heroism, it is likewise the traditional symbol of superior poetic achievement.

The opening verses also indicate the principal grounds for this victory. In one regard, the poet is a master of time. This notion is indelibly inscribed in the *exegi monumentum* topos that defines the poet's resolution *to build* a monumental temple like the Greeks and, above all (as the syntax of verse 2 plainly stresses), the *Romans*–i.e., Horace himself, the most illustrious 'builder' of imperishable poetic monuments of classical Rome. Later in the poem, this idea and the *exegi monumentum* theme otherwise arise in the repeated references to the corresponding impermanence of purely plastic monuments. At the privileged center point of the work, for example, the poet proposes a "Terme," or pillar, on which the admiral Gaspard de Coligny is painted as a Neptune who "fera semblant de faire armer / Noz escadrons François, soit pour donner bataille, / Soit *pour gaigner d'assaut quelque forte muraille*" (8:79, vv. 128-30).[98] It

---

[98] A similar allusion to camps and walls attacked and destroyed by the forces of Montmorency appears in vv. 45-48: "Là, les camps d'Attigny, & de Valenciennes /

is not until the antepenultimate stanza, however, that this point is expressed unequivocally:

> Ainsi, mon Mecenas, dans ce Temple de gloire
> Je mettray ces portraictz, sacrez à la Memoire,
> A fin que des longs ans les cours s'entresuyvants
> Ne foulent point à bas leurs honneurs survivans,
> Et que des CHASTILLONS la maison estimée
> Vive, maugré le temps, par longue renommée. . . .
>
> (8:82, vv. 197-202)

As if seized by a doubt that his preceding intimations will be properly understood, Ronsard at last insists explicitly that his poetic "Temple de gloire" will forever safeguard the Châtillon name and renown from the ravages of the passing years.[99]

Another factor in the victory of poetry over painting is the poet's deific ability to create entities of a distinctly miraculous nature. As the opening stanza likewise affirms, the poet will originate a temple and events that transcend the physical realm of experience. In the first case, he will produce a pure *marvel* ("la merveille"); in the second instance, he will institute the proceedings of a wholly *sacred* celebration ("une feste sacrée"). Thus, as emphasized in the ode *A son Luc* a decade earlier, the poet assumes a virtually divine status: he once again appears as the unparalleled *ami des Dieus* and *poeta vates*.

Like the poet's mastery over time, his quasi-divinity is more forcefully indicated at the end of the poem. In the penultimate stanza, Ronsard makes a refreshing modification to the traditional *poeta vates* theme by recasting the soothsayer as a poet-*sacrificulus*: a full-fledged 'sacrifier'[100] who, during a sacrificial rite that will complete

---

Seront peintz, & les murs de Bethune, & d'Avannes, / Ceux de Mont, & d'Aras, lesquelz il a cent fois / Epouvantez d'effroy, lieutenant de noz Roys" (8:75).

[99] Although this doubt would apply most properly to the *Temple de Messeigneurs*, it might likewise apply to all the narrative painting poems before 1555. For, in truth, the *Temple* is only the first work to make the *exegi monumentum* claim fully explicit. As our earlier analyses have shown, Ronsard pursues the idea of poetic immortality rather more metaphorically in the earlier narrative-painting poems. In a sense, then, the *Temple* may be said to pave the way for the more direct evocation of the *exegi monumentum* topos in *La Lyre*.

[100] I adopt the term and concept of "sacrifier" (i.e., the priest-like individual who "is obliged to become a god himself in order to be capable of acting upon them") proposed by Henri Hubert and Marcel Mauss in their study of sacrificial ritual, *Sacrifice: Its Nature and Function*, trans. W. D. Halls (London: Cohen & West Ltd., 1964), 20-22.

the "feste sacrée" promised earlier, assumes the sanctified role of intermediary between the living Châtillon and their deified fore-bears, the ancient spirits of Olympus, and the Heavenly Savior:

> Apres, dedans le Temple, imitant les Antiques
> Je feray sacrifice aux Espritz Olympiques,
> Aux Herôs le second, & le troisieme honneur
> Sera du sacrifice à Jupiter sauveur.
> Lors moy, le seul autheur d'un si divin office,
> Je feray dignement le premier sacrifice,
> Environné du peuple, à tes nobles Ayeux,
> Qui habitent l'Olympe assiz au rang des Dieux.
>   (8:83, vv. 217-24)

The godlike image of the poet as "seul autheur" of this holy office and (lest we forget) the extraordinary temple where it will transpire continues, with significant elaboration, into the final stanza. Here, Ronsard explains both *what* he will sacrifice and, more importantly, *why* he will do so. In addition to specifying the nature of the vic-tims he will offer up ("je vous sacrifie / Des ores, à vous tous, mon esprit & ma vie, / Mes Muses & ma plume" [8:84, vv. 241-43]), Ronsard reveals that the effects of this gesture should coincide with those he ascribes to the temple itself. In sacrificing his personal spirit and life, his own creative soul and the fruits of his pen, he ul-timately seeks to repay his generous patrons by affording them im-mortality–by conveying their praises throughout the world, better and better, always and forever: "Et sans me reposer, par les terres estranges / *Tousjours de mieux-en-mieux* j'envoiray les loüenges" (8:84, vv. 249-50: my emphasis). Accordingly, Ronsard takes one final opportunity to underscore the poet's mastery over time. In this instance, however, he simultaneously relates it to the poet's priv-ileged liaison with the Divine, his status as one "à qui les Soeurs se monstrent favorables" (8:84, v. 246). The emissary of the Muses can immortalize for the same reason that he can act as sacrifier: he is a virtual god among men, an 'author' in the absolute sense of the term.

The 186-verse ekphrasis of the temple ornamentation that fills the intervening three-quarters of the hymn exemplifies just how the poet comes to excel in these various regards. Two such means are poignantly demonstrated in the description of the picture of Odet de Coligny and the narrative stories to be figured upon his scarlet cardinal's robe:

> Je peindray sur ton chef un chappeau rougissant
> Puis au tour de ton col un roquet blanchissant
> Sur l'esclat cramoisy d'une robe pourprée,
> De mainte belle histoire en cent lieux diaprée:
> Là, d'un art bien subtil j'ourdiray tout au tour
> La Verité, la Foy, l'Esperance & l'Amour,
> Et toutes les Vertuz qui regnerent à l'heure
> Que Saturne faisoit au monde sa demeure.
> Sur ceste robe apres sera portraict le front
> De Pinde, & d'Helicon, & de Cirrhe le mont,
> Les antres Thespiens, & les sacrez rivages
> De Pimple, & de Parnasse, & les divins bocages
> D'Ascre, & de Libetrie, & de Heme le val,
> Et Phebus, qui conduit des neuf Muses le bal:
> Les Muses y seront elles-mesmes empraintes
> Que ta Vertu garda, lors qu'ell' estoient contraintes
> La France abandonner, ne prenant à-dedain,
> Quand plus on les moquoit, de leur tendre la main,
> Caressant leur present, voire & de leur promettre
> (O nouvelle bonté!) quelque fois de les mettre
> En paisible repos, pour les faire chanter
> Je ne sçay quoy de grand qui te doit contenter.
>
> (8:77-78, vv. 95-116)

A pair of vital lessons about the plenitude of poetic expression lie beneath the bombastic surface of this lengthy encomium. On the one hand, it is once again evident that poetry can signify all the orders of existence. In tacit agreement with the Scholastic theories of Aquinas and, especially, Dante, Ronsard reaffirms that, thanks to his reliance upon verbal language, the poet can give presence to physical realities as well as to conceptual and spiritual ideas. Moreover, he is able to accomplish this by employing all the modes of signification: literal, allegorical and symbolic. By means of what might be called the 'objective' variety of the purely literal mode of discourse, for example, the poet can readily call to mind the physical specificity of the Cardinal's biretta, rochet, and robe. Similarly, by employing the allegorical and symbolic modes of discourse in the references to Truth, Faith, Hope, and Love (in the first case) and to Saturn, Phebus-Apollo, the Muses, and the nine sacred sites of ancient music worship (in the second), he easily succeeds in representing the abstract subjectivity of Odet's religious and civic merits.

On the other hand, it is once more certain that the poet can consolidate these various levels of meaning and discourse and overcome the endless semantic deferral of the Hermetic drift. Despite the length, complexity, and (yes!) bombast of the passage, Ronsard eventually affords a unified and intelligible message about Odet de Coligny's character: he is supremely virtuous and a munificent leader in France's moral and artistic revival. This ability is metaphorically acknowledged in his promise *to weave* these ingredients *with the subtlest of artifice* ("d'un art bien subtil j'ourdiray . . ."). Although the act of weaving invariably requires the manipulation of multifarious threads, and hence a certain multiplicity, or *copia* (as Terrance Cave has duly observed [101]), that manipulation is fundamentally an integrative operation, a process whereby the many is reconfigured as the one, where the traces of artifice–the signs of mixture–are substantially reduced or utterly effaced in favor of a seamless whole.

The poet's expressive excellence is likewise enacted in the play of verbal tenses throughout the hymn. In no other poem thus far considered is this play so dynamic and significant. [102] The passage about the four white pillars that will frame the temple's central shrine to Anne de Montmorency provides an ideal (and typical) example:

> Là, pour servir d'entrée à ses vertuz premieres
> Je peindray tout cela qu'il feit dedans Mezieres,
> Compagnon de Bayard, & tout cela qu'il feit,
> Quand le grand Roy FRANÇOIS les Souïsses defeit.
> Là, les camps d'Attigny, & de Valenciennes
> Seront peintz, & les murs de Bethune, & d'Avannes,
> Ceux de Mont, & d'Aras, lesquelz il a cent fois
> Epouvantez d'effroy, lieutenant de noz Roys.

---

[101] Cave, "Ronsard's Mythological Universe," 170-71.

[102] While tense variations do indeed appear in the poems previously studied (as they do throughout the history of ekphrastic literature), the *Temple* stands apart for its role in exploiting the full range of temporal possibilities–past, present, and future.

Là sera peint aussi le Pas estroit de Suse,
Où dix mille Espagnolz se virent par sa ruse
Tuez, si qu'à un seul il ne fut pas permis
Retourner raconter la mort de ses amis.

(8:74-75, vv. 41-52)

Here, as elsewhere, [103] the relation between the future-tense verbs, used for describing the processes and anticipated visible results of the iconographic production, and the past-tense verbs, employed for explaining the intellectual (historical) meanings of those pictorial results, accomplishes two important effects. First, by deferring to a future time the existence of the temple as a signifier while simultaneously insisting that its signifieds are bound in the past, Ronsard figures a rift between the two. A void replaces the present of the narrative painting where the *visual* signifier would (presumably) retrieve its signifieds to become a meaningful sign. [104] Second, by successfully achieving the first effect, the poet gives unimpeachable proof that the *verbal* signifier can fill the semantic gap. Through their unique temporal flexibility, words can provide the meaning missing from the pictures. [105]

Thus, as in *Des peintures contenues dedans un tableau*, Ronsard contrasts the benefits of the poet's time-based verbal language with the liabilities of the painter's synchronic medium of images; and as before, he thereby dismisses one of the fundamental premises summoned by theorists like Leonardo in arguments for the superiority of painting. Only, in this case our laureate appears noticeably more confident than he is in the earlier poem. He takes a far greater delight in brandishing the temporal strengths of poetry than in decrying the corresponding impotence of painting. Moreover, this delight assumes an intimate connection between those strengths and the virtue of verbal imperishability. By demonstrating the ability of words to signify all the facets of time within an ekphrasis embedded in a poem that, from the very first verse, promises to reaffirm the

---

[103] Cf. the passage on the effigy of Gaspard I (vv. 17-22), and the "Avignon pillar" segment (esp. vv. 53-58 and 75-82).

[104] It is important to emphasize that the *Temple* is the only narrative-painting poem where present-tense verbs are so persistently displaced in this fashion.

[105] Brian Barron concludes that the prevalence of future-tense verbs serves only to underscore the "caractère abstrait des représentations artistiques du Temple" ("'Ut pictura poesis,'" 276).

principles set forth in the traditional *exegi monumentum* topos, Ronsard obliquely, yet surely, affiliates that ability with the power of the verbal art of poetry to be and make permanent.

This joyous confidence also underpins one of the most revealing details to be found in all of Ronsard's poetic incursions into the paragone. It emerges in the second stanza of the poem, the only true *vue d'ensemble* of the temple and its verbal-visual dialectic:

> Tout le Temple sera basty de marbre blanc,
> Où gravez en aerain j'attacheray de rang
> Tes Ayeulx elevez à l'entour des murailles,
> Qui tous auront escrit aux piedz de leurs medailles
> Leurs gestes & leurs noms, & les noms ennemys
> Des chevaliers qu'en guerre à mort ilz auront mis.
>
> (8:73, vv. 11-16)

Ronsard's insistence that the pictorially represented events and personages will be supplemented by scriptural identifications undoubtedly serves to intensify the *effet du réel* of his description. As Jean Cousin's *St. Mamas* tapestry plainly illustrates, such explanatory labels were indeed often appended to the narrative pictures of Ronsard's day. Moreover, as may be seen in the tapestry inspired by the same artist's depiction of the near drowning of the chaste huntress, Britomartis (one of the lesser known incarnations of Artemis-Diana from the Cretan mythological tradition [106]), a work included in the *History of Diana* series (1550-55) for Diane de Poitiers' castle at Anet, they were at times remarkably elaborate. An explanatory textual supplement of over eighty words (in both French and Latin) has been prominently woven into the strapwork of the *inquadratura* and the title panel at the top center of the piece (fig. 8). [107] More importantly, though, this detail should also recall the paragone-related implications of the laurel crown mentioned in the first stanza. By highlighting the presence of the titles, Ronsard draws attention to

---

[106] For more on this deity, see William Smith, ed., *Dictionary of Greek and Roman Mythology*, 3 vols. (Boston: Little, Brown and Co., 1859), 1:505-06.

[107] A brief history of this project and the Britomartis tapestry is presented in Béguin, *Fontainebleau*, 347-48. It is noteworthy that the other six tapestries of the collection, all representing the more widely known episodes in the story of Diana, receive a frame that is equally overrun by text. This fact could only have confirmed Ronsard's theory that, to a degree, all narrative pictures need such inscriptions to be comprehended.

FIG. 8: Jean Cousin the Elder, *The Drowning of Britomartis*, Château d'Anet, The New York Metropolitan Museum of Art, New York (Gift of the children of Mrs. Harry Payne Whitney, in accordance with her wishes, 1942 [42.57.1]. All rights reserved)

the referential emptiness of all pictorial works of art and the corresponding semantic plenitude of poetry, to the fact that poetry can fill that void with coherent and intelligible meanings.

* * *

Throughout the narrative-painting poems, then, Ronsard articulates a clear and vigorous bias against his counterpart in the pictorial arts. By every means at his disposal (including the astute manipulation of the paradoxes inscribed throughout the copious art-theoretical literature he inherits from Plato, Aristotle, and their intellectual heirs), he repeatedly rejects the arguments by which painting would make its claim for supremacy in the hierarchy of the arts. Even the most (traditionally) compelling virtues of pictorial signs (their naturalness and synchronousness) are shown wanting next to the marvelous powers of words (their referential and temporal versatility, and thus their ability to subdue the endless semiosic drift). The painter and his brush are simply no match for the poet and his pen.

Or so it seems. For inevitably embedded within Ronsard's poetry-privileging professions is an abiding anxiety about, or envy of, the contemptible painter and his images. The poet is caught in the contradictory double bind, the predicament of having a desire to surpass the other that inscribes a conscious or unconscious recognition that the other is 'worthy' of being surpassed–*worthwhile* in some essential, unassailable way.

While this bind is most often confined to the interstices of the poems we have examined, it does produce certain indelible traces. In *La defloration de Lede*, for example, it might well explain the insistence on the naturalness of the sea scene on Leda's basket:

> La mer est painte plus bas,
> L'eau ride si bien sur elle,
> Qu'un pescheur ne nîroit pas
> Qu'*elle ne fust naturelle*.
> (2:72, vv. 89-92: my emphasis)

An envy of the painter might likewise explain the reference, in *Le ravissement de Cephale*, to the likeness to life of the earth image on Neptune's cloak: "Au vif traitte i fut la terre" (2:134, v. 25), or the allusion, in *La Lyre*, to the anticipated satisfaction of the (virtual) spectator's expectations of naturalness upon seeing the lyre's depiction of Apollo at the feast: "En le voyant vous diriez . . ." (15:29, v. 305).[108]

In general, however, such comments ring more ironic than true. Even the fact that images are engraved upon the poetry symbols (the musical instruments) in *A sa guiterre* and *La Lyre* encodes a privileging of the poetic. Rather than denote an alliance of the arts founded upon an implicit sense of mutual respect, it underscores the reliance of the visual on the verbal. Whereas the guitar and lyre enjoy an ontological autonomy that transcends their painted decorations, the decorations cannot exist without the 'foundation' afforded by those instruments. Hence any intimation of praise is again substantially subverted by the poet's overwhelming efforts to promote the priority of poetry.

Substantially, that is, except in the *Temple de Messeigneurs*. In this case, the trace of admiration (and thus the double bind) is somewhat more resilient precisely because the poet assumes the role of absolute "autheur" of his poetic and pictorial artworks. In so doing, he necessarily accepts (or desires) a mastery over the two principal varieties of signs: those that are conventional and diachronic (the verbal) and those that are natural and synchronic (the visual).

Paradoxically, the tokens of this admiration (and the bind) first show forth in the stanza immediately following the 'titles' passage. Here Ronsard pays explicit tribute to the accuracy and vitality of his proposed marble effigy of Odet's father, the Maréchal de France, Gaspard (I) de Coligny:

> A part, vers la main dextre, appuyé sur sa lance
> Ton Pere, qui jadis fut Marechal de France,
> Sera *vivant* en marbre, & tellement le traict
> De sa face premiere *au vif* sera portrait,
> Qu'on luy recongnoistra *vivement* en la pierre
> La mesme audace au front, qu'il eut jadis en guerre.
>
> (8:73, vv. 17-22; my emphasis)

---

[108] Cf. also the description of the depiction of Marsyas: "*Vous le verriez* lentement consommer . . ." (15:31, v. 332: my emphasis).

Four stanzas later, a comparable lifelike quality is ascribed to the image of Anne de Montmorency and his battle against the Spanish at Avignon that will be vividly imprinted ("vivement imprimée": v. 53) on the second pillar to flank the Commander's altar:

> Les chevaux & les gens y seront *si bien faictz*,
> Et les murs d'Avignon *si au vif* contrefaictz,
> Et luy *si bien gravé* d'un visage semblable,
> Qu'on ne le dira feint, mais *chose veritable*.
>
> (8:75, vv. 59-62; my emphasis)

At last Ronsard seems willing to acknowledge openly a possible equality between the conventional signs of poetry and the natural signs of painting. It appears that the pictorial arts may even claim a special expressive advantage over poetry in respect to material reality: they may come extremely close to the "chose veritable," the real physical *thing* that they represent. Again, however, such a deference is rarely so explicit in the vast majority of Ronsard's narrative-painting poems.

In the verses that evoke portraits, on the other hand, this respect is more noticeably and consistently in evidence. Although our laureate's overall enthusiasm about the preeminence of poetry does not diminish, he is distinctly more inclined to accept the virtues of painting. And with that acceptance comes a clearer sense of Ronsard's entanglement in the double bind, his ambivalence toward the art of his rival the painter.

CHAPTER THREE

THE POEMS ON PAINTED PORTRAITURE

> Aussi l'art qui imite Nature, ne se soucie guiere
> des autres parties, quand il veut bien represanter
> ou retraire une personne. On se contante de pein-
> dre ou talher le visage, pour la totalle ou princi-
> palle marque de cet individu. Car vous lisés-là qui
> c'act, non-moins que s'il etoit ecrit.
>
> (Laurent Joubert, "Epistre," *Traité du Ris*, 1579)

The early European Renaissance found portraiture among the
least respected, and hence least common, art forms to which a
painter could apply his brush. Due in part to the promulgation of
the overt and implied criticisms of philosophers like Aristotle and
Plotinus,[1] in part to the rejection of pagan idolatry by Church Fathers such as Clement of Alexandria, Tertullian and St. Augustine
(a renunciation subsequently revived by the Iconoclasts of the
eighth and ninth centuries[2]), in part to the pervading Christian
ethic of self-abnegation and spiritual idealism,[3] the painting of *real*
men and women–i.e., individuals whose historical existence is either factually verifiable or plausible to the imagination–came to lose

---

[1] Again, these criticisms are essentially theoretical, bearing primarily on the relation of portraits to inaction (for Aristotle) and corrupt material reality (for Plotinus). See above, Chapter One, 48-49, 68-69.

[2] See Chapter One, 50 and n. 38.

[3] In artistic terms, this idealism is otherwise reflected in the decree of the Council of Nicaea II in 787 that effectively required that the composition of all subjects
be defined by the Church, that all figures conform to predetermined types. See
John Walker, *Portraits: 5,000 Years* (New York: Harry N. Abrams, Inc., 1983), 68-
69.

much of the prominence it had assumed in Antiquity. Whereas portrait sculptures had continued to flourish in the funerary monuments of the Middle Ages (which received the full approval of
Catholic dogma, as may still be witnessed at the Basilica of St.
Denis and in countless other medieval religious edifices across Europe),[4] most portrait *paintings* had been relegated to the margins,
literal and figurative, of the more esteemed pictorial artworks of
Western society. In Northern Europe, this predicament is typified
in donor portraits like the one featuring Nicolas Rolin, the Chancel-
lor of Burgundy, by the Flemish master, Rogier Van der Weyden
(ca. 1399-1464).[5] Rather than appear autonomously, as an indepen-
dent object worthy of consideration on its own merits, this late-me-
dieval painting is consigned to the left-wing, exterior panel of the
Last Judgment altarpiece of the Hôtel-Dieu at Beaune (ca. 1443-51)
(fig. 9). In keeping with the majority of portraits produced between
late Antiquity and the Renaissance, Rolin's image is allowed to exist
only contingently, as an adjunct to a picture, or set of pictures,
whose subject matter has the official sanction of the reigning political and religious institutions.[6]

   As the early humanists succeeded in imprinting the antiquarian
ethoi of naturalism and individualism on the Western psyche,[7] how-

---

   [4] Walker, *Portraits*, 63-77.
   [5] Van der Weyden often undertook commissions for Philippe le Bon and the
Burgundian court during their frequent visits to Brussels.
   [6] The contingency of portraiture is likewise exemplified by the donor portraits
on the outer panels of Jan Van Eyck's altarpiece of *The Adoration of the Lamb*
(1432) (from which Van der Weyden is believed to have taken inspiration for the
exterior of his Beaune *Last Judgment*) as well as Van Eyck's portrait of Rolin flank-
ing the *Virgin of Autun* (mid-1430s) for Notre Dame at Autun (Louvre: inv. 1271).
Although it is true that both Flemish artists, as well as the most famous French-
born painter of the fifteenth century, Jean Fouquet, also left portraits of the autonomous kind (e.g., Van der Weyden's *Portrait of a Young Woman* and Fouquet's
Portrait of a Man with a Glass of Wine), such pictures were far from the rule. It is
also important to recall that the redemption of portraiture occurred later in France
than in the Netherlands, and that the vogue of portrait painting in Italy (which Fouquet had the opportunity to study during his Roman sojourn in 1445-48) had come
into being on the heels of the Italian Renaissance, nearly a full century earlier. See
Lorne Campbell, *Van der Weyden* (New York: Harper & Row, 1980); Walker: *Portrait*, 104 ff; Henri Bouchot, *L'Exposition des primitifs français: la peinture en France
sous les Valois*, 3 vols. (Paris: Librairie Centrale des Beaux-Arts, n.d.). On the evolution of the 'donor' species of portraiture, see Pope-Hennessy, *Portrait*, 257-300.
   [7] For more on this development, and especially the rise of the notion of individualism as it derives from the theories of the late-classical and early modern Neoplatonists, see William Kerrigan and Gordon Braden, *The Idea of the Renaissance* (Bal-

FIG. 9: Rogier Van der Weyden, *The Last Judgment* altarpiece (exterior)
(ca. 1443-51) Hôtel-Dieu, Beaune

ever, the painting of distinct personalities enjoyed a remarkable return to favor. By the second third of the sixteenth century seemingly everyone embraced the ancient custom, reported by Pliny and others, of commissioning pictures of themselves and their kin to document familial lineage and confirm personal merit.[8] Even the disparaging Neoplatonic pronouncements of Giorgio Vasari and Michelangelo could not reverse the rising status of portraiture. Despite the efforts of the esteemed Italian theorist-artists to convince 'true' painters that this pictorial genre was a waste of time and talent because it (ostensibly) requires a slavish copying of the sitting subject's imperfect physicality, and hence promotes a rejection of ideal beauty,[9] an ever-growing number of artist workshops busily turned out images of anyone who could afford their services, from the wealthiest princes to the most ordinary tradespeople. So widespread did the practice become that, in a revealing letter of July 1545, Pietro Aretino was moved to enjoin Leone Leoni to refrain from portraying "the faces of those who are scarcely known to themselves, and still less to others" ("le facce di coloro che appena son noti a se stessi, non che altrui"). Above all, Aretino wished his sculptor friend to eschew the "infamy" of the century, "which so willingly allows mere tailors and butchers to appear in painting" ("A tua infamia, Secolo, che sopporti che, sino a' sarti, et i baccaj' appaiano là vivi in pittura."). [10] Such complaints notwithstanding, as the remark on painted faces in the 1579 *Traité du Ris* of the royal physician and humanist theorist of laughter, Laurent Joubert (1529-

---

timore: Johns Hopkins University Press, 1989), 101-15. See also the comments of François Lecercle, who more reductively ascribes the rise of portraiture to the new secularism of the early humanists: *Chimère*, 52-53.

    [8] Pliny refers to and describes "the existence of a strong passion for portraits in former days" ("imaginum amorem flagrasse quondam"). He also alludes to similar reports of this fervor by Marcus Varro and Cicero's friend, Titus Pomponius Atticus: *Historia naturalis* 35.2-4, esp. 266-68. See also, Pope-Hennessy, *Portrait*, 65-100.

    [9] Such Neoplatonic attacks clearly inscribe the Plotinian criticism according to which portraits would be slaves to the corruptible matter ($\H{\upsilon}\lambda\eta$) of created things ($\gamma\varepsilon\gamma\text{ov}\acute{o}\varsigma$) (i.e., the sitting human subject) (see Chapter One, 69). For more on Vasari's and Michelangelo's theories, and the disparity between the social and intellectual respectability of portrait painting during the Renaissance, see Campbell, *Renaissance Portraits*, 22-24, 150-51.

    [10] Quoted in Lecercle, *Chimère*, 52-53. This situation changed little throughout the century, as may be inferred from Paolo Lomazzo's reprise of the same idea in the chapter, "Composizione di ritrarre dal naturale," of his 1585 *Trattato dell'arte* (see Lecercle, ibid., 51, n. 3).

1582), saliently suggests, the Renaissance would become a virtual golden age of the painted portrait. [11]

The prominence of this art form is similarly apparent in the poetry of Pierre de Ronsard. Contrary to the claims of Jean Plattard, who insists that our author has no genuine interest in pictures of individual human sitters because they lack the spirit, voluptuousness, and conceptual versatility so dear to his aesthetic sensibilities, [12] Ronsard exhibits a profound and enduring fascination with portraits. He evokes them at least as frequently as narrative paintings, and likewise at all stages of his career. But what are the reasons for this preoccupation?

It would be unwise, if not impossible, to ascribe Ronsard's concern to any single cause. Certainly, the prevalence of his portrait poems follows, to some degree, from the extraordinary popularity of this painting genre in mid-sixteenth-century France. Ronsard acknowledges his awareness of this vogue (among others [13]) in the *Hymne de France*:

> Noz imagers ont la gloire en tout lieu
> Pour figurer soit un homme, ou un Dieu,
> De si tres pres imitans la nature,
> Que l'oeil béant se trompe en leur peincture
>
> (1:32-33, vv. 181-84)

By the time these verses appeared in 1549, it was evident the "imagers" of France had attained a "gloire" our laureate was powerless to overlook.

Equally relevant, however, are the properly literary factors. On the one hand, Ronsard takes inspiration from a variety of poetic

---

[11] Countless scholars of art history and literature have already made this assertion. See, for example, Louis Dimier, *Histoire de la peinture de portrait en France au XVIe siècle* (Paris: Librairie Nationale d'Art et d'Histoire, 1924-1925); Anthony Blunt, *Art and Architecture*, 116; Lecercle, *Chimère*, 51; Campbell, *Renaissance Portraits*.

[12] See Chapter Two, 87-89.

[13] The allusion to figures of "un Dieu" also reflects the poet's recognition of another popular genre of painting of the period: the mode of representing mythological and allegorical figures (which falls outside of the strict definition of portrait art employed by most art historians and throughout the present study). Other sources of French glory to receive special attention in this hymn include recent accomplishments in mathematics, city and monument building, and of course, poetry and music (vv. 169-95).

antecedents. Among these are the numerous portrait poems of Anacreon of Teos and his followers (known primarily through the editions and translations of Henri Estienne, Josse Badius, and Jean Brodeau [14]), as well as the picture-like character descriptions of the medieval *descriptio personae*, whose successful passage from the early *chansons de geste* and chivalric romances into the idiom of the Renaissance poets is otherwise epitomized by another important literary model: Lodovico Ariosto's celebrated depiction of the beautiful Alcina in *Orlando furioso* 7. [15] On the other hand, Ronsard clearly makes the most of the unique practical benefits of the poetic portrait. Besides presenting him a convenient occasion to externalize the psychological drama provoked within the lovelorn poet persona by the elusive or absent lady of his desires, verbal portraiture has the advantage of fitting felicitously into the most diverse assortment of poems. Just as personality pictures in paint can fit upon surfaces as large as a wall or as small as a medal or a coin, [16] those in words can take up a hundred-line elegy as readily as they can abide within the fourteen verses of a sonnet.

Perhaps the most important reason behind the prevalence of painted portraits in Ronsard's oeuvre, though, is the same one that explains his great many poems on narrative paintings: this art form permits the author to engage the most far-reaching issues confronting all artists. It once more allows him to reflect upon the sta-

---

[14] Ronsard became familiar with Anacreon primarily by way of Henri Estienne's 1554 edition of the *Anacreontea*. This impact is made explicit in his *Odelette a Corydon* of the 1555 *Meslanges*: "Je vois boire à Henry Estienne, / Qui des enfers nous a rendu / Du vieil Anacreon perdu / La douce Lyre Teïenne . . ." (6:175-76, vv. 27-30). The Vendômois also owed important debts to the editions of the *Greek Anthology* produced by Josse Badius (1531), Jean Brodeau (1549), and Estienne (1566). These influences are explored in meticulous detail in Silver, *Evolution*, 1:107-28, and James Hutton, *The Greek Anthology in France* (Ithaca, 1946), esp. 350-74.

[15] Marcel Raymond identifies Jean-Antoine de Baïf's *O douce peinture amiable* of the 1552 *Amours de Meline* (in Charles Marty-Laveaux, ed., *Evvres en rime de Ian Antoine de Baif*, 1 [Geneva: Slatkine, 1965], 28-30) as yet another primary source for Ronsard's portrait: *L'Influence de Ronsard sur la poésie française (1550-1585)*, 2 vols., 2nd ed. (1927, rpt.; Geneva: Droz, 1965), 1:143-44. Regarding the influence on Ronsard of Ariosto's *descriptio* and that of other early modern Italian authors, see McGowan, *Ideal Forms*, 165-66.

[16] See, for example, Titian's 1548 *Emperor Charles V on Horseback* (332 x 279 cm.) in the Museo del Prado (Madrid) (Campbell, *Renaissance Portraits*, 237, plate 258), and Leone Leoni's 1560 medal of Michelangelo (diameter 5.9 cm.) in the Victoria and Albert Museum (London) (Pope-Hennessy, *Portrait*, 210, plate 230).

tus of the real, the capacity of human understanding, and the relative ability of poets and painters to give a meaningful presence to the realities within their physical, emotional, intellectual, and spiritual grasp. In a sense, he is seduced by the philosophical, semiotic, and aesthetic opportunities to which portrait poems inevitably give rise.

Yet how Ronsard surrenders to this temptation, and more importantly, what positions he finally articulates, are matters that the foregoing study of the narrative-painting poetry can only begin to anticipate. While maintaining a definite bias for his own verbal art form, the laureate finds virtues in the painted portrait that cannot be impugned. This paradoxical attitude obtains in various ways throughout the poetry on portraiture, but nowhere does it strike more profoundly than in the longest and most acclaimed portrait ekphrasis of his career: the description of a full-length nude picture of Cassandre that the poet would commission from "Janet" in the *Elegie à Janet, peintre du roi* of the 1555 *Meslanges*.

I. The *Elegie à Janet*: A Dilemma of Ambivalence [17]

The one common truth to be gleaned from the copious criticism engendered by the *Elegie à Janet* is that the title divulges little about the 192 decasyllabic verses that follow it. The *coeur* of the work goes far beyond its metatextual *habit*: the poem is much more than an elegiacal homage to François Clouet (ca. 1515-72), the renowned portrait artist who, in 1541, assumed both the prestigious post of "peintre et varlet de chambre du roi" and the *nom de guerre* "Janet" from his famous portraitist father, Jean Clouet (ca. 1485-1541). [18]

---

[17] The following analysis of the *Elegie à Janet* recapitulates and expands the conclusions originally published in my article, "A Poem to a Painter: The *Elegie à Janet* and Ronsard's Dilemma of Ambivalence," *French Forum* 12 (1987): 273-87.

[18] The original Janet (also "Jeannet," "Jehannet," "Jamet," and "Jehamet"), Jean Clouet, is celebrated by such important contemporary authors as Clément Marot, in his *Epître au roi sur la traduction des psaumes de David* (1539), Etienne Jodelle, in the *Recueil des inscriptions, . . . ordonnées en l'hostel de ville à Paris* (1558), and André Thevet, *Pourtraicts et vies des hommes illustres* (1584). For more on the histories of son and father, see Peter Mellen, *Jean Clouet: Complete Edition of the Drawings, Miniatures and Paintings* (London: Phaidon Press Ltd., 1971); Blunt, *Art and Architecture*, 66-70, 116-19; Louis Dimier, *Histoire de la peinture*

This is not to say that title-driven readings have never been advanced. Several scholars have discerned nothing but applause in Ronsard's remarks about Clouet. This position has prompted the identification of certain (ostensible) correspondences between the round and exaggerated forms in the poet's picture and those that appear in such Clouet masterpieces as the *Diane de Poitiers* portrait (ca. 1571) at the National Gallery in Washington, D.C. (fig. 10). It has also drawn renewed attention to contemporary commentaries from the likes of Marc-Antoine de Muret, whose gloss on the *Elegie* confirms that Janet was commonly considered a "Peintre tres excellent . . . qui, pour representer vivement la nature, a passé tous ceux de nostre aage en son art." [19]

For others, however, Ronsard makes no significant statement about this artist. Notwithstanding the stylistic homologies detected by the former group of readers, the latter critics have subscribed to the notion, succinctly heralded by Jean Plattard, that (on balance) the poet's portrait of Cassandre "cadre mal avec les caractères de l'art de Janet." [20] Among the seventy-one pieces that Clouet is judged to have left us, [21] for example, full-length female nudes appear exclusively in his allegorical *Diane au bain* of the Musée de Rouen (fig. 11): a work that not only fails to qualify as a portrait (in the strict sense), but also dates from approximately 1558, hence

---

française des origines au retour de Vouet: 1300 à 1627 (Paris: Librairie Nationale d'Art et d'Histoire, 1925), 67-72; L. Dimier, *Portrait*, 6-31, 47-59; Henri Bouchot, *Les Clouet et Corneille de Lyon* (Paris: Librairie de l'Art, 1892); Comte de Laborde, *La Renaissance des Arts à la Cour de France*, 3 vols. (New York: Burt Franklin, 1850), 1:13-150.

[19] Marc-Antoine de Muret, *Premier Livre des Amours*, in *Commentaires au premier livre des Amours de Ronsard*, ed. Jacques Chomarat, Marie-Madeleine Fragonard, Gisèle Mathieu-Castellani, *Travaux d'Humanisme et Renaissance* 207 (Geneva: Droz, 1985), 119. Cf. also Muret's remarks on sonnet CCXVI, "Telle qu'elle est, dedans ma souvenance" (sonnet CCVIII, in the Laumonier edition [5:154-55]): "Janet, peintre du Roy, homme, sans controverse, premier en son art" (ibid., 94). Foremost among the modern literary critics who have offered such readings are Richard A. Sayce, Jean Adhémar, Helmut Hatzfeld, and Henri Chamard (see Introduction, n. 7). In the interest of completeness, it should be noted that these critics have broadened their examinations to include reflections on the apparent relations between Ronsard's descriptions and the distinctive features of sixteenth-century pictorial mannerism.

[20] Plattard, "Les Arts," 484.

[21] According to Louis Dimier, this corpus includes fifty-four drawings, thirteen paintings, and four miniatures: *Portrait*, 111-32.

Fig. 10: François Clouet, *Diane de Poitiers* (ca. 1571), National Gallery of Art, Washington, D.C. (1961.9.13, Samuel H. Kress Collection, 1997)

FIG. 11: François Clouet, *Diane au bain* (1552-1558?), Musée des Beaux-Arts, Rouen (Réunion des Musées Nationaux)

some four years after the composition of the *Elegie* in 1554.[22] Readers of the second type have therefore proposed that all allusions to Clouet are merely generic, that the thirty-three imperatives and five apostrophes directed to "Janet" (in the two 1555 editions[23]) would in fact denote any or all of the major figure painters and sculptors of Ronsard's period. Further and more importantly, they have concluded that the poem is above all a drill in poetic description, an exercise devised to evidence the laureate's ability to emulate the ancient, medieval, and early modern masters of the verbal portrait.[24]

Certainly, each point of view has its merits. While statements like Muret's provide a strong reason to concede that François Clouet is a primary object of the poet's meditations, there can be little doubt that Ronsard also pays homage to the powers of poetry and the tradition of poetic portraiture that transcends any commentary on a single painter. In a sense, then, the poem both *is* and *is not* about the title's "peintre du roy." Just how this is so, however, remains to be illuminated. Despite the abundant scholarly attention the *Elegie* has garnered in recent decades, it is still unclear when and to what end the discourse on François Clouet intersects that on poetry.

* * *

---

[22] Roger Trinquet first proposes the 1558 designation for the *Bain* in his "L'Allégorie politique au XVIe siècle dans la peinture française, ses Dames au Bain," *BSHAF* (1967): 1-16. Trinquet's theory is subsequently supported by Béguin (*L'Ecole de Fontainebleau*, 54-57). For more on the dating of the *Elegie*, see below (esp. n. 41).

[23] These numbers decrease somewhat in the subsequent, shorter versions of the poem. In the 1584 edition, for example, Janet is named only four times, and he is the object of only twenty-seven direct imperatives.

[24] The most important and indisputable models for the *Elegie* include Anacreon's *Portrait of His Mistress* and *Portrait of Bathyllus* (*Odes* XXVIII and XXIX), the medieval *descriptio puellae*, Ariosto's portrait of Alcina, the blason tradition popularized by Clément Marot, and Ronsard's own early ode to Jacques Peletier, *Des beautez qu'il voudroit en s'amie*. Among the principal proponents of this point of view (with inevitable variations in emphasis) are Jean Plattard, "Les Arts," 484; Laumonier, *Oeuvres*, 6:152, nn. 2-3, and 182, n. 2 (see also his *Ronsard poète lyrique*, 504); Raymond Lebègue, "La Pléiade et les Beaux-Arts," 117; Henri Weber and Catherine Weber, *Les Amours* (Paris: Garnier, 1963), 607-09; Yvonne Bellenger, "Les poètes français," 434-36; Françoise Joukovsky, "L'*Elegie à Janet* de Ronsard, portrait 'mental,'" in *Le Portrait*, ed. Joseph-Marc Bailbe (Rouen: Université de Rouen, 1987), 21-36 (see also her *Bel objet*, 99).

As it happens, the very disparities between the known artwork of Clouet and the poetically encoded portrait of the *Elegie* guide us to an answer. Ultimately these discrepancies are the most conspicuous indices of the irony that gives primary definition to the confluence of Ronsard's complementary commentaries. In the final analysis the praise to the king's portrait painter (and to painted portraiture in general) is equivocal: it is an encomium that very nearly implodes under the weight of words and examples that otherwise stress the potency of poetry.

The irony is immediately apparent in the paradoxical evolution of the first ten verses. Although the poet's initial call to Janet to render the perfect beauties of Cassandre would seem to attest to an overall faith in the painter and his art, his subsequent warning against an "art menteur" speaks to a deep-seated crack in that confidence:

> Pein moi, Janet, pein moi je te supplie
> Dans ce tableau les beautés de m'amie
> De la façon que je te les dirai.
> Comme importun je ne te supplirai
> D'*un art menteur* quelque faveur lui faire,
> Il sufist bien si tu la sçais portraire
> Ainsi qu'elle est, sans vouloir deguiser
> Son naturel pour la favoriser,
> Car la faveur n'est bonne que pour celles
> Qui se font peindre, & qui ne sont pas belles.
>
> (6:152, vv. 1-10: my emphasis)

In relation to the hyperbolic rhetoric of love that overlays all the discourses of the poem, this caution serves simply to accent the beloved's consummate beauty. It affirms that no amount of "lying art," or deceptive artifice, can improve upon her loveliness. Yet in the narrower context of Ronsard's comments on portraiture and poetry, the same prohibition recognizes that Janet is not only predisposed to distort the truth, but also in need of guidance from the poet to resist that unfortunate penchant. This vital incrimination, which has no counterpart in the principal literary models for the elegy, is reinforced by a more fundamental misgiving. With the proviso of verse 6 ("si tu la sçais portraire . . ."), the laureate once again departs from his sources in order to suspend confirmation that the painter would ever be competent to portray Cassandre as she truly is ("Ainsi qu'elle est").

Not surprisingly, any candid repudiation of this ability is deferred in order to promote the inescapability of that conclusion. Keeping to the tactic he inaugurates in the earlier narrative-painting pieces, Ronsard sets out to emphasize the inadequacies of *pictura* by *demonstrating* the extraordinary strengths of *poesis*. A sampling of the ensuing head-to-toe instructions to Clouet exposes the mechanisms of this endeavor. The directions for Cassandre's hair in the second stanza set the pattern:

> Fai luy premier les cheveus ondelés
> Noüés, retors, recrepés, annelés,
> Qui de couleur le cedre representent,
> Ou les demesle, & que libres ils sentent
> Dans le tableau, si par art tu le peus,
> La mesme odeur de ses propres cheveus.
>
> (6:152-53, vv. 11-16)

In formulating this description (and all those that come after) as a set of commands ("Fai luy . . . Ou les demesle . . ."), Ronsard does more than pay tribute to his various literary antecedents. He also achieves essentially the same effect produced, through the play of future- and past-tense verbs, in the *Temple de Messeigneurs*. Like that contemporary hymn, the *Elegie* illustrates the ability of the poet to give presence to realities well in advance of the painter. Only, in the present instance the credit goes to the special modal flexibility of words. Thanks to the ability of verbal signs to express imperatives, Ronsard succeeds in recreating his beloved's hair (and other splendors) before Janet's brush can touch the canvas.

The poet's challenge to portray the odor of Cassandre's hair, "La mesme odeur de ses propres cheveus," circumscribes an additional distinction of poetry. On one level this invitation is but another trace of Ronsard's debt to the ekphrastic portraits of the past. The reader is instantly reminded of the hair description in Anacreon's verses to the "master of the Rhodian art" in the sixth-century-B.C. *Portrait of His Mistress*: "First paint me then her flowing hair / Both soft and black; and if the wax / Be able *let it breathe perfume*." [25] On a different level the call to reproduce a smell func-

---

[25] *Odes* 16, vv. 6-8 (my emphasis), in *The Anacreontea and Principal Remains of Anacreon of Teos*, trans. and ed. Judson France Davidson (New York: Dutton, 1915), 95. See also H. and C. Weber, *Les Amours*, 607, n. 3.

tions to distinguish the synesthetic versatility of poetry from the monesthetic limitations of painting. While *verba* are probably no better than *imagines* at inducing actual olfactory sensations, their conceptual essence allows them to convey more easily the various effects of such impressions upon the mind and spirit. Thus to denote an "odeur" in words disrupts nothing. Like the option to portray the lady with locks undone, this maneuver substantially enhances the erotic appeal of the description. Conversely, as the repetition of the conditional "si" in verse 15 reveals, the poet distrusts the transperceptual grasp of the painter's "art" (artifice). For Ronsard, pictures consist of natural signs that are bound more or less exclusively to the realm of the visible. Although the painter can readily configure the visually perceivable appearance of the act of smelling,[26] he is hindered from signifying the deep emotional or cognitive responses to an olfactory stimulus.[27]   •

The preeminence of poetry over painting receives further support in the exceptional alternative offered at the middle of the sizain.[28] By employing the disjunctive "Ou," Ronsard succeeds in denoting a set of parallel realities and experiences: one staging the lady with tightly tied curls and ringlets, as she might appear for formal court gatherings and public occasions[29]; the other featuring the

---

[26] Cf. the early sixteenth-century French tapestry depicting the sense of smell in the *Dame à la Licorne* series at the Musée de Cluny in Paris: Francis Salet, *La Tapisserie française du moyen-âge à nos jours* (Paris: Vincent, 1946), pl. 38. Here the sense in question is rendered both symbolically and in gesture: in the first case, by the rose that the lady has selected from a basket of flowers to attach to her crown (presumably for its fragrance); in the second instance, by a small monkey on her right, who has chosen another flower from the same basket and holds it directly under his nostrils, leaving no doubt as to the object's primary attraction.

[27] Cf. Dante's approach to synaesthesia and the "visibile parlare" in *Purgatorio* 10 (Chapter One, pp. 61-62).

[28] Once again, Ronsard departs from his principal models, which take a distinctly conjunctive approach to itemizing the beloved's corporal virtues. Indeed, even the early prototype of this work, the ode to Peletier, *Des beautez qu'il voudroit en s'amie* (Laumonier, *Œuvres*, 1:3-8), presents only two cases of option (once regarding the odor of the lady's breath; another time, in respect to what her hands can do). In the last poem, however, the poet makes no explicit attempt to imitate painting.

[29] As we know from the contemporary literature (e.g., Rabelais' description of the *religieuses* at the Abbey of Thélème in *Gargantua* 56, and the accounts of period fashion from the likes of Brantôme) and the iconographic record (including the images produced at Fontainebleau and, of course, François Clouet's own portraits), the women of the period typically wore their hair in tight curls and frizzed (or beneath wigs so styled), and nearly always accessorized with some form of headgear. See Roger Gaucheron, ed., *Recueil des Dames* (Paris: Payot, 1926); Henri Bouchot, *Les Femmes de Brantôme* (Paris: Quantin, 1890), esp. 67-68, 115.

mistress with tresses unraveled and free, a veritable Botticellian Venus, as the poet-lover might know her in the most intimate circumstances.

We ought not to surmise, however, that the *Elegie à Janet* thereby marks a retreat from the ideal of conceptual unity promoted in the poems about narrative painting. Despite its multiplicity of meanings, the verbal portrait maintains a unifying semantic outline precisely because those meanings proliferate disjunctively–in such a way that *only one* meaning (or 'disjunct') may obtain per context. To say that a thing 'T' has qualities 'X' *or* 'Y' is ultimately to affirm that, while 'X' and 'Y' are among the possible attributes of 'T', in any given circumstance 'T' has *one, but not both*, of the qualities 'X' and 'Y'. Thanks to the disjunctive ability of verbal language, therefore, Ronsard may be said to have his semantic cake and eat it too: he creates a 'portrait' that anticipates an ideational diffusion as it retains a conceptual unity, acknowledges the semiosic drift while subduing its powerful tow.

In contrast, the connotation of multiple realities poses a host of difficult or irresoluble problems for the painter. Fettered by the inherent naturalness and synchronousness of visual signs, François Clouet would be obliged to adopt a conjunctive mode of representation. In attempting to comply with Ronsard's directions, the portrait painter would be required to depict two Cassandres within the same frame, each modeling a different coiffure, or perhaps to multiply the lady's presence by surrounding her with a miscellany of mirrored surfaces, as Vasari reports Giorgione to have done in the show of "fine whim and caprice" ("bellissimo ghiribizzo e capriccio") that won him success in a dispute for artistic supremacy with some sculptors of his day.[30] In either scenario, not only would Janet violate the conventions of decorum rigorously observed in formal court portraiture, but he would surrender to the Hermetic flow by subverting the referential cohesion of his painting.

The importance of the last forensic strategy is otherwise apparent in the prevalence of option proposals throughout the *Elegie*.

---

[30] "Dipinse uno ignudo che voltava le spalle et aveva in terra una fonte d'acqua limpidissima, nella quale fece dentro per riverberazione la parte dinanzi; da un de' lati era un corsaletto brunito che s'era spogliato, nel quale era il profilo manco, perché nel lucido di quell'arme si scorgeva ogni cosa; da l'altra parte era uno specchio, che drento [sic] vi era l'altro lato di quello ignudo . . .": Giorgio Vasari, *Le Vita de' più eccellenti pittori, scultori et architettori*, ed. Rosanna Bettarini and Paola Barocchi, 6 vols. (Florence: Studio per Edizioni Scelte, 1966-87), 3:46.

Among the twenty-five body-part descriptions that comprise the poem, eight–hence about a third–contain one or more offers of choice.[31] Moreover, all save one of these cases propose options that transcend the purely visible physical states presented in the hair passage. Except for the portrait of the "autre chose" (vv. 157-62), where Ronsard preserves a sense of visceral eroticism by allowing the nakedness of the beloved's member to be fully unobscured or ("Si ce n'estoit") cloaked in a diaphanous veil of silk that might engage the poet's intro-piercing phallic gaze ("affin qu'on l'*entrevoie*": my emphasis), these descriptions shift swiftly into the figurative. Capitalizing upon the unique virtue of verbal signs to signify analogies, Ronsard is able to relate the "beautés" of his human subject to the larger world of nature and the gods and goddesses of mythology.

The move to offer a choice among nature-based analogues is exemplified in the instructions for Cassandre's "oreille." After reviewing the visually discernible material attributes of the ear–its shape, size, structure, and color: properties of particular concern to every Renaissance painter[32]–Ronsard expands his description by likening the hue that radiates through the lady's veil to that of a lily contained in a crystal receptacle or a rose freshly enclosed in a glass:

> Apres fai lui sa rondellette oreille
> Petite, unie, entre blanche & vermeille,
> Qui sous le voile aparoisse à l'egal
> Que fait un lis enclos dans un cristal,

---

[31] For the purposes of this calculation, I have deliberately ignored certain problematic elements of Ronsard's portrait, either because they are ancillary to Cassandre's corporal charms (viz., the "crespe noir" [vv. 17-22]: a fact that may well have motivated the suppression of this passage in 1560), or because they are more properly subsumed within other body features (viz., the "venes . . . muscles & les ners" beneath the skin of the breasts [vv. 137-40]).

[32] Cf. the three visible properties of space-line ("spatio-linea"), composition ("compositione") and color ("colori") that Alberti lists among the painter's primary concerns in the *Della pittura* (81-82). Cf., also, the ten attributes of the eye ("10 ofiti dell'ochio")–darkness, light, solidity and color, form and position, distance and propinquity, motion and rest ("tenebre . luce corpo e colore . figura e sito . remotione . propiquita . moto . e quiete")–itemized by Leonardo in his introduction to the *Trattato* (*The Notebooks of Leonardo da Vinci*, ed. Jean Paul Richter [1883; rpt. New York: Dover, 1970], 23). No less revealing is the underlying design according to which modern editors have organized Leonardo's original manuscripts. Richter, for example, has divided them into chapters on linear perspective, light and shade, perspective and disappearance, color theory, perspective and color, and proportions and movements of the human figure.

Ou tout ainsi qu'aparoist une rose
Tout fraichement dedans un verre enclose.

(6:155, vv. 65-70)

As before, Ronsard elicits a set of realities beyond the representational domain of the painter. Taking full advantage of the simile, he plainly and succinctly evokes a set of conceptual impressions that reflect his own subjective responses. Thus we learn not only that the ear would evince the fragile, evanescent delicacy of a freshly cut flower, but in accordance with Western traditions of symbolism surrounding the lily and the rose, it would also arouse competing thoughts of Cassandre's seraphic purity and carnal sexuality. And as to the veil she would be wearing (an item initially noticed in the third stanza, vv. 17-22), a similarly paradoxical reaction is anticipated. Typically consisting of a light opaque fabric, a garment of this kind was used primarily to conceal or shelter the hair and ears. In painting, then, this object could at best be depicted as François Clouet has done in his unforgettable rendering of princess Marie Stuart in the mourning veil she donned after the untimely demise of her young husband, François II (fig. 12). [33] Poetry, on the other hand, suffers no such limitations. Indeed, in the mind's eye and words of the lover-poet the veil becomes either as transparent as crystal or as brittle as glass, and hence something quite separate from what it can be in the corporeal eye and material paint of the portrait artist. [34]

---

[33] In fact, Clouet's drawing presents Marie Stuart in a white veil whereas, according to Ronsard's description in verse 17, Cassandre's veil would be a "crespe noir." For other renderings by Jean and François Clouet of ladies in veils and other head coverings, see Raoul de Broglie, "Les Clouet de Chantilly: Catalogue illustré," *Gazette des Beaux-Arts* (May-June, 1971): 305-28. We shall return to the painting of Marie Stuart in the pages that follow.

[34] Ronsard makes a similar use of the alternative comparisons that would reflect the beauties of Cassandre's cheeks (vv. 81-84) and lips (vv. 105-10). Joined by the images of milk, a carnation, and a red sea coral, the lily and the rose are again the vehicles by which the poet infuses Cassandre's visible physical beauties with a number of transcendental qualities: a prurience that would be pure ("une rose . . . sur du laict") or a purity that would be prurient (a "lis qui baise un oeillet rougissant"); a dangerousness ("la rose . . . flambante au printemps sur l'espine") or an inaccessibility (the "coural vermeil . . . au fond de la marine"); and an overarching sense of universality with each incursion into the macrocosm of nature. For additional examples of milk imagery, which is more commonly associated with the alluring chromatic or nourishing properties of the breast, see the *Ode à Jean Dorat* (1:136, vv. 4-6), the *Ode à Macée* (1:202, vv. 31-36), and the blason-style sonnet CLX, "Ces flotz

FIG. 12: François Clouet, *Marie Stuart en deuil blanc* (ca. 1560), Paris (cliché
Bibliothèque Nationale de France)

The directives for the "beau sourci voutis" (6:154, vv. 39-46)
contain two additional challenges to the painter that divorce Cassandre even further from her physical ontology. In one regard, Ronsard imbues his nature-based analogue with a more expansive spatial measure and a definite orientation in time: "que son pli tortis /
Semble un croissant qui montre par la nue / Au premier mois sa
vouture cornue" (6:154, vv. 40-42). In place of the essentially atem-
poral, discrete physical objects of the prior comparisons, the poet
proposes a fully developed landscape (or skyscape) having a clear
seasonal bearing: the lady's eyebrow should resemble not just any
crescent moon, but one that shines through the clouds of a night
sky in the "premier mois" of January.[35]

The landscape analogy appears elsewhere in the poem as well.
But as we discover from the choices offered to describe Cassandre's
"greve" (shin) in the penultimate stanza, it is also subject to significant modifications:

> . . . fay lui la greve plene,
> Telle que l'ont les vierges de Lacene,
> Alant lutter au rivage connu
> Du fleuve Eurote, ayans le cors tout nu,
> Ou bien chassans à meutes decouplées
> Quelque grand cerf es forets Amiclées.
>
> (6:159-60, vv. 169-74)

As supplementary evidence of the preeminence of poetry in the hierarchy of the arts, Ronsard now endows the landscape with a def-

---

jumeaulx de laict bien espoissi," of the 1552 *Amours* (4:152-53). As for other carnation, coral, lily, and rose analogies, cf. sonnet VI, "Ces liens d'or, ceste bouche ver-
meille" (4:10), and sonnet XXIII, "Ce beau coral, ce marbre qui souspire," of the
1552 *Amours* (4:26-27).

[35] In fact, expansions of the nature analogue occur initially in the descriptions
of Cassandre's "beau front" and the "beau rubi" she would wear in the middle of
the "greve" (part) separating her hair and forehead (vv. 29-38). In the former case,
Ronsard likens the smoothness of the brow to the sleeping surface of the ocean in a
windless calm ("tel qu'est la pleine marine / Quand tant soit peu le vent ne la mu-
tine / Et que gisante en son lit elle dort / Calmant ses flots sillés d'un somme
mort . . ." [6:153, vv. 29-32]). In the latter instance, he compares the rays emitted
by the ruby over the furrow of the lady's hairline to moonbeams glowing upon the
untrodden snow that has fallen to the bottom of a valley ("ainsi qu'on voit de nuit /
Briller les rais de la lune qui luit / Dessus la nege au fond d'un val coulée, / De trace
d'home encore non foulée . . ." [6:153-54, vv. 35-38]). Other examples of expanded
nature analogies may be found in the representations of the nose (esp. vv. 79-80)
and the neck (esp. vv. 117-18).

inite geographical and historical/legendary dimension. Fulfilling the potential of verbal language to achieve denotative precision through its proper nouns, he specifically relates the beloved's shin–and Cassandre herself–to the histories and legends of the Spartan virgins of Lakedaimon ("Lacene") who would wrestle naked on the banks of the Eurotas River and hunt stags in the forests of Amiklai. Moreover, by submitting this analogy for a feature that is earlier classified among "le reste / De ses beautés, *qui ne m'est manifeste*" (6:157, vv. 125-26: my emphasis),[36] Ronsard subtly recalls the poet's vatic gifts. He cleverly reemphasizes the unique '*in*-sight' of the poet previously recognized in the ode *A son luc* and narrative-painting poems like *La defloration de Lede*: the privileged ability of the "ministre des dieux" to see the truths beneath and beyond the *habit* of the visible material world.

A second peculiarity of the "sourci" passage is its leap from the tangible domain of physical nature into the conceptual universe of mythology. As an alternative to the landscape, the poet bids Janet to fashion the beloved's eyebrow after the semicircular bow of the mythological Cupid: "Ou si jamais tu as veu l'arc d'Amour, / Pren le portrait dessus le demi tour / De sa courbure à demi cercle close, / Car l'arc d'Amour & lui n'est qu'une chose . . ." (6:154, vv. 43-46). This invitation would seem to suppose the poet and the painter are equally qualified to conceptualize and configure Love's curvilinear weapon. However, by imposing the condition that Janet draw upon a prior visual experience ("si jamais tu as veu l'arc d'Amour"), the proposal ultimately precludes such an ideational parity. Since the imaginary world of Cupid and his bow is not available to the bodily eye, this condition can never be met.[37] Accordingly, the

---

[36] This group includes eight body features in all: the lady's *tétins, épaules, ventre, nombril, autre chose, cuisses, greve*, and *pieds*.

[37] This is not to say that early modern artists never attempted such depictions. On the contrary, Cupid had long been, and continued to be, a favorite subject for painters and sculptors, and Ronsard was well aware of the fact. Cf. his imitations of the *Anthologie grecque* in sonnet VI of the 1555 *Continuation des Amours* (7:122); in the *Chanson*, "Quiconque soit le peintre. . .," of the 1569 *Sixiesme livre des Poëmes* (15:120-21); the *Stances* of the 1578 *Amours d'Eurymedon et de Callirée* (17:146-47, vv, 55-60); and the *Cartel pour les Chevaliers des Flammes* of the 1584 *Œuvres* (18:116, vv. 33-44). Nevertheless, in all of these cases the pictorial representations of Cupid are never truly offered as models. For more on the images of Cupid during Antiquity and the Renaissance, see Panofsky, *Studies in Iconology*, 95-128 and Plates 69-106.

mythological alternative not only preordains Janet's failure, but it tacitly charges that failing to the defect of portrait painting historically decried by the Neoplatonic philosophers and art theorists: its slavish reliance on the empirically accessible model.[38] By contrast, the mere inclusion of this proposition testifies eloquently to the extensive epistemological and semiotic capabilities of the poet. It gives unimpeachable proof that the latter can comprehend and signify an idea as readily as a thing, the immaterial as well as the material.

But as so often before Ronsard is unwilling or unable to rely on a single display of the poet's powers. This fact becomes especially salient with the quadruplication of mythological similes in the ensuing segment on Cassandre's eyes:

> Que l'un soit dous, l'autre soit furieus,
> Que l'un de Mars, l'autre de Venus tienne,
> Que du benin toute esperance vienne,
> Et du cruel vienne tout desespoir:
> Ou que l'un soit pitoiable à le voir,
> Come celuy d'Ariadne delessée
> Aus bord de Die, alors que l'incensée,
> Voyant la mer, de pleurs se consommoit,
> Et son Thesée en vain elle nommoit.
> L'autre soit gay, come il est bien croiable
> Que l'eut jadis Penelope louable,
> Quand elle vit son mari retourné,
> Aiant vint ans loing d'elle sejourné.
>
> (6:154-55, vv. 52-64)

Undoubtedly the first four verses owe a debt to the description of Bathyllus' eyes in the *Portrait* to that handsome Samian youth by Anacreon: "Let them be dark and bright and keen, / And let them breathe desire; / From Venus take their wanton sheen, / From Mars their earnest fire" (vv. 13-16).[39] Nonetheless, Ronsard clearly attains a complexity absent from the poem of his ancient predecessor. Whereas the Teosian summons the images of Venus and Mars to describe traits that are visually perceptible and operationally related, a luminosity and burning that one could presumably observe si-

---

[38] See Chapter One, 68-69; and above 166 and n. 9.
[39] Anacreon, *The Anacreontea*, 98.

multaneously in the same eye, the Vendômois evokes them to designate characteristics that are fundamentally abstract and mutually
exclusive, a benignity and a cruelty that are only cognitively perceivable and destined to reside independently, in one eye or the
other, at any single moment. Thus, well before the option is mentioned explicitly, Ronsard realizes much the same effect that he accomplishes, by way of the disjunction, in the hair stanza at the beginning of the *Elegie*. In requiring a body feature (here the eye) to
assume two disparate or antithetical dispositions, he advocates a
feat that would undermine the visual integrity of a conventionally
painted portrait while it assures the completeness, and hence unity,
of his own poetically rendered picture. Moreover, as in the eyebrow
passage, he uses mythology to present truths that transcend the
world of sensory experiences. It therefore seems improbable that
Ronsard could add anything more to his endorsement of poetry
with the introduction of the choice in verse 56.

Nevertheless, our laureate again finds a means to refine and re-
inforce his position. For in the end that alternative more clearly distinguishes the kinds of meta-sensory realities under the poet's
purview. In the first four verses, these realities are the contradictory
emotions that Cassandre provokes in her love-torn admirer. They
are the impressions of gentleness and harshness that the poet knows
personally–those that bring him "esperance" or "desespoir" in his
quest for amorous gratification. In the nine verses that remain they
are the psychological conditions of the lady herself. With noticeably
longer appeals to the mythological love stories about Ariadne's
painful separation from Theseus and Penelope's happy reunion
with Ulysses, Ronsard actualizes the poet's more extraordinary ability to apprehend and translate the intangible realities of the
Other–the states of maddening grief and joyous relief in Cassandre's soul to which only God and his privileged poetic intermediary
may gain access.

The numerous instances of option serve a vital function within
the paragone-related discourse that propels the *Elegie à Janet*. They
are the most common means by which Ronsard *enacts* the superiority of verbal signification. As in the first stanza, though, the Pléiade
laureate may achieve a similar result through irony or, in certain
cases, by enlisting the diachronic virtues of his art.

Both effects are conveniently conjoined at the center of the
poem, in the dizain devoted (appropriately enough) to the corpore-

al source of words, the lady's "bouche." Initially, the poet works ironically:

> Helas, Janet, pour bien peindre sa bouche
> A peine Homere en ses vers te diroit
> Quel vermeillon egualer la pouroit,
> Car pour la peindre ainsi qu'elle merite,
> Peindre il faudroit celle d'une Charite.
>
> (6:156, vv. 90-94)

The concession to Janet's inability to reproduce the exact vermillion of Cassandre's "bouche" is merely another ploy in the poet's rhetoric of self-exaltation. The painter's failure can have no satisfactory justification. The fact that this color would be barely describable by the divine Homer, or require the painting of a "Charite," the embodiment of grace and beauty, is no defense. On the contrary, the portraitist's ineptitude is all the more reproachable precisely because, in truth, the Greek bard *would* find the appropriate verses (albeit "a peine"), and the poet of the present poem *does* recreate the perfection of his beloved 'Grace', mouth and all. What is worse, the painter would muddle the very task his art most aptly prepares him to fulfill. By misrepresenting that cinnabarine hue, Janet would break faith with the countless theorists of aesthetics and painting, from Plato on, for whom the mastery of the chromatic universe continues to be a defining advantage of painting.[40]

In the second half of the dizain, Ronsard revisits the special benefits of poetic diachrony. Extending the concepts he introduces in *Des peintures contenues dedans un tableau*, and laying the ground for those he will elaborate, a few months later, in the *Temple de Messeigneurs*,[41] the Pléiade laureate makes the inherent temporal powers of poetry a key to the expressive force and beauty of that art form:

---

[40] Cf. Ronsard's intimations about color in *Des peintures* and the *Defloration de Lede* (Chapter Two, 103, 147 and n. 36).

[41] Although the composition of the *Elegie* has yet to be dated with precision, it was most likely written after the appearance of Henri Estienne's edition of the *Anacreontea*, in March 1554, and before the first printing of the *Meslanges*, on 22 November 1554. Accordingly, the work would probably have preceded by at least six months the *Temple de Messeigneurs*, whose *terminus a quo* Laumonier convincingly places after April 1555. For more on Ronsard and Anacreon, see above, n. 14.

Pein la moy donc qu'elle semble parler,
Ores sourire, ores embasmer l'air
De ne sçay quelle ambrosienne haleine.
Mais par sur tout fai qu'elle semble pleine
De la douceur de persuasion.

(6:156, vv. 95-99)

Like the disjunctive "ou" and its equivalents, the coordinated "ores
. . . ores" of verse 96 permits an offer of problematic alternatives. It
allows the poet to prescribe multiple states of appearance that Janet
would be either disinclined or unable to illustrate: the illusions of
speaking and smiling (neither of which emerges as a typical element
in Clouet's pictures) and the semblance of exuding Cassandre's am-
brosial breath (another olfactory effect outside the denotative possibilities of conventional portraiture). What stands out here, however, is the affiliation between those options and the notion of a
presentation over time. The paired adverbs clearly indicate that the
mouth should not only seem to speak, but *at a different moment*,
appear to smile, and *at a later point*, embalm the air with a heavenly
scent. These terms thereby wed the idea of semantic plenitude to a
diachronic mode of deployment, and thus to one of the most basic
attributes of words and poetry. In the end, the consummate verbal
art of the poet would be able to produce the portrait of Cassandre
that is most truly "*pleine* / De la douceur de persuasion."

As in *Des peintures* and the *Temple*, then, the temporal essence
of poetry becomes a principal premise in Ronsard's argument for
the superiority of poets over painters. Indeed, given the placement
of the "ores" in verse 96, which coincides with the exact middle of
the poem in all printings before 1560, that essence may rightly be
regarded as the cynosure of the inter-art commentaries in the
Elegie.

For the reason why this poetic quality should dominate all others, Ronsard's preoccupation with the theories anchoring Leonardo's evidence for the primacy of painting once more suggests an answer. Like the *baudrier* sextet at the midpoint of *Des peintures*, the
centering of the "ores" in the *Elegie* may inscribe a rebuttal to the
Florentine's obsessive praise for pictorial simultaneity. However,
unlike the reply in the earlier poem, whose foremost concern is the
semantic absence plaguing the synchronous signifiers of the painter,
the present response would highlight the semantic and aesthetic

fullness that ennobles the time-based signifiers of the poet. Reviving the *pictura loquens* ('speaking picture') notion of poetry that attracted the vigorous opposition of Leonardo, Ronsard makes his portrait 'talk' on every level. Notwithstanding the request that the lady in paint should "semble[r] parler," and the subsequent announcement, in the final verse of the poem, that "Bien peu s'en faut qu'elle ne parle à moy" (6:160, v. 192), the fact persists that Janet's *pictura* remains *muta*. Its voice is doomed to eternal immanence–forever to *seem* ("semble[r]") and to be *almost* ("peu s'en faut"). [42] By contrast, the lady in words is 'speech' personified. She verbalizes meaning in every manner and facet of her being, visible and nonvisible–and paradoxically, before the slightest utterance should leave her lips.

The diachrony of words is likewise an ally of true beauty. Drawing implicitly upon Aquinian and Dantean notions about the sense of plenitude inscribed in the beautiful, Ronsard is able to associate beauty with the verbal diachrony that actualizes the plenitude of poetry and, in the same gesture, to counter the harmony-based principle of Neoplatonic aesthetics that allows Leonardo to draw his conclusion about the concinnity ("concento") of painting. [43] While present from the earliest versions of the *Elegie*, this affiliation attains its greatest thematic prominence when the evocation of the "Charite," the archetype of the highest beauties (v. 94 in 1555 and 1557), secures the midpoint (v. 86) of the shorter, 172-verse edition that first appears in 1567.

* * *

At the same time the *Elegie* advances this eloquent case for the supremacy of poetry, however, it also encodes a profound admiration for Janet that speaks to Ronsard's underlying ambivalence toward portraiture and his embroilment in the contradictory double

---

[42] Ronsard manifestly takes his lead from the concluding verse of Anacreon's *Portrait of His Mistress*: "Arrête, arrête, je te vois, ô portrait, tu vas parler." However, where the latter author uses the near future tense to make a speaking portrait seem not only possible but inevitable, Ronsard implies a permanent deferral of voice. Barron comes to a similar conclusion in his dissertation (381).

[43] The relevant theories of Aquinas and Dante are reviewed in Chapter One, 49-63; similarly, on the Neoplatonic principle adopted by Leonardo, see Chapter One, 80-81.

bind. In the broadest way this conflict of desires manifests itself as it does in the *Temple de Messeigneurs*. In both poems the subject's endeavor to establish superiority, and so alterity, simultaneously entails a wish for resemblance to the object Other. The competitor poet aspires to assume an 'authorship' of the pictorial artwork that inscribes a concomitant wish to arrogate the artistry and visual signification of the rival painter.

Unlike the *Temple*, though, the *Elegie* suspends any conclusive declaration of praise. In the hymn all insinuated tributes to painting engage future-tense verbs that impart a sense of inevitability to the acclaim. While envisioning the Avignon pillar of the Montmorency shrine the poet makes it clear that the hair and people there configured "*seront* si bien faictz" (8:75, v. 59). In the *Elegie*, on the other hand, any possible adulation is deferred by an indefinite 'nearly-but-not-quite', as in the matter of the portrait's "almost" speaking mouth, or it is relegated to a distant hypothetical or unreal by a network of 'ifs'.

The latter maneuver is epitomized in the instructions for Cassandre's "nez." The connotations of praise are submerged and effectively abrogated in the contrary-to-fact hypothetical of the past conditional: "Mais pour neant *tu aurois fait* si beau / Tout l'ornement de ton riche tableau, / *Si tu n'avois* de la lineature / De son beau nez bien *portrait* la peinture . . ." (6:155, vv. 71-74: my emphasis). Not only is the existence of the "riche tableau" a matter of uncertainty, but *if* it were not, and Janet had managed to produce such an artwork, then he would have done so for naught *if* he had otherwise failed to capture the true contour of the lady's beautiful nose. Nevertheless, disappointment is virtually guaranteed by the ensuing stipulation that the feature be at once "gresle, long, aquilin, / Poly, traitis" and, what is worse (thanks to the landscape analogy), that it be situated "Parmi la face, ainsi comme descend / Dans une pleine un petit mont qui pend" (vv. 75-76; 79-80).

In the *Elegie à Janet* the admiration for the pictorial arts shows less in what the poet says than in what he decides not to aver. Thus, although that esteem is less immediately accessible than in the *Temple*, it is in fact more influential upon the overall forensic posturing toward the paragone debate in the *Elegie*.

This influence is exposed in the editorial fate of the extraordinary twelve lines that start the sixteen-verse final stanza:

Ha, que fais-tu? tu gaste ton ouvrage.
Tu faus, Janet, à peindre son visage,
Le paignant mal tu pers de ton renom:
Vien, sui mes pas au logis de Brinon,
Là tu verras, dans un coin de sa salle
Une peinture aus déesses egale,
Qu'il fist tracer par la main des amours
Pour sa Sidere, afin que tous les jours
En la voiant eust souvenance d'elle:
Je veus du tout que m'amie soit telle.
Ne lui pein donc, Janet, ne pis ne mieux,
Le front, le nez, la bouche, ni les yeux.

(6:160, vv. 177-88)

This refreshingly frank rebuke of Janet and his (anticipated) artwork provides explicit justification for the apprehension the poet articulates at the beginning of the poem. The painter is more than predisposed to "un art menteur": he is fully guilty of that error since the visual portrait falls short of depicting the complete range of Cassandre's attributes *ne pis ne mieux* than they truly are. Moreover, it has none of the mnemonic capabilities the poet so cherishes in the "peinture" that Ronsard's patron, the "conseiller au Parlement de Paris" Jean Brinon, is reported to have commissioned in homage to his beloved Sidere. This is not to admit that some anonymous painter has succeeded where Janet could not; rather, as before, the portraitist falters where the poet prevails. In stipulating that the preferred artwork is "*Pour* sa Sidere" at the opening of verse 184 (located, like other key phrases, at the exact middle of the stanza in which it appears [here the concluding stanza, vv. 177-92]), the poet opposes Janet's portrait to the "peinture" (in the figurative sense) that is the *Meslanges* itself. The collection is, after all, *for* Brinon and his lady, as Ronsard clearly announces in the *Odelette* dedicated "A Jean Brinon & à sa Sidere" that introduces the second 1555 edition: "Car puis qu'Amour vous veut lier / Ensemble, il vous faut dedier / Mon livre à tous deus . . ." (6:268, vv. 7-9).[44]

---

[44] The same dedication, "A Jean Brinon, & à sa Sidere," accompanies the opening ode, *A sa lyre*, of the first 1555 edition of the *Meslanges*. This interpretation is further supported by the use of the equivocal verb "tracer" (v. 183), which often denotes the scriptural process itself, as may be seen in sonnet CLXVII of the 1552 *Amours*: "Donne moy l'encre, & le papier aussi: / En cent papiers tesmoingz de mon souci, / Je veux *tracer* la peine que j'endure" (4:159, vv. 9-11: my emphasis). From another perspective, it is probable that Ronsard would have referred to a painting '*de* sa Sidere' (*of* Sidere) had he wished to designate another portrait in paint.

Notwithstanding their singular force and interest, verses 177-88 are peremptorily expunged from all editions and printings of the *Elegie* beginning in 1560. [45] This deletion may follow, in some measure, from the passing of Brinon in March 1555 and, later, from the relocation of the poem in the 1560 *Premier livre des Amours*. The denunciation invariably loses a certain relevance when one of its principal referents disappears and the collection to which it belongs has no firm affiliation with the councilor's (or anyone else's) name. [46] Nevertheless, although such circumstantial changes might require a revision or (at most) a deletion of the Brinon and Sidere remarks in verses 180-86, [47] they would hardly justify the suppression of the *art menteur* rebuke in verses 177-79 and 187-88.

There are two remaining theories that might explain this development. First, perhaps Ronsard decided that this final complaint clashed rhetorically and aesthetically with the preceding 176 lines of the poem. It is true that the last attack is significantly bolder than the foregoing program of subtle ironies and innuendos. It is no less true, however, that audacious concluding climaxes, or "pointes," are a regular feature of Ronsard's poetry. The climactic poet-*sacrificulus* episode highlighted in our examination of the *Temple de Messeigneurs* is but one of numerous instances. Moreover, it is apparent that these twelve verses resonate thematically with the other paragone-connected comments in the work. The reprise of the "art menteur" idea from the opening stanza even furnishes a satisfying–and for Ronsard, representative–circular structure to the whole.

---

[45] In fact, this controversial passage was to remain lost in editorial oblivion until Paul Laumonier brought it to light in his article, "Deux cent vingt vers inédits de Ronsard," published in the *Revue de la Renaissance* in 1903 (4:210).

[46] See Barron, "'Ut Pictura Poesis'," 373. Even though many of Ronsard's colleagues contributed to the liminal and post-liminal pieces of the *Amours*, and Marc-Antoine de Muret was its acknowledged commentator since the 1553 edition, there is no explicit dedicatee of the work.

[47] There is room for disagreement on this point as well since, in fact, Brinon's name is equally resilient in other transported poems of the *Meslanges*. Cf. the *Elegie du verre* (6:165-71), subsequently moved into the *Premier livre des Poëmes* and the *Elegies*; *L'Hinne de Bacus* (6:176-90), transferred to the *Hymnes*; the *Ode: L'Arondelle* (6:199-201), resituated in the *Cinquième livre des Odes*; and *La Chasse* (6:231-42), transported to the *Troisième livre des Poëmes*. For more on Ronsard and Brinon, see Laumonier, *RPL* 133-37.

This leaves the second theory. In essence, it may be that Ronsard could no longer restrain the double bind; the admiration in his ambivalence toward the rival Other has forced him to reject the vehement censure of the *Elegie*. Indeed, if the beginning of the 1567 *Elegie* to Marie Stuart is any indication, Ronsard may have eventually been moved to procure a copy of Clouet's *Marie Stuart en deuil blanc* (fig. 12), or to imagine he has done so, and to accord it a place of honor in his study:

> Comme un tableau vivement imprimé
> J'ay toutesfois pour la chose plus rare
> (Dont mon estude & mes livres je pare)
> Vostre portrait qui fait honneur au lieu,
> Comme un image au temple d'un grand Dieu.
>
> (14:152-53, vv. 5-9)[48]

Of course, we can only conjecture as to the motives for Ronsard's presumed new appreciation, though this opinion would unquestionably bring him closer to the popular bias of the day. As Marc-Antoine de Muret's remarks (cited previously) poignantly demonstrate, Clouet was indeed considered a "tres excellent" painter of unsurpassed artistic ability. Despite his close association with the personalities and affairs of the court, however, Ronsard would scarcely have followed the multitude for the mere sake of fitting in. His myriad condemnations of literary and social fashion throughout his career bespeak the independence of his spirit and convictions.[49] If Ronsard yielded to a deep-seated appreciation of the portraitist and his works, it was almost certainly because the popular view inscribed truths he could neither miss nor deny. Perhaps the laureate came at last to accept for Clouet and portraiture what Leon Battista Alberti had said about painters and their art over a century earlier: "Painting contains a divine force which not only makes absent men

---

[48] For Jean Adhémar ("Fontainebleau," 345; and *Les Clouet*, 30) and Marcel Raymond (*La Poésie française*, 41), this testimony seems to suffice as a statement of fact. We shall return to this elegy below.

[49] Cf. the "Au Lecteur" to the 1550 *Quatre premiers livres des Odes* (1:43-50), and, of course, the *Remonstrance au Peuple de France* (11:63-106). For more on the political satire of Ronsard and his Pléiade brothers and an analysis of the Vendômois' criticisms of the court for its part in fueling the religious tensions in France after 1560, see Weber, *Création*, esp. 79-86, 102-06, 587-88; Daniel Ménager, *Ronsard: Le Roi, le poète et les hommes* (Geneva: Droz, 1979).

present, as friendship is said to do, but moreover makes the dead seem almost alive." [50]

Ronsard expresses sentiments reminiscent of Muret's and Alberti's in the second quatrain of sonnet CCVIII of the 1553 *Amours*; only, here we discover a surprising shift in the poet's attention:

> Un seul Janet, honneur de nostre France,
> De ses craions ne la portrairoit mieus,
> Que d'un Archer le trait ingenieus
> M'a peint au coeur sa vive remembrance.
>
> (5:155, vv. 5-8)

This declaration would seem to relate Ronsard's irrepressible respect for Janet less to the artist's painted works than to his sketches. [51] In fact, such esteem for portraits in charcoal and earthtone colored chalks was hardly uncommon. [52] Catherine de Médicis, for example, was one of the most ardent supporters of face drawings. She repeatedly engaged court portraitists, including our Janet, to render her family and herself in this manner (cf. figs. 13-15). Indeed, around 1570 the Queen commissioned François Clouet to assemble over five hundred portrait crayons–including several of his own drawings, but also scores of pieces by his father and their many (often anonymous) followers and assistants–in an album that would subsequently constitute one of the major monuments to French Renaissance portraiture in any medium: the Lord Carlisle

---

[50] "Tiene in sé la pittura forza divina non solo quanto si dice dell'amicizia, quale fa gli uomini assenti essere presenti ma più i morti dopo molti secoli essere quasi vivi . . . " (¶ 25 [44]; 63). It is also true, of course, that this remark constitutes an important reprise of the literary *exegi monumentum* topos. We shall return to this implication below.

[51] This is not to suggest that sonnet CCVIII presents a wholly favorable view of such portraiture. On the contrary, before 1578 this poem is essentially a stage for the *exegi monumentum* theme, which traditionally highlights the superior ability of poetry to immortalize its subjects. We shall return to this poem and other *exegi monumentum* pieces in the pages that follow.

[52] Henri Bouchot, *Les Clouet*, 18-38; Etienne Moreau-Nélaton, *Chantilly: crayons français du XVIe siècle* (Paris: Librairie Centrale des Beaux-Arts, 1910), 5-69; Dimier, *Portrait*, 1:93-94; Dimier, *Peinture*, 73; Dimier, *French Painting in the Sixteenth Century*, tr. Harold Child (London: Duckworth, 1904), 242-48. See also Armand Fourreau, *Les Clouet* (Paris: Rieder, 1929), 52-55; Jean Adhémar, *Les Clouet et la cour des rois de France* (Paris: Bibliothèque Nationale, 1970), 12-13; Blunt, *Art and Architecture*, 116 and 155.

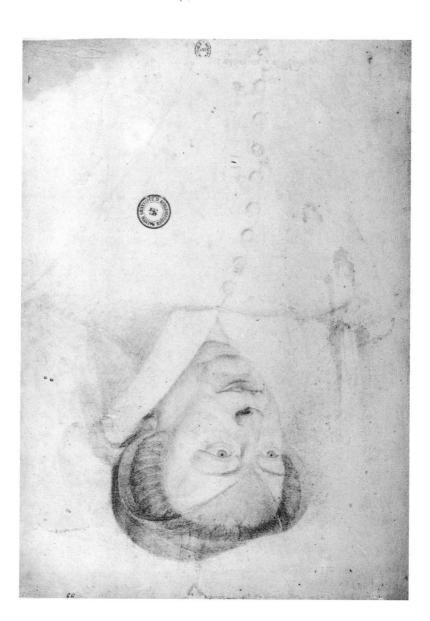

FIG. 13: François Clouet, *Catherine de Médicis* (ca. 1560), Paris (cliché Bibliothèque Nationale de France)

FIG. 15: François Clouet, *Marguerite de Valois* (ca. 1560), Paris (cliché Bibliothèque Nationale de France)

FIG. 14: François Clouet, *Charles IX* (1561), Paris (cliché Bibliothèque Nationale de France)

collection of the Musée Condé at Chantilly.[53] As a result of such support, during the last quarter of the century (hence after Clouet, albeit to an important degree because of him) portrait sketches came fully into their own. Rather than continue in their customary role as cartoons, preliminary designs in the service of (and subordinate to) the *painting* process, they grew to be appreciated and commissioned as autonomous products of the finest pictorial artistry.

Still, the foundations of this unexpected appreciation remain a mystery. Which properties of Janet's sketches might incline the poet to extol such works openly in sonnet CCVIII and to abandon the forthright reproaches to the portraitist in the *Elegie*? Again Ronsard's reticence reduces us to speculation, yet clearly this art form enjoys one distinctive advantage over painting: drawings can be completed quickly, and can therefore most readily capture a person *au vif*, as he or she appears from one instant to the next, and thus as if truly animate. This benefit was apparent to Catherine de Médicis, who as Queen Mother expressly demanded that the crayons of her children be done "au vif, sans rien oblier de leurs visaiges."[54] Likewise, at the end of the last century, Henri Bouchot, the art historian-librarian of the Bibliothèque Nationale who first attempted to restore order to the confusions surrounding the Clouets and their followers, proffers the following observation:

> "A vrai dire, le crayon était dans le travail de François Clouet la partie intéressante. C'était aux crayons de couleur qu'il traitait ses premières esquisses *d'après le modèle*, parce que cette manière de procéder demandait une pose moins longue et un moindre déploiement d'accessoires. Le peintre d'alors ne recevait pas dans son atelier, il se rendait à domicile, croquant sur un

---

[53] See Moreau-Nélaton, *Chantilly*, 33-69, and his *Catherine de Médicis et les Clouets de Chantilly* (Paris: Firmin-Didot, 1926), 4-15. See also, Dimier, *Portrait*, 89; and Adhémar, *Les Clouet*. Most of Catherine de Médicis' drawings, from the Chantilly reserves and beyond, were artfully reproduced and published in Ronald Gower, *Three Hundred French Portraits, Representing Personages of the Courts of Francis I, Henry II, and Francis II* (London: Sampson Low, Marston, Low & Searle, 1875). The other major compilation of French Renaissance portrait drawings is traditionally called "les Clouet du Cabinet des Estampes." This collection consists of some 569 pieces from various sources, including the famous *Album Lécurieux* (named after its nineteenth-century owner, the painter Jacques-Joseph Lécurieux), which features some fifty crayons from the Clouet workshop that the Queen Mother once intended for a friend at court. See Adhémar, ibid., 9-11.

[54] Moreau-Nélaton, *Chantilly*, 26.

bout de table le personnage impatient de se savoir terminé. . . . Cette priorité reconnue du croquis au crayon lui donne une importance particulière; *c'est le premier jet, l'idée toute neuve, sans retouches ni reprises.*" [55]

Continuing Bouchot's work nearly forty years later, Louis Dimier embellishes this point by emphasizing the immediacy-based accuracy of Clouet's sketches:

> Dans la seule partie du dessin il mérite les plus grands éloges. Une véritable profondeur de science s'y allie à une mesure parfaite. Dans le tracé du visage, et de toutes les parties dont se compose cet objet unique de l'observation d'un peintre, on trouve à François Clouet la capacité d'un spécialiste, en qui le long usage de l'art a fait s'accumuler le trésor de l'expérience. *La proportion des traits, la mise en place de toutes les parties déliées, fuyantes et mobiles du visage, la recherche attentive des relations plus subtiles qui donnent au gros des formes la solidité et l'aptitude à façonner la physionomie ou le type, vont chez lui à la perfection.* [56]

Different from the paintings, which are many times the works of the master's apprentices and often only the studio-made color copies of the original crayons (as in the case of the portraits of Elisabeth d'Autriche: figs. 16-17), [57] Clouet's drawings are created by his own hand and executed *sur le vif*, in the presence of the living model. They therefore show all the perceivable facets of that subject, what Joubert might call "la totalle ou principalle marque de cet individu," from the manifold dimensions of the person's most prominent facial features to the subtlest physiognomic manifestations of his or her fleeting mental and emotional attitudes.

Of course, there is no definitive proof that Ronsard judged Janet's drawings in this way, or that he ever truly preferred them to the artist's paintings. The deletion of verses 177-88 in 1560 suggests simply that the Pléiade laureate could no longer endure the criticisms expressed therein. It seems he finally comes to recognize an unembellished veracity, and so a 'presence', in Clouet's portraits—

---

[55] Bouchot, *Les Clouet*, 24 (my emphasis).
[56] *Portrait*, 1:94 (my emphasis). Cf. Fourreau, *Les Clouet*, 54.
[57] See Moreau-Nélaton, *Chantilly*, 62-64; and Dimier, *Portrait*, 72.

FIG. 16: François Clouet, *Elisabeth d'Autriche* (1571) (drawing), Paris (cliché Bibliothèque Nationale de France)

FIG. 17: François Clouet: *Elisabeth d'Autriche* (1571) (painting), Louvre, Paris (Réunion des Musées Nationaux)

whether drawn or painted–that meets the qualifications laid out at the opening of the poem. Thus, in the end, Ronsard's ambivalence toward Janet and his pictures appears to provoke an unmistakable shift in his writing; the poet's underlying appreciation for his portraitist rival seems at last to leave a vital textual trace.

II. A PRESENCE OF EKPLEXIS

This reading of the *Elegie* finds further corroboration elsewhere in Ronsard's oeuvre. A trace of admiration, and hence strong ambivalence, is likewise detectable in his other poetic allusions to portraitists and their art. But wherein lie the 'truths' of portraits that the Pléiade laureate cannot ignore?

Ronsard's words on portraiture in his earliest ode *A son Luc* are especially revealing in these regards. As his remarks confirm the perenniality of a special affection toward that art form, they simultaneously intimate the basis for that opinion:

> Sus Muses sus, celebrez moi le nom
> Du grand Apelle immortel de renom,
>   Et de Zeuze qui paignoit
>   Si au vif, qu'il contraignoit
> L'esprit ravi du pensif regardant
> A s'oublier soi mesmes, ce pendant
>   Que l'oeil humoit à longs trais
>   La douceur de leurs portrais.
>
> (2:160, vv. 81-88)

Thanks to the unflagging popularity of Pliny the Elder's art-historical commentaries in Book Thirty-Five of the *Historia naturalis*,[58] the hyperbolic praises of Zeuxis (fifth-fourth centuries B.C.) and Apelles (fourth-third centuries B.C.)[59] were a commonplace in early modern deliberations on the arts. No humanist reflection on the

---

[58] The *Historia* became known to Renaissance humanists primarily through the numerous incomplete *vetustiores* of the Middle Ages, the 1469 Venetian *editio principeps* of Johannes de Spira and the adaptations of Pliny's most memorable stories in the widely read works of Cicero, Quintilian, Dionysius of Halicarnassus, and Lucian. For more on the history of Pliny's masterpiece, see Sandys, *Classical Scholarship*, 1:654 and 2:97, 103.

[59] *Historia*, 35.36.61-66, 79-97.

practice of pictorial representation was complete without a mention of one or both of their revered names.[60] And although both artists were well known for their achievements in narrative painting (cf. *Des peintures*, v. 2), their Renaissance reputations derived primarily from the qualities and principles they applied in their legendary lost masterpieces of portraiture–most notably, the *Helen of Troy*–designed by Zeuxis after the attributes of five beautiful maidens of Croton, and the *Aphrodite Anadyomene* (or *Venus Rising from the Sea*), in which Apelles stages the goddess of love at the moment she wrings the seawater from her hair.[61] Initially, then, it is tempting to ascribe little credibility to the laudatory evocation of these ancient artists in *A son Luc*. Ronsard seems merely to pay requisite deference to a well worn literary and cultural topos.

The same remarks on portraiture assume a far greater significance, however, when reconsidered against the observations on narrative painting in the very next stanza. Whereas the latter inscribe a strong sense of negative irony (in the ways described previously[62]), the former raise no discernible reservations. There is no immediate indication that the laureate harbors anything but the greatest enthusiasm for Zeuxis and Apelles. Hence, if only by their divergence, these comments invite a less cynical reading of their sincerity: they suggest a sense of true admiration for these exemplary artists and the portraiture they perfected. And yet it is likewise true that the portrait passage cannot be completely divorced from the attacks on narrative pictures that follow. By assuming the postposition, the latter strictures become the concluding statement upon painting as a whole, and so a reminder that painted portraits are not wholly exempt from such denunciations. As in the *Elegie à Janet*, then, the poet's estimation of portraiture proves ineluctably equivocal, simul-

---

[60] Cf. Alberti, *Della pittura*: "Libro Terzo," ¶ 53 (92), ¶ 56 (96-98) and passim; Leonardo, *Tr.* 19 (Richter, 58) and *Tr.* 21 (Richter, 59); Dolce, *Aretino*, 2 (86-87), 12 (106-07), 24 (130-31), 28 (138-39), 34-35 (150-53); Giorgio Vasari, "Lettera di Giovambattista Adriani a Giorgio Vasari," in *Le Vite* (Bettarini, vol. 1), 179-227; Rabelais *Quart livre* 17 and *Cinquiesme livre* 40; Castiglione, *Cortegiano* 1.28 (50), 1.51-53 (85-87); Montaigne, *Essais* 3.8.932b.

[61] *Historia* 35.36.64,66 and *Historia* 35.36.79-97, respectively. See also, Dolce, *Aretino*, 28 (138-39). On the special significance of these and other lost artworks in Renaissance art theory, see Lecercle, *Chimère*, esp. 56-62 and n. 18; Muret's comment on Ronsard's "Quand au matin..." (*Commentaires*, 23). Cf. McGowan, *Ideal Forms*, 197; Gombrich, *Heritage*, 17 (on Apelles' "Splendor").

[62] See Chapter Two, 90-96.

taneously positive and negative, and thus fundamentally imbued with the ambivalence that marks Ronsard's entanglement in the double bind of his conflicting mimetic desire.

Quite unlike the *Elegie*, though, the ode *A son Luc* also provides clues about the laudable characteristics at the heart of this ambivalence. While confirming the importance of an accurate resemblance to life, the capability of the portrait to represent a subject "au vif" (as Janet's pictures do), this poem makes it clear that the underlying reason transcends the appreciation for the aesthetic of natural-sign mimesis established by Plato and Aristotle and implemented by Renaissance artists and art theorists like Alberti and Leonardo. [63] What intrigues Ronsard is less the portraitist's gift for duplicating a sitter's physical animation–the sensible and intelligible attribute that Aristotle calls *enargeia* (ἐνάργεια) in the context of his meditations on the representational achievements of Homer (*Rhetoric* 3.11.2-4)–than the affective consequence of that gift: the portrait artist's ability to create images that *enthrall and astonish the mind and spirit*, or in the poet's words, artworks that "contraign[ent] / L'esprit ravi du pensif regardant / A s'oublier soi mesmes." [64] Ronsard thereby draws attention to a fundamental similarity between portraits and poems. In contrast to the commentaries on narrative painting, which stress the inferiority of the painter's objects to those of the poet, the present verses highlight a response to portraiture that would match the reaction to poetry described some thirty lines earlier in the ode. Like the best poems, the finest portraits can ignite a sense of awe or stupefaction in their audience: "Mais Dieu juste qui dispense / Tout en tous, les fait chanter / . . . / *Pour le monde épouvanter*" (2:158-59, vv. 49-52: my emphasis).

Beyond anything we anticipated in our analysis of the *Elegie à Janet*, then, the preoccupation of Ronsard's remarks on portraiture in *A son Luc* would seem to coincide with a primary interest of the

---

[63] See above, Chapter One, 74 ff.

[64] We may compare this remark to Ronsard's reflection on the contemporary portraitists of France in his 1549 *L'Hymne de France* (also cited above): "Noz imagers ont la gloire en tout lieu / Pour figurer soit un homme, ou un Dieu, / De si tres pres imitans la nature, / *Que l'oeil béant se trompe en leur peincture*" (1:32-33, vv. 181-84: my emphasis). Once again the emphasis falls on the affective impact of the naturalism that these artists can achieve: the measure of their mimetic accuracy is their ability to astound the viewer. It is also fitting that, in the multiple editions of the poem that appear between 1554 and 1573, the first hemistich of verse 184 is revised to read "Que l'oeil *ravi*."

so-called 'Longinus'. In chapter fifteen of his ground-breaking treatise *On the Sublime* (Περὶ Ὕψος), this enigmatic Greek literary theorist of the first century A.D.[65] focuses on the gravity, majesty, and
excitement of poetry that succeeds in inducing vivid "images"
(φαντασίαι),[66] or "mental pictures" (εἰδωλοποιἳας), in the reader. For Longinus, these epistemological reactions are produced
when words are filled with inspiration and profound emotion (ἐν-
θουσιασμοῦ καὶ πάθους)–i.e., as they achieve *enargeia* (ἐνάργεια),
or vivid physical imitation, and most especially (in the matter of poetry), a sense of *ekplexis* (ἔκπληξις), or enthrallment:

> Weight, grandeur, and energy in writing are very largely pro-
> duced, dear pupil, by the use of "images." (That at least is what
> some people call the actual mental pictures.) For the term Imag-
> ination is applied in general to an idea which enters the mind
> from any source and engenders speech, but the word has now
> come to be used predominantly of passages where, inspired by
> strong emotion, you seem to see what you describe and bring it
> vividly before the eyes of your audience. That imagination means
> one thing in oratory and another in poetry you will yourself de-
> tect, and also that the object of poetry is to enthral, of prose
> writing to present things vividly, though both indeed aim at this
> latter and at excited feeling. (15.1-2)[67]

With the ode *A son Luc* Ronsard has not only marked out his own
poetic sympathies for this response-oriented emotionalist aesthetic,
but he has extended the notion to apply, when appropriate, to the
non-verbal art of pictorial portraiture.

It is doubtful that Ronsard could actually have read Longinus'
pronouncements by the time he was composing this ode in 1541-
43. Although the first known manuscript of *On the Sublime* was a
tenth-century document (identified as Parisinus 2036) that was almost surely being copied during the late fifteenth century, a wide
dissemination of the work in early modern Europe did not occur

---

[65] A review of the inconclusive theories on the identity of Longinus is presented
by D. A. Russell in his translation, *'Longinus': On the Sublime* (Oxford: Clarendon
Press, 1964), pp. xxii-xxx.

[66] Russell prefers the translation 'visualizations' (*Sublime*, 120).

[67] Longinus, *On the Sublime* in *Aristotle: "The Poetics"; "Longinus": "On the
Sublime"; Demetrius: "On Style,"* trans. William Hamilton Fyfe (London: William
Heinemann Ltd., 1932), 170-71.

before Francesco Robortello's machine-printed *editio princeps* of 1554, Διονυσίου Λογγίνου ρήτορος περὶ ὕψους βιβλίον.[68] For his earliest conception of ekplexis, then, Ronsard was probably indebted to a more accessible set of metaphysical, epistemological, and aesthetic commentaries. At one point or another nearly every major philosopher and art theorist would address the issue of 'enthrallment' when reflecting on the nature of human associations with God and the realm of higher truths. In Plato, for instance, this idea is inseparably inscribed in the ecstasy (ἔκστασῃ) the true poet would be able to accomplish by virtue of his divine madness (μανίας) (*Phaedrus* 245; *Ion* 533-34), or in the case of the painter, in the 'pleasure' (ἡδονὰς) made possible by that artist's special affinity with sight, light, and the visually perceivable properties of the beautiful (*Philebus* 51; *Gorgias* 474).[69]

Building upon these notions, the Neoplatonic philosophers commonly include astonishment among the *sine qua non* of the genuine aesthetic experience. In *Ennead* 1.6.4, for example, Plotinus specifically evokes ekplexis as one of the distinguishing signs of our soul's proximity to true beauty and the perfection of the divine: "These experiences must occur whenever there is contact with any sort of beautiful thing, *wonder and a shock of delight* and longing and passion and a happy excitement."[70] And as witnessed in our

---

[68] It should nevertheless be noted that, according to Robortello, Longinus' work was previously unknown: "opus hoc redivivum, antea ignotum, opera industriaque sua e tenebris in lucem eductum atque expolitum": cited in *Longinus on the Sublime*, ed. W. Rhys Roberts (2nd ed.; Cambridge: University Press, 1907), 247. Eventually, however, Renaissance editors would produce nearly a dozen versions of the essay. But again, none of these would appear until the latter half of the sixteenth century–whether in the Greek transcriptions of P. Manutius (1555) and F. Portus (1569), or in the translated versions of D. Pizzimenti (1566) and P. Pagano (1572) (both in Latin), or of G. da Falgano (1575) (in Italian). On the history of Longinus' essay, see Russell, *Sublime*, xlii-l; Sandys, *Aesthetics*, 1:288-93, 2:141; Roberts, *Sublime*, 247-61.

[69] See Chapter One, 43 and n. 19. We should never lose sight of the fact that Longinus himself was profoundly influenced by Plato, Aristotle, the Academicians, and the Peripatetics (cf. his commentaries on Plato in *Sublime*, 12.2-13.1, 32.5 and passim; on Aristotle, in *Sublime*, 32.3). The influence of the Academicians and Peripatetics is perhaps less direct, coming through the filters of models like Cicero and Dionysius of Halicarnassus. For more on the conceptual foundations of Longinus' essay, see W. Rhys Roberts, *Greek Rhetoric and Literary Criticism* (New York: Longmans, Green and Co., 1928), 122-50.

[70] "θάμβος καὶ ἔκπληξιν ἡδεῖαν καὶ πόθον καὶ ἔρωτα καὶ πτόησιν μεθ' ἡδονῆς": Plotinus, *Ennead*, 1:244-45: my emphasis.

previous investigation of the aesthetics of the fifteenth-century Florentine Academy, Marsilio Ficino would also emphasize this effect–otherwise denoted by the terms 'to ravish' (*rapere*) and 'rapture' (*raptio*)–in the definition of beauty he sets forth in his *Commentarium in Convivium*: "It is that charm of virtue, or of form or
sounds which calls and ravishes the soul through thought, sight, or
hearing that is most justly called beautiful." [71]

Leonardo da Vinci reserves a comparably privileged place for
this virtue. Much like his Pléiade counterpart a half century later,
he includes ekplexis–now subsumed in the locution, 'spellbinding
admiration' ("istupenda ammiratione")–among the highest achievements of painted portraiture. Unlike the poet of *A son Luc*, however, the painter-theorist also posits a basis for that accomplishment.
As in his deliberations on a lover's reactions to a portrait of his
beloved's angelic face in *Trattato* 21, [72] Leonardo regards enthrallment as a necessary consequence of the harmonious concinnity
("armonico concento") that results because a pictorial image can
present itself to the eye simultaneously ("in uno medesimo tempo"),
with its multifarious parts conjoined in proportions proper to the
essence of the beautiful. [73]

---

[71] Cf. above, Chapter One, 72 and n. 100. See also, Leone Ebreo's notion of
'enrapturing' ("dilettare") in the *Dialoghi d'amore*: "Among the objects of the external senses there are things which are good, useful, gentle, and pleasant, but that
grace, which *enraptures and moves the soul* to special love and which is called beauty, is not found in the three material senses of taste, smell, and touch, but only in
the objects of the two spiritual senses, sight and hearing . . ." ("Negli oggetti di tutti
i sense esteriori si truovano cose buone, utili, temperate e delettabili; ma grazia che
diletti e muova l'anima a proprio amore [qual si chiama bellezza] non si truova negli
oggetti de li tre sensi materiali, che sono il gusto, l'odore e il tatto, ma solamente
negli oggetti de'due sensi spirituai, viso e audito . . ."): Tatarkiewicz, *History*, 3:124-
25, n. 15 (my emphasis).

[72] See Chapter One, 80-81.

[73] Alberti also introduces the idea of enthrallment, albeit less forcefully than
Leonardo, in the second book of the *Della pittura* (¶ 40). It is represented as a goal
of the copiousness, variety, and (later) movement that a painter should achieve in
any "istoria": "The 'istoria' which merits both praise and admiration will be so
agreeably and pleasantly attractive that *it will capture the eye of whatever learned or
unlearned person is looking at it and will move his soul* . . ." ("Sarà la storia, qual tu
possa lodare e maravigliare, tale che con sue piacevolezze si porgerà sì ornata e
grata, che *ella terrà con diletto e movimento d'animo qualunque dotto o indotto la
miri* . . ."): Spencer, 75; Grayson, 68 (my emphasis). For more on Alberti's conception, see below.

Despite the multitude of potential intermediary sources there can be no doubt that, in the last analysis, Ronsard's sympathies are fundamentally Longinian. This coincidence becomes particularly evident in the 1565 *Abbregé de l'art poëtique françois* and the posthumous (1587) preface to the *Franciade* of 1572, both of which appear well after Robortello's edition of Longinus' treatise. The poet's impassioned calls for "conceptions hautes, grandes, belles, & non trainantes à terre," in the first essay (14:5-6), and "conceptions grandes & hautes," in the second (16:347), precisely parallel the Greek theorist's petition for "the general effect of dignity and eleva- tion" (ἡ ἐν ἀξιώματι καὶ διάρσει σύνθεσις) at the beginning of *Sublime* 8. Indeed, combined with the idea of enthrallment from *A son Luc*, these appeals emerge as virtual transliterations of what Longinus comes to identify as the two "congenital," or "natural" (αὐθιγενεῖς συστάσεις), sources of the "sublime" (ὑψηγορία): "full-blooded ideas" (τὸ περὶ τὰς νοήσεις ἁδρεπήβολον) [74] and "the inspiration of vehement emotion" (τὸ σφοδρὸν καὶ ἐνθουσι- αστικὸν πάθος). [75]

A. *From Shadows to Metamorphoses*

The ekplexis-based ambivalence toward portraiture of *A son Luc* is equally discernible in the *Amours* of 1552. In the latter case, however, the duality is dispersed among the only four poems of the collection to refer to a figure painting that would have an objective presence outside of the love-struck poet's heart or soul. [76] According to Marc-Antoine de Muret, sonnets IX, XXXIV, CVI, and CXXIV explicitly or implicitly evoke "un portrait de sa Dame," Cassandre, by the multi-talented humanist and friend to Ronsard and all the Pléiade authors, Nicolas Denisot du Mans (1515-1559), known af- fectionately by the anagrammatic sobriquet, "Conte d'Alsinois," or simply "Conte." [77]

---

[74] Russell translates this as the "grasp of great thoughts": Longinus, *Sublime*, 86.

[75] *Sublime* 8.1 (140-41). As Isidore Silver has put it, "Ronsard's ultimate under- standing of the nature of poetry . . . was to resemble that of 'Longinus' in every fun- damental respect": Silver, *IER*, 2:343 (cf. 2:323, 343, and 335-36 [n. 103]).

[76] It should be noted that the "image peinte" of Cassandre is most often as it is in Petrarch, namely, a picture of the beloved in the poet's soul.

[77] Muret, *Commentaires*, 5. As for the issue of Denisot's rapport with Ronsard

It is dubious that the picture in question ever truly existed. The portrait is probably no more real than the rendering of Cassandre by François Clouet or, for that matter, than the vast majority of painted artworks elicited in Ronsard's poetry. Nevertheless, in addition to his successes as a teacher, linguist, and author of devotional poems like the *Noëls* (1545) and the *Cantiques* (1553), the Conte enjoyed considerable notice for his abilities as a calligrapher, a cartographer, and especially, a painter of portraits. Renaissance authors and modern art historians unanimously extol his artistic gifts. From Jean Antoine de Baïf and François Grudé, Sieur de la Croix du Maine, during the sixteenth century, to Henri Bouchot and Louis Dimier in more recent times, all are of the opinion, succinctly stated by Muret, that Denisot was "excellent en l'art de Peinture." [78] Thus,

---

and his followers, two theories have been advanced. On one side, Clément Jugé has proposed that the Conte became an ardent opponent of the Pléiade poets when he expressed an aversion to their polytheistic mythology in his 1553 *Cantiques* (*Nicolas Denisot du Mans [1515-1559]: Essai sur sa vie et ses oeuvres* [Geneva: Slatkine, 1969], 79-108). On the other side, Marcel Raymond has convincingly argued against the adversary theory. Regarding the apparent attack on mythology in the *Cantiques*, for example, he notes that "Denisot, quoi qu'il dise, est loin de rejeter l'héritage des Anciens; à l'encontre de Babinot, plus authentiquement chrétien, il use de la mythologie chaque fois qu'il aperçoit en elle une légende, un symbole, qui puissent s'appliquer à son propos; et surtout il enrichit son style d'un grand nombre d'expressions qu'il admire chez Ronsard" (*Influence*, 336-37). In addition, Raymond reminds us that the "pièces liminaires" for this work were composed by some of the same men Denisot was supposed to have alienated, including Etienne Jodelle, Remy Belleau, and Marc-Antoine de Muret (335). Finally, he points out the strong influence that Denisot's poem had upon Ronsard's own *Hercule Chrestien* (8:207-23), a piece first published in the 1555 *Hymnes*, but which was begun shortly after the appearance of the *Cantiques*.

[78] Muret, *Commentaires*, 5. Cf. the poetic commentaries by Baïf in the final stanza of his "O douce peinture amiable" in the *Premier livre des Amours de Meline*:

> Heureux sois tu, & soit heureuse
> La docte main industrieuse
> Qui te peignit de ces couleurs,
> O dous confort de mes douleurs.
> Jamais ne soit que tu ne vives,
> Portrait, & les couleurs naives,
> De qui mon Denisot t'a peint,
> Sans que l'age t'oste le teint.

(Marty-Laveaux, 1:29, vv. 69-76). See also the flattering judgment pronounced by La Croix du Maine (as cited by Jugé): "Il a été estimé . . . surtout très excellent à la peinture, principalement pour le crayon. Car auparavant qu'elle fut en si grand usage entre les François, comme elle est aujourd'hui, il étoit estimé le premier de son temps pour un qui n'en faisoit pas profession autrement que par plaisir" (*Nicolas Denisot*, 40). For the opinions of later art historians, see Dimier, *Portrait*, 60-61; and Bouchot, *Les Clouet*, 54-58.

although the only picture assigned to him with any certainty is the figure of Marguerite de Navarre adorning the verso of the title page to his 1551 *Tombeau de Marguerite de Valois Reine de Navarre* (fig. 18) (to which Ronsard was a multiple contributor),[79] scholars have willingly accepted that the Conte could have readily fashioned a splendid portrait of Cassandre. They have even suggested that it was he, and not Jean Cousin,[80] who supplied the designs for the profile-bust engraving of the poet and his mistress displayed on the frontispiece of the first editions of the *Amours* (fig. 19), and further, that Ronsard may be alluding to the Cassandre medallion in the four Denisot portrait sonnets.[81]

Be that as it may, there can be no dispute that, collectively, these works offer conflicting notions of portraiture strongly redolent of the *Elegie à Janet*. On the negative side, sonnets XXXIV and CXXIV again exploit the dependence of painted portraits on the material and, conversely, the capacity of poetry to articulate feelings and ideas. In this respect, they may also be read as the inspirations

---

[79] Commemorating the death of the queen of Navarre in 1549, this work features the panegyrical poetry of Denisot's English pupils, the Seymour sisters, along with pieces by "plusieurs des excellentz Poëtes de la France," including three odes and a "hymne triomphal" by Ronsard. Although it was originally published in 1550, under the Latin title: *Annae Margaritae Janae sororum virginum heroidum Anglarum, in mortem divae Margaritae Valesiae Hecatodistichon*, it is only the 1551 version that contains the mentioned engraving and the following attribution to Denisot: "Nulla ut parte sui perire posset / Margareta: comes reduxit illam / De busto Alsinous, tibique lector / Ut fruare dedit: nihil deesse / Praeter verba potest: roga libellos, / Illi pro Domina sua loquentur" (3:40, my emphasis). Louis Dimier raises a question as to what this attribution actually designates: the engraving itself (as Henri Bouchot proposes) or one or more of the drawings or paintings of Marguerite found in the portrait collection at Chantilly (the solution Dimier prefers) (*Portrait*, 60-61). For my part, I find Dimier's refinement of Bouchot not only convincing, but also conducive to the present argument since, in the end, the Chantilly drawings display a level of artistry diluted in the book engraving (cf. Broglie, "Les Clouet de Chantilly," 305, Plates 204, 205). Finally, it should be noted that Denisot may have also painted a portrait of Olivier de Magny's beloved Marguerite, which affords the title and subject of one of the 1554 *Gayetez*, "Au pourtraict de sa Marguerite faict d'apres le naturel par le Comte d'Alsinois." For more on the latter work, see Muret's note to sonnet IX (3) and Laumonier, *RPL*, 85, n. 2.

[80] The first documentation of this attribution appears in Jean-Michel Papillon's *Traité historique et pratique de la gravure en bois*, 2 vols. (1766: rpt. Paris: Editions des Archives Contemporaines, 1985), 1:204. During the nineteenth century, this theory was resurrected by Achille de Rochambeau in his *Famille de Ronsart: recherches généalogiques, historiques et littéraires sur P. de Ronsard et sa famille* (1868: rpt. Nendeln, Liechtenstein: Kraus Reprint, 1973), 119.

[81] See H. and C. Weber, *Les Amours*, 510, n. 3; Charles Guérin, *Odes*, 314 (Ode 11, n. 10).

FIG. 18: Nicolas Denisot, *Marguerite de Navarre* (1551), *Tombeau de Marguerite de Valois Reine de Navarre* (verso of the title page), Paris (cliché Bibliothèque Nationale de France)

FIG. 19: Nicolas Denisot, "Ronsard and Cassandre," Frontispiece of the 1553 *Amours*, Paris (cliché Bibliothèque Nationale de France)

for the two epigraphical quatrains by Jean Antoine de Baïf that gloss the frontispiece medallions, whether the object is Cassandre:

> L'Art la Nature exprimant
>   En ce pourtraict me faict belle
>   Mais si ne sui-je poinct telle
> Qu'aux escrits de mon amant.

or Ronsard himself:

> Tel fut Ronsard, autheur de cest ouvrage,
> Tel fut son oeil, sa bouche et son visage,
> Portraict au vif de deux crayons divers:
> Icy le Corps, et l'Esprit en ses vers. [82]

Like Ronsard's sonnets, Baïf's epigraphical verses contrast the elemental physicality of visual images with the essential conceptuality of poetry.

Unlike Baïf, however, our laureate invests his reflections with a share of philosophical and mythological authority. In sonnet XXXIV ("Las, je me plain de mille & mille & mille . . ."), for example, Ronsard inserts criticisms of a manifestly Platonic and Neoplatonic flavor. Among the targets of the poet's Petrarchan-style complaints against his "beaulté cruelle" is a portrait of the lady, presumably the work by Denisot first mentioned in sonnet IX (to which we shall return), that is "inutile" because it affords a mere shadow of the original: "Puis je me plain d'un portraict inutile, / *Ombre du vray* que je suis adorant . . ." (4:37, vv. 5-6: my emphasis). Certainly, Ronsard has taken a measure of inspiration from his future Pléiade colleague, Pontus de Tyard. The Mâconnais' sonnet LXV ("J'estois pensif, melancoliq, et sombre . . .") of the 1549 *Erreurs amoureuses* evokes a no less disappointing 'shadowy' portrait of a perfectly beautiful mistress: "Il ne m'osa promettre d'avantage / De retirer de ses beautez, que l'*ombre*. / . . . / Puis ayant peint l'*ombre*, me dit ainsi / Contente-toy seulement de ceci. . . ." [83] In this instance, the

---

[82] H. and C. Weber, *Les Amours*, 15.

[83] Ponuts de Tyard, *Œuvres Poétiques Complètes*, ed. John C. Lapp (Paris: Librairie Marcel Didier, 1966), 68-69, vv. 7-8, 12-13: my emphasis. Pontus makes the same point in the inscription, "l'ombre de ma vie," that accompanies the Flaman's engraving of Pasithée printed after the title page of the *Erreurs* (see the Conclusion and fig. 20).

promised pictorial "ombre" would feature Tyard's beloved Pasithée, and the artist in question ("Il") is the "Flaman" (v. 3), Corneille de Lyon (ca. 1500/1510-ca. 1574), the Flemish-born court portraitist who became the chief rival of Jean and François Clouet outside of Paris.

For both Ronsard and Tyard, the assault on the pictorial "ombre" undoubtedly takes its principal lead from Plato's meditations on the shadowy status of all mimetic arts in *Republic* 7 and 10, and Plotinus' reprise of those considerations in *Ennead* 1.8.[84] What is more, Ronsard's emphasis on a portrait that is "inutile" (useless) plays plainly upon grievances against the relative inability of pictures to fulfill an edificatory function: reproaches voiced, on various occasions and in an assortment of ways, by not only Plato and the Neoplatonists, but also Aristotle and his Scholastic heirs.[85]

Sonnet CXXIV ("De ceste doulce & fielleuse pasture . . .") ascribes a still more universal value to these criticisms by equating the poet's reaction to the portrait with the sufferings of the mythological Narcissus:

> Car ce bel oeil, qui force ma nature,
> D'un si long jeun m'a tant faict epasmer,
> Que je ne puis ma faim desaffamer,
> Qu'au seul regard d'*une vaine peinture*.
> Plus je la voy, moins souler je m'en puis,
> *Un vray Narcisse* en misere je suis. . . .
> (4:121-22, vv. 5-10: my emphasis)

The closest intertext of this poem is the forty-fifth sonnet of Petrarch's *Rime sparse* ("Il mio adversario in cui veder solete . . .").[86]

---

[84] Cf. Chapter One, 42, 69. See also Plato, *Laws* 889A (in Tatarkiewicz, *History* 1:137, n. 40).

[85] The edificatory function is inscribed in the ancient aesthetic concept of "utile," according to which the value of a work of art depends largely, and in varying degrees, on its ethical utility–its capacity to foster good moral thought and behavior–and its hedonistic function–its ability to promote pleasure and happiness (cf. Chapter One). The latter purpose seems to preoccupy the poet in the present circumstance.

[86]
> Il mio adversario in cui veder solete
> gli occhi vostri ch'Amore e 'l Ciel onora
> colle non sue bellezze v'innamora
> più che 'n guisa mortal soavi et liete.

However, whereas the Narcissus is the "Donna" (Laura) of Petrarch's poem, he is the poet himself in Ronsard's sonet. Furthermore, the reflective surface in which Narcissus risks annihilation is no longer a mere "specchio" (mirror); rather it is a "vaine peinture" of Cassandre, a spiritually vacuous portrait of the lover's other half that will prove as fatally dissatisfying as the soulless simulacrum of the self-absorbed Boeotian youth of ancient mythology.[87]

A less conspicuous influence might also be Alberti's personal account of the origin of painting in the "Libro secondo" of his treatise on painting:

> I say among my friends that Narcissus who was changed into a flower, according to the poets, was the inventor of painting. Since painting is already the flower of every art, the story of Narcissus is most to the point. What else can you call painting but a similar embracing with art of what is presented on the surface of the water in the fountain?[88]

> Per consiglio di lui, Donna, m'avete
> scacciato del mio dolce albergo fora:
> misero esilio! avegna ch' i' non fora
> d'abitar degno ove voi sola siete.
>
> Ma s'io v'era con saldi chiovi fisso,
> non dovea specchio farvi per mio danno
> a voi stessa piacendo aspra et superba.
>
> Certo, se vi rimembra di Narcisso,
> questo et qual corso ad un termino vanno—
> ben che di sì bel fior sia indegna l'erba.

(My adversary in whom you are wont to see your eyes, which Love and Heaven honor, enamors you with beauties not his but sweet and happy beyond mortal guise.

By his counsel, Lady, you have driven me out of my sweet dwelling: miserable exile! even though I may not be worthy to dwell where you alone are.

But if I had been nailed there firmly, a mirror should not have made you, because you pleased yourself, harsh and proud to my harm.

Certainly, if you remember Narcissus, this and that course lead to one goal–although the grass is unworthy of so lovely a flower.)

Petrarch, *Petrarch's Lyric Poems: The "Rime sparse" and Other Lyrics*, trans. and ed. Robert M. Durling (Cambridge, Mass.: Harvard University Press, 1976), 110-11.

[87] Although Petrarch's verses retain the distant possibility that the beloved lady may eventually find pleasure in a human speculum (the poet himself, who envisions a quid pro quo with his "adversario," the inanimate mirror), Ronsard's sonnet stages a gazing lover beyond all hope of gratification.

[88] "[U]sai di dire tra i miei amici, secondo la sentenza de' poeti, quel Narcisso convertito in fiore essere della pittura stato inventore: ché già, ove sia la pittura

It is as if Ronsard were deconstructing all the positive facets of Alberti's analogy. Far from reaffirming the regeneration topos of the ancient myth, the idea that Narcissus perishes in order to be resurrected as a flower, the French author stresses its themes of agony and destruction, the notion that the Boeotian youth (now the lovelorn poet) suffers and eventually dies from his obsessive dependence on an image. Moreover where Alberti would highlight the superior gratification to be gained from painting, the consummate delectability that makes it the "flower of every art," Ronsard emphasizes the dissatisfaction a picture can cause: "Plus je la voy, moins souler je m'en puis." Finally, in antithesis to the art theorist's insinuation that a mirror-like surface can inscribe the fullness of the world it reflects, the Pléiade laureate insists that his superficial painted facsimile is supremely "vaine" (hollow).

In counterpoint to the two negative poems, sonnets IX and CVI inscribe a decidedly complimentary attitude toward the Cassandre portrait. In the latter piece, Ronsard seems to have joined the most celebrated art theorists of the Renaissance in supporting the intellectual basis of pictorial portraiture:

> Haulse ton aisle, & d'un voler plus ample,
>   Forçant des ventz l'audace & le pouvoir,
>   Fay, Denisot, tes plumes esmouvoir,
>   Jusques au ciel où les dieux ont leur temple.
> Là, d'oeil d'Argus, leurs deitez contemple,
>   Contemple aussi leur grace, & leur sçavoir,
>   Et pour ma Dame au parfait concevoir,
>   Sur les plus beaulx fantastique un exemple.
> Moissonne apres le teint de mille fleurs,
>   Et les detrampe en l'argent de mes pleurs,
>   Que tiedement hors de mon chef je rue:
> *Puis attachant ton esprit & tes yeulx*
> *Dans le patron desrobé sur les dieux*
> *Pein, Denisot, la beaulté qui me tue.*
>
> (4:104-05: my emphasis)

While modeled after Petrarch's famous *rima* in praise of Simone Martini, "Per mirar Policleto," which similarly reports the artist's

---

fiore d'ogni arte, ivi tutta la storia di Narcisso viene a proposito. Che dirai tu essere dipignere, altra cosa che simile abracciare con arte quella ivi superficie del fonte?" (¶ 26 [46]; 64).

ascent into heaven to find the paradigm for a picture of the poet's mistress, Ronsard's verses add a theoretical dimension absent from the Italian poem. They would even recall the fifteenth- and six- teenth-century art treatises of Cennino Cennini, Alberti, Leonardo, and Ludovico Dolce as well as Castiglione's discourse on painting in Book One of the *Cortegiano*. In particular, the final tercet resur- rects the rebuttals of such essays against the ancient and early mod- ern philosophers who routinely excluded painting from the ranks of the intellectually based *artes liberales* on the grounds that it was an *ars mechanica*, an art form produced primarily through manual labor.[89] For the poet of sonnet CVI, portrait painting has overcome this inferior classification: it merits inclusion among the august Lib- eral Arts—at least, that is, when it originates in the mind ("esprit") and the sight ("yeulx") of a preeminent artist like Nicolas Denisot.

Perhaps the most memorable defense of portraiture in the 1552 *Amours*, however, is the one embedded in sonnet IX:

> Le plus toffu d'un solitaire boys,
>   Le plus aigu d'une roche sauvage,
>   Le plus desert d'un separé rivage,
>   Et la frayeur des antres les plus coys:
> Soulagent tant les soupirs de ma voix,
>   Qu'au seul escart de leur secret ombrage,
>   Je sens garir une amoureuse rage,
>   Qui me raffolle au plus verd de mes moys.
> Là, renversé dessous leur face dure,
>   Hors de mon sein je tire une peinture,
>   De touts mes maulx le seul allegement,
> Dont les beaultez par Denisot encloses,
>   Me font sentir mille metamorphoses
>   Tout en un coup, d'un regard seulement.

(4:13-14)

Whereas the harsh Petrarchan landscapes catalogued in the open- ing quatrain are the cathartic spaces that would provide the poet a

---

[89] See Chapter One, 74 ff (and n. 105). See also, Cennino Cennini, *Il Libro dell'Arte*, 1.1 (ed. and trans. Daniel V. Thompson, Jr., 2 vols. [New Haven: Yale University Press, 1932], 1:2, 2:1-2); Alberti, *Della pittura* ¶ 28 (Spencer, 66-67; Grayson, 50-52); Dolce on the "dignità della Pittura": *Aretino*, 11-15 (105-13); Cas- tiglione, *Cortegiano*, 1.49-52, 81-86. Cf. also, Ronsard's comments on narrative painting in *A son Luc* (see Chapter Two, 95).

comforting haven from "*une* amoureuse rage" (as they do for the
Tuscan laureate's tortured venerator of the cold-hearted Laura), [90]
Denisot's portrait affords him the only relief from "*touts* [s]es
maulx." This compliment is surprising not merely for its all-inclu-
siveness, but especially because it is antithetical to Ronsard's customary complaints against the painter's art. Paradoxically, it proceeds from many of the same bases set forth by such premier
paragone rivals as Leonardo da Vinci. Reminiscent of the Florentine in *Trattato* 21, the Pléiade laureate endorses the ability of portrait painting to contain the "beaultez" of Cassandre's angelic face
all at once, "encloses" [91] and "Tout en un coup, d'un regard seulement."

Furthermore and again like Leonardo, the poet commends the
ekplexis that results from this quality. He credits the special pain-
relieving property of portraits to the ability of those artworks to
ravish. For Ronsard, however, that virtue translates less as an experience of ecstatic admiration and joy, what Leonardo calls "istupenda ammiratione e gaudio incomparabile," [92] than as a sensation of
"mille metamorphoses." Although suggestive of the endlessly destructive mutations suffered by the Medusa-struck or Acteon-like
poet-lover of Petrarch's *Rime*, [93] Ronsard's metamorphoses precipitate an impression of perpetual inner churning that stands out as
spiritually salubrious and profoundly desirable.

The attainment of this metamorphosing enthrallment may also
be the ultimate measure of both painting and poetry. Ronsard
strongly hints at this possibility in a commentary on Denisot's Cassandre portrait in the ode *Au Conte d'Alsinois* of the *Cinquiesme
livre des Odes* (published "ensemble" the first *Amours* in September or October 1552). Initially the encomium to the Conte's
painterly and poetic "fureur double" (v. 29) presents a neat and
even-handed opposition between the mimetic perfection of Denisot's pictures and the unsurpassed emotive impact of his verses:

---

[90] Cf. *Rime sparse*, 259, "Cercato ho sempre solitaria vita."

[91] Although this adjective might first seem to evoke the "petit espace" decried
in the narrative painting passage of *A son Luc* (see Chapter Two, 95), it in fact denotes a more temporal than spatial concision. In this regard it might coincide with
Leonardo's lengthy insistence, again in *Trattato* 21, that a pictorial portrait is more
harmonious than a poetic one because it is *not* revealed "bit by bit" ("à parte à
parte"). See Chapter One, 80-82.

[92] See Chapter One, 81.

[93] Cf. *Rime* 23 and 51. For more, see Durling's prefatory essay (26-33).

Mais où est l'oeil qui n'admire
Tes tableaux si bien portraictz,
Que la Nature se mire
Dans le parfaict de leurs traictz?
Où est l'oreille bouchée
De telle indocte espesseur
Qui ne rie, *estant touchée*
De tes vers plains de doulceur?

(3:178-79, vv. 33-40: my emphasis)

By the penultimate stanza of the ode, however, the poet not only blurs the distinctions between painting and poetry, but he clearly subordinates all mimetic achievements to the affective ones:

Mais, ô Denisot, qui est-ce
Qui peindra les yeulx traictifz
De Cassandre ma Deesse,
Et ses blondz cheveux tortifz?

Lequel d'entre vous sera-ce,
Qui pourroit bien colorer
La magesté de sa grace
Qui me force à l'adorer?
Et ce front dont elle abuse
Ce pauvre Poëte amant,
Son riz (ains une Meduse)
Qui tout me va transformant!

(3:182, vv. 93-104)

It is significant that the queries about the emotive powers come to occupy twice as many verses as the questions about physical mimesis and, further, that they comprise the poem's last explicit word on Denisot's talents.[94] In this fashion the ode *Au Conte d'Alsinois* goes

---

[94] As Laumonier has speculated (6:227, n. 2), the last allusion to this picture may in fact appear in the *Ode à Cassandre* (written in 1554) of the 1555 *Meslanges*. As in sonnets XXXIV and CXXIV of the 1552 *Amours*, however, the "peinture" is never expressly attributed to Denisot. It should also be noted that the ode *Au Conte d'Alsinois* was probably written before the *Amours* (most of whose pieces were composed in early 1552). It might therefore be proposed that the mere existence of the portrait sonnets would constitute evidence of Ronsard's favorable bias toward Denisot's painterly talents. In truth, however, the ode to the "Conte" has been impossible to date, so such a conclusion is at best tentative. Moreover, as we have seen, the sonnets are fundamentally ambivalent on the status of portraits. Thus even if *Au Conte d'Alsinois* had been completed before the *Amours* poems, the questions it poses remain open, and the parity it establishes between portraits and poems remains unchallenged.

beyond the ninth *Amour* and *A son Luc* in signaling the primacy of a Longinian ekplexis in Ronsard's aesthetic universe. It is also meaningful that the inquiries are never answered. By deferring any conclusion Ronsard allows that portraits and poems may be able to accomplish many of the same ends–including (we now realize) the paramount effect: an experience of psycho-emotional enthrallment, a veritable Medusean transformation, like that produced by the Mortal Gorgon evoked in Lucian's account of the petrifying effects needed for an accurate portrait of the stunning Panthea in the *Εικονες* (*Essays in Portraiture*).[95]

Taken together, the Denisot portrait sonnets of the 1552 *Amours* and the ode *Au Conte d'Alsinois* add much to our understanding of the ambivalence toward figure painting we have detected in the *Elegie à Janet* and the ode *A son Luc*. On the critical side, they revive the views that would privilege the complaints against the overall hollowness of visual signs promulgated in ancient mythology, the idealist philosophies of Plato and the Neoplatonists, and Ronsard's own reflections on narrative painting. On the adulatory side, they register notions that would closely resemble the principles advanced by ardent proponents of painting such as Alberti and, especially, Leonardo da Vinci. Like these art theorists, Ronsard applauds the ability of visual portraiture to ravish while ascribing that marvelous effect to the synchrony and concinnity of pictorial images: the very qualities he takes so eagerly to task in the two anti-portrait sonnets of the *Amours* and (lest we forget) the *Elegie, A son Luc,* and the poems on narrative pictures.

B. *Of the Shades of Portraits that Enthrall*

Ronsard's other evocations of painted portraits are comparably ambivalent. Openly contemptuous pieces are regularly countervailed by works that commend; indeed on occasion reproach and compliment merge almost seamlessly within the verses of one and the same poem. And again the pronouncements of praise typically highlight the ability of portraiture to precipitate a transformative enthrallment. Yet often this aptitude is conceptually shaded in order to dramatize other controversial attributes–concomitant ca-

---

[95] See especially *Εικονες*, 1-3.

pacities that are hardly recognized in the previous portrait poems, yet which remain objects of intense interest for Ronsard and all the major players in the early modern paragone debate.

One such capacity intersects the central concern of the *exegi monumentum* topos. In some instances Ronsard allows that the best portrait painters may 'transform' the inanimate into the animate, the dead into the living, and so wield a god-like power to immortalize the people they represent.[96] This possibility is first articulated at the beginning of the *Epitaphe de François de Bourbon, Conte d'Anguian* of the 1550 *Second livre des Odes*, a panegyric penned soon after the hero of the 1544 battle at Cerisoles was fortuitously dispatched by "un coffre jeté par une fenêtre . . . à la Rocheguyon" on 23 February 1546:[97]

> D'Homere grec la tant fameuse plume,
> Ou de Timante un tant fameus tableau,
> Durant leurs jours avoient une coutume
> D'arracher vifs les hommes du tumbeau.
>
> Je vous di ceus qui leur plaisoit encores
> Resusciter en depit de leur nuit
> Oblivieuse, ores par l'encre, & ores
> Par la couleur, eternisant leur bruit.
>
> (1:234, vv. 1-8)

In the spirit of ut pictura poesis, theorists of poetry and painting were frequently moved to associate a timeless bard like Homer with an excellent artist of Antiquity or their day. In the main, however, the comparisons were carefully restricted to matters of conception and style. In a comment on the proper way to depict the movement of women, for example, Alberti paraphrases Quintilian to point out that Homer's *dispositio* directly influenced Zeuxis' *compositione*: "The movements and poses of virgins are airy, full of simplicity with sweetness of quiet rather than strength; even though to Homer, whom Zeuxis followed, robust forms were pleasing even

---

[96] On the history of this topos, see Ernst Curtius, *European Literature and the Latin Middle Ages*, trans. Willard R. Trask (Princeton: Princeton University Press, 1973), 476-77, and my article, "Pictorial Concerns in the Ronsardian *Exegi Monumentum*," *The Sixteenth Century Journal* 24 (1993): 671-83, esp. 672.

[97] This incident is recorded in a note in Nicolas Richelet's *Commentaire des Odes de Ronsard* (1604) and is reprinted by Laumonier in *RPL*, 58, n. 2.

in women." [98] Analogously, Lodovico Dolce quotes a passage from Ariosto's *Orlando Furioso* as evidence that, in order to denote Alcina's inner character, the Ferraran poet uses color descriptions whose subtlety recalls the refinement of Titian's *colorito*:

> the painter's function consists in imitating, with the appropriate distinctions, the inherent character of any object there may be.

> *Over her delicate cheek there spread its way*
> *A color blended out of rose and may.*

> Here Ariosto puts in the coloring, and shows himself to be a Titian in the way he does this. [99]

On the politically and economically more sensitive issues of durability and 'immortalizability', on the other hand, inter-art equations are noticeably scarce. Acutely aware that the capability to overcome the oblivion of death was a principal basis on which wealthy patrons decided their awards of position and riches, most Renaissance art commentators scrupulously biased their remarks to favor one artistic medium over all others. Notwithstanding an occasional profession of parity from a painting advocate like Alberti ("Painting contains a divine force which . . . makes the dead seem almost alive"), the majority of visual-art theorists proceeded as Leonardo does when, in *Trattato* 19, he decrees painters to be the "grandchildren of God" ("nipoti à dio") by virtue of the permanence their paintings may attain once applied upon copper surfaces. [100] And the proponents of poetry were equally inclined to play favorites. Following the precedents set by Horace, Pindar, Propertius, and Lucian, [101] these advocates commonly endorsed monuments in words

---

[98] "Siano alle vergini movimenti e posari ariosi, pieni di semplicità, in quali piuttosto sia dolcezza di quiete che gagliardia, bene che ad Omero, quale seguitò Zeosis, piacque la forma fatticcia persino in le femine" (¶ 44 [78]; 80). Cf. Quintilian, *Institutio*, 12.10.5.

[99] "[L]'ufficio del Pittore è d'imitare il proprio di qualunque cosa con le distintioni, che si convengono. '*Spargeasi per la guancia delicata / Misto color di rose e di ligustri.*' Qui l'Ariosto colorisce, & in questo suo colorire dimostra essere un Titiano": Lodovico Dolce, *Aretino* 25 (132-33).

[100] See Chapter Two, 138-39.

[101] Cf. Horace, *Carminum Liber*, 3.30 (cited above) and 4.8-9; Pindar, *Pythia* 1 and 3, *Isthmia* 2 and 6, *Nemea* 4, 5, 7, 8 and 9; Propertius, *Carmina*, 3.2; and Lucian, Εικονες (*Essays in Portraiture*), § 23.

over those in bronze and paint, as Ariosto does at the start of *Orlando Furioso* 33, where writers are thanked ("mercé degli scrittori") for insuring the lasting fame of Tymagoras, Apelles, and other luminary artists of the plastic media.[102]

The opening quatrains of the *Epitaphe de François de Bourbon* depart boldly from this practice. Ronsard overtly equates "plume" and "tableau" in terms of their powers to snatch men from the infinite obscurity of the tomb. What is more, by making Homer a peer of Timanthes, the legendary Ionian portraitist of the fourth century B.C., Ronsard singles out portraiture as the genre of painting endowed with this ability while simultaneously intimating that this advantage relates to the potential of portrait artists to depict and stir intense feelings. Without dispute, Timanthes qualifies as one of the greatest painters of Antiquity in this regard, due especially to the exceptional rendering of Menelaus' grief in his legendary painting of the sacrifice of Iphigenia.[103] Quintilian offers a concise account of Timanthes' achievement in the *Institutio Oratoria*:

> Timanthes, who was, I think, a native of Cythnus, provides an example of this in the picture with which he won the victory over Colotes of Teos. It represented the sacrifice of Iphigenia, and the artist had depicted an expression of grief on the face of Calchas and of still greater grief on that of Ulysses, while he had given Menelaus an agony of sorrow beyond which his art could not go. Having exhausted his powers of emotional expression he was at a loss to portray the father's face as it deserved, and

---

[102] "Tymagoras, Parrhasius, Polignote, / Timant, Protogenes, Apollodore, / With Zeuxis, one for skill of speciall note: / Apelles eke, past all the rest before: / Whose skill in drawing, all the world doth note / And talke of still (to writers thanks therefore) / Whose works and bodies, time and death did wast, / Yet spite of time and death their fames do last . . ." ("Timagora, Parrasio, Polignoto, / Protogene, Timante, Apollodoro, / Apelle, più di tutti questi noto, / e Zeusi, e gli altri ch'a quei tempi fôro; / di quai la fama [mal grado di Cloto, / che spinse i corpi e dipoi l'opre loro] / sempre starà, fin che si legga e scriva, / mercé degli scrittori, al mondo viva . . ."): Ludovico Ariosto, *Sir John Harington's Translation of "Orlando Furioso" by Lodovico Ariosto,* ed. Graham Hough (Carbondale: Southern Illinois University Press, 1962), 391; *Orlando Furioso,* ed. Santorre Debenedetti, vol. 3 (Bari: Gius. Laterza & Figli, 1928), 1.

[103] For more on Timanthes, see Mary Hamilton Swindler, *Ancient Painting from the Earliest Times to the Period of Christian Art* (New Haven: Yale University Press, 1929), 234-35.

solved the problem by veiling his head and leaving his sorrow to the imagination of the spectator. [104]

Inspired by such reports, Alberti holds up Timanthes' *Iphigenia* as a paradigm of "istoria" (or "storia"), the most honorable effect of painting characterized by the capacity to impress the beholder with a sense of monumentality and drama: [105]

> First of all I think that all the bodies ought to move according to what is ordered in the *istoria*. In an *istoria* I like to see someone who admonishes and points out to us what is happening there; or beckons with his hand to see; or menaces with an angry face and with flashing eyes, so that no one should come near; or shows some danger or marvellous thing there; or invites us to weep or to laugh together with them. Thus whatever the painted persons do among themselves or with the beholder, all is pointed toward ornamenting or teaching the *istoria*. Timantes of Cyprus is praised in his panel, the Immolation of Iphigenia, with which he conquered Kolotes. He painted Calchas sad, Ulysses more sad, and in Menelaos, then, he would have exhausted his art in showing him greatly grief stricken. Not having any way in which to show the grief of the father, he threw a drape over his head and let his most bitter grief be imagined, even though it was not seen. [106]

---

[104] "Ut fecit Timanthes, opinor, Cythnius in ea tabula, qua Coloten Teium vicit. Nam cum in Iphigeniae immolatione pinxisset tristem Calchantem, tristiorem Ulixen, addidisset Menelao, quem summum poterat ars efficere, maerorem, consumptis adfectibus, non reperiens, quo digne modo patris vultum posset exprimere, velavit eius caput et suo cuique animo dedit aestimandum" (2.13.13): *Institutio Oratoria of Quintilian,* ed. and trans. H. E. Butler, 4 vols. (London: William Heinemann, 1933), 1.294-95. Cf. Pliny, *Historia* 35.36.73-74; Cicero, *Oratorio,* 22.74; Valerius Maximus, 8.2. *Ext.* 6.

[105] John Spencer analyzes this innovative concept in the introduction to his translation of Alberti's treatise (*On Painting*, 23-28).

[106] "Parmi in prima tutti e' corpi a quello si debbano muovere a che sia ordinata la storia. E piacemi sia nella storia chi ammonisca e insegni a noi quello che ivi si facci, o chiami con la mano a vedere, o con viso cruccioso e con gli occhi turbati minacci che niuno verso loro vada, o dimostri qualche pericolo o cosa ivi maravigliosa, o te inviti a piagnere con loro insieme o a ridere. E così qualunque cosa fra loro o teco facciano i dipinti, tutto apartenga a ornare o a insegnarti la storia. Lodasi Timantes di Cipri in quella tavola in quale egli vinse Colocentrio, che nella imolazione di Efigenia, avendo finto Calcante mesto, Ulisse più mesto, e in Menelao poi avesse consunto ogni suo arte a molto mostrarlo adolorato, non avendo in che modo mostrare la tristezza del padre, a lui avolse uno panno al capo, e così lassò si pensasse qual non si vedea suo acerbissimo merore" (¶ 42, 72-74; 78). Dolce likewise cites Timanthes' feat as an example of true invention ("vero inventione") and propriety ("convenevolezza") in painting: *Aretino* 20 (122-23).

Ronsard undoubtedly knew of these and other accolades (including Du Bellay's allusion to "la ruse de ce noble peintre Tymante" in his *Dédicace* to Jean du Bellay at the beginning of the *Deffence et Illustration de la langue francoyse*),[107] and in the earliest versions of the *Epitaphe* he might well have welcomed their capacity to infuse the inter-art equation with an affective dimension that would complement the response-oriented aesthetic of emotions introduced in *A son Luc*. Nevertheless, eventually that emotionalist sense is superseded by a concern for the objective naturalism of great portraiture. This shift is prominently evidenced in 1555, when the first two verses of the *Epitaphe* are modified to read: "D'Homere grec l'ingenieuse plume, / Et de Timant' les *animés* tableaus" (my emphasis). Stressing the infusion of *anima*–i.e., physical and spiritual vitality, or literally, the 'breath' of the body and the soul–into the picture, Ronsard redirects the focus to the immortality of the human subject depicted and thereby restores attention to the central consideration of the *exegi monumentum* topos: the ability of poets and plastic artists to resuscitate the personalities they represent from the oblivious night of death ("Resusciter en depit de leur nuit / Oblivieuse").

Much the same perspective is assumed in sonnet XIII, *Au Roy Henri II*, of the 1559 *Second livre des Meslanges*:

> Quand entre les Cesars j'aperçoy ton ymage,
> Decouvrant tout le front le laurier revestu,
> Voyez (ce di-je lors) combien peut la vertu,
> Qui fait d'un jeune Roy un Cesar davant l'age.
>
> Ton peuple en ton portraict revere ton visage,
> Et ta main qui n'aguere a si bien combatu,
> Faisant combatre autruy, quand l'Anglois abatu
> A ta France rendit son ancien rivage.
>
> Ce n'est pas peu de cas que d'estre portrait, Sire,
> Entre les vieux Cesars, qui ont regi l'empire,
> Comme toy valeureux, magnanimes & justes.
>
> Ce signe te promet, grand Roy victorieux,
> Puisque vif on t'eleve au nombre des Augustes,
> Que mort tu seras mis là haut entre les Dieux.
>
> (10:78-79)

---

[107] Joachim Du Bellay, *La Deffence et Illustration de la langue francoyse*, ed. Henri Chamard (Paris: Marcel Didier, 1948), 7.

Like the twenty other *courtisanesque* sonnets of the second *Meslanges* (all composed "long temps davant la mort du Roy" in June 1559 [10:3]), this work reserves one level of meaning to winning the poet "faveur . . . caresse & bon visage"[108] from the king and his wealthy and powerful entourage. This purpose engenders the encomium to Henri's virtue and military prowess in the quatrains and, in the tercets, the insistence on the perpetuity of the king's magnanimity and valor–a durability actualized (at least partly) by the inscription of these qualities into the poet's time-resistant verses. On a different level, though, the sonnet *Au Roy* acknowledges a commensurate immortalizing potential in painted portraiture. Further, as in the *Epitaphe*, one of the principal contributors to that ability is the affinity of figure painting for rendering a subject true to life, "Puisque *vif* on t'eleve au nombre des Augustes . . ." (my emphasis).[109] Beyond the issue of naturalism, however, Ronsard also pays tribute to the ease with which this art form can signify the *promise* of immortality. This semiotic feat is adeptly realized through a judicious attribution of vestments and social affiliations. By crowning Henri's forehead with the laurel vine of ancient royal majesty and situating him amid a gathering of "vieux Cesars," the portrait artist produces a visual "signe" that is equal to the poet's words in denoting a promise of the French monarch's god-like imperishability.[110]

Important as these poems may be, the majority of pieces to compare the 'immortalizability' of verses and portraits contradict these sentiments in order to remain steadfast to the spirit of the traditional Horatian *exegi monumentum* topos. Ronsard again reveals his ambivalence toward portraiture by affirming that poetry would be fundamentally more perpetuating than painting, and for many of the theoretical reasons articulated elsewhere.

---

[108] Sonnet XXI, *Imitation de Martial* (10:86, v. 7).

[109] The nominal complement of the adjective "vif" is admittedly equivocal. The qualifier can reasonably modify either of the nouns in the preceding verse: the "Roy" who is still 'alive' at the time the poem was written, or the portrait-*signe* that depicts him with such vividness and animation.

[110] Laumonier has interpreted the object of this acclamation somewhat differently. In a note to the first quatrain, he proposes that Ronsard evokes a "portrait de Henri II qu'un peintre avait par flatterie fait placer parmi ceux des Cesars romains dans une galerie du Louvre ou d'un autre palais" (10:78, n. 2). Although the painting in question may well have hung in a gallery of the sort Laumonier has described, verses 9-10 indicate that the Caesars are likewise depicted at Henri's sides, within the same picture frame.

The 1550 ode *A Charles de Pisseleu, Evesque de Condon* (composed soon after the dedicatee's promotion to bishop in 1545) embraces and revitalizes the most customary complaint against the plastic arts:

> Que nul papier dorennavant
> Par moi ne s'anime sans mettre
> (Docte Prelat) ton nom davant
> Pour donner faveur à mon mettre.
>
> C'est lui qui mieus te fera vivre
> Qu'un portrait de marbre attaché,
> Ou qu'une medaille de cuivre
> Mise à ton los dans un marché.
>
> (1:226-27, vv. 1-8)

The attack on a perishable portrait in marble establishes Ronsard's debt to the *exegi monumentum* tradition of the Ancients. It is particularly reminiscent of Horace's *Donarem patteras grataque commodus* (*CL* 8), which singles out the impermanence of the marble treasures by Scopas of Paros, the Attic sculptor of the fourth century B.C. who, like his painter contemporary Timanthes, received notice for portraying and igniting profound emotions.[111] On the other hand, the reference to the "medaille de cuivre / Mise à ton los" draws these inter-art reflections into the paragone debate of Ronsard's own day. The allusion to a portrait on a copper coin invariably recalls and challenges Leonardo da Vinci's nineteenth *Trattato*, where the Florentine specifically praises the indestructibility of a "picture . . . upon *copper*" ("pittura . . . sopra *rame*").[112]

The denunciation of transitory plastic portraits becomes more timely still in sonnet CCVIII of the 1553 *Amours*. Here Ronsard

---

[111] Of course, the comment likewise echoes Horace's condemnations of weather- and time-battered pyramids in his famous *Exegi monumentum aere perennius* (*CL* 3.30) (see Chapter Two, 138). Cf. also Propertius' attack on all stone monuments in his *Carminis interea nostri redeamus in orbem*: "neither the Pyramids built skyward at such cost, nor the house of Jove at Elis that matches heaven, nor the wealth of Mausolus' tomb are exempt from the end imposed by death. Their glory is stolen away by fire or rain, or the strokes of time whelm them to ruin crushed by their own weight . . ." ("neque Pyramidum sumptus ad sidera ducti, / nec Iovis Elei caelum imitata domus, / nec Mausolei dives fortuna sepulcri / mortis ab extrema condicione vacant. / aut illis flamma aut imber subducit honores, / annorum aut ictus pondere victa ruent . . .") (*Elegiarum* 3.2, vv. 19-24): Propertius, *Propertius*, trans. H. E. Butler (Cambridge: Harvard University Press, 1952), 180-81.

[112] See Chapter Two, 138-39.

identifies the manipulator of corruptible artistic materials as the illustrious "Janet" (François Clouet) himself:

> Telle qu'elle est, dedans ma souvenance
>   Je la sen peinte, & sa bouche, & ses yeus,
>   Son dous regard, son parler gratieus,
>   Son dous meintien, sa douce contenance.
> Un seul Janet, honneur de nostre France,
>   De ses craïons ne la portrairoit mieus,
>   Que d'un Archer le trait ingenieus
>   M'a peint au coeur sa vive remembrance.
> Dans le coeur donque au fond d'un diamant
>   J'ai son portrait, que je suis plus aimant
>   Que mon coeur mesme. O sainte portraiture,
> *De ce Janet l'artifice mourra*
>   *Frapé du tans, mais le tien demourra*
>   *Pour estre vif apres ma sepulture.*
>
> (5:154-55: my emphasis)

Notwithstanding the accolades of the second quatrain, Janet suffers the flaw of every plastic artist: he employs a medium whose physicality is destined to decay under the blows of the inexorable temporal tides.

The 1550 ode *A René d'Urvoi* (written between 1545 and 1549) takes the assault substantially further. Besides decrying the fragility of plastic memorials, this tribute to Ronsard's schoolmate from the days at the Collège de Coqueret returns to impugn the semantic ineptitude of such artworks, their incapacity to give lasting presence to truths of the conceptual variety:

> Ma painture n'est pas mue
> Mais vive, & par l'univers
> Guindée en l'air se remue
> De sus l'engin de mes vers.
> . . . .
> Les vers sans plus t'ejouissent,
> Mes vers donq je t'ofrirai,
> Les vers seulement jouissent
> Du droit que je te dirai.
>
> Les Colonnes elevées,
> Ne les marbres imprimés

De grosses lettres gravées,
Ne les cuivres animés,

Ne font que les hommes vivent
En images contrefais,
Comme les vers qui les suivent
Pour témoins de leurs beaus fais.

(2:148-50, vv. 5-8, 29-40)

Whereas the words about elevated columns, imprinted marbles and animated coppers reemphasize the physical mutability of the plastic arts as a whole, the comments on men "contrefais" in images and a painting that is "mue" (mute) specifically reiterate the criticisms against the ideational absence of painted portraits and the pictorial arts. The first term reprises the pejorative sense of *contrefaire* found in *Des peintures contenues dedans un tableau*, where the word designates a misleading and defective imitation. The second term not only revives Simonides' *pictura poesis muta* and the implicit denunciations of the pictorial arts expressed by the Aquinian Scholastics, but it also anticipates *Des peintures* in taking exception to all those who, like Leonardo da Vinci, would deny or defend the inherent muteness of painting. The Pléiade laureate might well be refuting the Florentine's redemption of dumb portraits in *Trattato* 19: "though poetry is able to describe forms, actions, and places in words, the painter employs the exact images of the forms and represents them as they are."[113]

Two other *exegi monumentum* poems deliver similar incriminations. The emphasis falls again on the relative impermanence of dumb portraits in the *Contr'Estrene, au Seigneur Robert de la Haye* of the 1552 *Cinquiesme livre des Odes*. A mute canvas or copper coin culminates the list of presents Ronsard would offer to Robert de la Haye "pour estrener / La foy de nostre amour premiere" (vv. 76-77), a friendship kindled near the end of 1551 when the neo-latin poet and lawyer of the Parlement de Paris published a resounding tribute to Du Bellay and the Pléiade leader:

Ou si j'estois assez subtil,
Pour animer par un outil

---

[113] "[S]e la poesia s'estende con le parolle a figurare forme, atti e siti, il pittore si moue con le proprie similitudini delle forme a contrafare esse forme" (1:57). Cf. Chapter One, 76-77, 82-83 and Chapter Two, 101.

> La toille muette, ou le cuivre:
> Mon art t'offriroit ses presens,
> Mais ces dons là contre les ans
> Ne te scauroyent faire revivre.

> Pren donc mes vers qui vallent mieux. . . .
>
> (3:169, vv. 85-91)

The profession of modesty ("si j'estois assez subtil") does more than endear Ronsard to his dedicatee. It also underscores the semantic superiority of the poet's verses by denoting an incorporeal concept (humility) that the painter's vision- and matter-bound "toille muette, ou le cuivre" would be hard pressed to signify without an allegorical mediation. But even if that confession were absent, the ode fully merits De la Haye's god-like "bonté haulte." Although imperfect, the poem can "faire revivre" his friend throughout the ages. A painted or engraved portrait, on the other hand, can offer no lasting life. Such an artwork is doubly destined to decay: it is the material product of an "outil," a mutable artifact fashioned through mere manual labor; worse still, it is "muette," without a voice to sing the praises of de la Haye's highest qualities.

The connection between the perishability and semantic limitations of pictorial portraits appears once more, though with no explicit mention of muteness, at the beginning of the 1555 *Troisiéme livre des Odes*, in the ode *Au Roy Henri II* written in 1554, thus contemporaneously with the *Elegie à Janet*. With the penultimate stanza Ronsard drops any pretense of objectivity to reveal a political reality motivating many (or perhaps all) of the paragone-related commentaries in his oeuvre: his need for royal financial support in order to pursue his own poetic ambitions. In this instance, the poet entreats Henri II to keep an unfulfilled promise to subsidize his *Franciade*, the epic story tracing the political and cultural feats of France since the days of Henri's legendary ancestor, Francus, the son of Hector of Troy:

> Donques pour engarder que la Parque cruelle
> Sans nom t'ensevelisse en la nuit éternelle,
> Toujours ne faut avoir à gage des maçons
> Pour transformer par art une roche en maisons,
> Et toujours n'acheter avecques la main pleine
> *Ou la medale morte, ou la peinture vaine.*

Mais il faut par bienfaits & par caresse d'yeus
Tirer en ta maison les ministres des Dieus,
Les Poëtes sacrés, qui par leur écriture
Te rendront plus vivant que maison ni peinture.

(7:32, vv. 137-46: my emphasis)

The implications of the adjective "vaine" at the rhyme of verse 142 are critical. More than connote 'hollow', by its opposition to the adjective "pleine" at the rhyme of the preceding verse, or 'lifeless', by its parallel with the adjective "morte" at the caesura six syllables earlier, "vaine" must be understood in terms of both ideas. With respect to the meaning of the noun it modifies, "la peinture," this adjective compels two complementary readings. On the one hand, painting is 'hollow', or worthless, because it is subject to physical decay, or death. This interpretation conforms to the *exegi monumentum* topos promoted in the Horatian, Pindaric, and Propertian traditions. On the other hand, a painting is "morte," or lifeless, because it is 'hollow', or referentially vacuous (as in sonnet CXXIV of the 1552 *Amours*), unable to express the kind of virtues listed among the topics of the "Franciade" at the end of the poem:

Ma Franciade tienne, où la Troïenne race
De Francus ton ancestre, où les faits glorieus
De tant de vaillans Roys qui furent tes aïeus,
Où mesmes tes vertus y luiront évidantes,
Comme luisent au ciel les étoilles ardantes
Sortant de l'Ocean.

(7:33, vv. 158-63)

These are the foremost metaphysical qualities of the living human essence, those that glow as brilliantly as the burning stars of the highest cosmic heavens–properties pertaining to the *sine qua non* of the portrait that would seem truly alive.

Outside of any direct appeal to the immortality issue, Ronsard expands on the nature of pictorial 'hollowness' in yet another piece about painted portraiture from 1554, the *Ode à Cassandre* that first appeared with the *Elegie à Janet* in the 1555 *Meslanges*. In effect, this Petrarchan-style love poem serves as a gloss to all the versified indictments against the emptiness of figure painting. Its focus is a picture of the poet-lover's anguished and moribund bodily shell, a work ostensibly offered as a gift to the cold-hearted Cassandre in the hope of attracting her affections by first piquing her sympathetic "merci":

> En vous donnant ce pourtraict mien
> Dame, je ne vous donne rien:
> . . . .
> Car ce n'est rien de voir, Maistresse,
> La face qui est tromperesse,
> Et le front bien souvent moqueur,
> C'est le tout que de voir le coeur.
> Vous voyriés du mien la constance,
> La foi, l'amour, l'obeissance,
> Et les voyant, peut estre aussi
> Qu'auriés de lui quelque merci,
> Et des angoisses qu'il endure. . . .
>
> (6:227-29, vv. 1-35)[114]

Ronsard now applies to pictorial portraiture much the same criticism he levies against narrative painting in *La defloration de Lede* and *La Lyre*: it is doomed to signify false or incomplete exteriors (the *dehors*–here the "face" and "front"). [115] For this reason the painted portrait both reveals and *is* a "rien," an empty 'nothing' that fails to expose the inner truth, the poet-lover's "coeur" of constancy, faith, love, obedience, and anguish–qualities to which the present ode, and thus the verbal art of poetry in general, would manifestly enjoy the most sweeping access. Ronsard thereby echoes a reproach against figure painting voiced, some five years earlier, in Joachim Du Bellay's *Deffence et Illustration*. In the chapter warning against the treasonous business of translating poetry (1.6), the Angevin likens the ineptitude of the translator who would dare to reencode the unique "energie" and "esprit" of a poet's "divinité d'invention," or genius, to the inability of the portrait painter who

---

[114] According to Laumonier, the poet would be seeking to exchange this picture for the portrait of Cassandre by Denisot evoked in the 1552 *Amours* (6:227, n. 2). In truth, there is no textual evidence to suggest that Ronsard seeks anything but the lady's elusive favors.

[115] See Chapter Two, 143-50.

would foolishly attempt to represent a person's "ame" by replicating his or her mere "cors." [116]

* * *

With the new political, social, and professional realities of the 1560s, on the other hand, Ronsard makes fewer and less developed appeals to the *exegi monumentum* topos. His earlier preoccupation with the relative 'immortalizability' of the arts is substantially restrained, and to a degree invalidated, following the deaths of Henri II (1558) and François II (1560), the start of Catherine de Médicis' two and three-quarter year regency (December 1560-August 1563) for her second son, Charles IX, the escalation of religious "troubles" in 1560 and 1562, and the resulting postponement of the *Franciade* project, one of the principal motivators for engaging the immortality issue (as noted previously). These influential events receive particular attention in *Les Trois Livres du Recueil des nouvelles Poësies* of 1564. Perhaps the most vivid meditation on their impact is the one Ronsard stages in the *Compleinte à la Royne Mere du Roy* of the second book, a poem written during the anxious days immediately after the first civil war in March 1563 and before the close of Catherine's regency on 15 August of that year. An apostrophe to a judgmental posterity emphasizes how the death of Henri II ended all foreseeable hope of royal support for the *Franciade*, and consequently, how the poet is now obliged to pursue other poetic agendas and themes. As Ronsard delicately explains it with the help of a transparent travel metaphor, he must "[s']en partir d'icy / Pour trainer autre part [s]a plume & [s]on soucy / En estrange pays, servant un autre Prince" (12:184, vv. 251-53). [117]

---

[116] "Mais que diray-je d'aucuns, vrayement mieux dignes d'estre appellés traditeurs que traducteurs? veu qu'ilz trahissent ceux qu'ilz entreprennent exposer . . . : qui, pour acquerir le nom de scavans . . . se prennent aux poëtes, genre d'aucteurs certes auquel, si je scavoy' ou vouloy' traduyre, je m'adroisseroy' aussi peu, à cause de ceste divinité d'invention qu'ilz ont plus que les autres, de ceste grandeur de style, magnificence de motz, gravité de sentences, audace & varieté de figures, & mil'autres lumieres de poësie: bref ceste energie, & ne scay quel esprit, qui est en leurs ecriz, que les Latins appelleroient *genius*. Toutes les quelles choses se peuvent autant exprimer en traduisant, comme un peintre peut representer l'ame avecques le cors de celuy qu'il entreprent tyrer apres le naturel": Du Bellay, *Deffence*, 39-41.

[117] Ronsard proceeds more explicitly in the verses immediately following this metaphor: " 'Souvent le malheur change en changeant de province. / Car que feray je icy sans ayde & sans suport? / L'espoir qui me tenoit se perdit par la mort / Du

In fact the commentaries on portraiture from this period call at several scarcely explored thematic *pays*. At the same time each reflection highlights a heretofore peripherally discerned facet of the response-centered idea of enthrallment, each one does so in overtly equivocal terms, as if to signal the poet's commitment to remaining ambivalent toward the value of portraits.

One such representation comes to light in the third book of the same *Nouvelles Poësies*, in the *Discours amoureux de Genevre* that Ronsard seems to have written between July 1561 and July 1562, at the height of his love affair with the brown-eyed blond "Genevre." [118] Of course this elegy of 488 alexandrine verses does much more than describe a picture. The work is primarily the aging poet's narrative account of the events attending and following his *innamoramento* with Genevre one sultry evening at the end of July.

While bathing in the Seine to escape the "chaut violent" of the waning day, a similarly 'waning' Ronsard spies a young lady with an "oeil brun" and "deux tresses blondes" dancing on the nearby shore. Refilled with an "ardeur infine" that belies his "plus vieil, plus froid & plus grison" exterior, he is roused to abandon his watery cloak in order to join, "Tout nud," in the lady's irresistible dance and to deliver a kiss to her hand before abruptly plunging back into the river in an effort to extinguish his "premier feu nouveau." This tactic proves vain, however, as the lady's eyes have filled his heart with a fire that rages throughout the ensuing night and day and compels him to seek her out to confess his affection (12:257-59, vv. 5-60).

The next evening the poet rediscovers his beloved at the door of her house. Deprived of his remaining "pauvre raison" by Cupid's implacable arrows, the love-struck Ronsard strives to earn Genevre's "mercy" by promising to become a "serviteur fidelle" who will render her a suitably "grand honneur" (12:259-62, vv. 61-116). The lady is unmoved, however, for as the poet explains, her amorous flame was forever extinguished with the life of her recently

---

bon Prince Henry, lequel fut l'esperance / De mes vers, & de moy, & de toute la France'" (12:184-85, vv. 254-58). Cf. the laureate's answer to his protestant calumniators (notably Jacques Grévin and Florent Chrestien) in the *Epistre au Lecteur* of the same *Nouvelles Poesies* (12:3-24).

[118] For more on the identity of Genevre, see Michel Simonin, *Pierre de Ronsard* (Paris: Fayard, 1990), 226-29. See also Laumonier's note (12:256, n. 2), his Introduction (12:ix-xiii), and *RPL* 211.

deceased lover. Rejected and confused, Ronsard returns home and
cries incessantly for four days until, on the fifth day, he resolves to
see Genevre one last time. Convinced that the lady must have failed
to recognize his true identity, the poet goes back to her home and
promptly announces his name and the professional and personal
credentials he hopes will win her over (12:262-64, vv. 117-60).
Scarcely more impressed, the mourning woman responds to his
clarifications with sighs and tears that finally induce the poet-narrator to cede the narrative charge to Genevre herself. The latter
thereupon commits 284 verses to a response that bares her own sad
story: the tale of a six year love affair abruptly cut off, nine months
earlier, by the death of her young *amant*, her other soul, from a fatal
attack of hydropsy (12:264-75, vv. 161-444).

It is at the numerical middle of this intradiagetic anecdote that
Ronsard embarks on an ekphrastic excursus evoking a portrait that
the expiring lover offers to Genevre as a memento of his vital form
and undying love:

> Mais las! puisque mon corps, lequel t'a bien aymé,
> Sera tantost sans forme en poudre consumé,
> Pour souvenance au moins garde bien ma peinture,
> Où sont tirés au vif les traits de ma figure:
> La voyant tu pourras de moy te souvenir,
> Et souvent dans ton sein cherement la tenir.
>   Et luy diras: Peinture, ombre de ce visage
> Qui mort & consumé encores me soulage,
> Que tu m'es douce & chere, ayant perdu l'espoir,
> Si ce n'est par la mort de jamais te revoir.
> O beau visage feint! feinte teste & plaisante!
> De rien sinon de toy mon cueur ne se contente!
> Ton faux m'est agreable & ton vain gracieux,
> Et seulement de toy se contentent mes yeux.
>   (12:270, vv. 301-14)

The ambivalence in this representation is unmistakable. Among its
virtues, the portrait once more achieves a special physical accuracy:
the facial features painted are "tirés au vif," modeled accurately
after the traits of the lover's own living visage. Moreover, thanks to
that accuracy, which infuses the work with an essential mnemonic
utility, the portrait will be affectively provocative. Along with fos-
tering an approbative aesthetic assessment ("O *beau* visage . . .": my

emphasis), it will arouse a variety of deep emotional responses in the viewer. According to the dying lover, Genevre will eventually find the image "plaisante," and especially it will render *soulagement* and *contentement* for her eye and heart. It will therefore stir the senses and the soul much like the portraits by Zeuxis applauded in *A son Luc* and the painting of Cassandre by Densiot celebrated in the earliest *Amours*.

Among its failings, on the other hand, the portrait is still just a simulacrum. As in the 1554 ode *Au Roy Henri II*, the 1554 *Ode à Cassandre*, sonnets XXXIV and CXXIV of the 1552 *Amours,* and the *Elegie à Janet* (before and after 1560), the picture provides only an "ombre" of the man's face. It displays a mere "visage feint" which, although "agreable" and "gracieux," is semantically "vain" and ontologically "faux"–i.e., devoid of the inner qualities that define the real lover's essence–and thus a spurious version of its referent in the world. It is doubtless for this reason that, in the end, the grieving Genevre finds no enduring solace in this picture and is forced to admit to Ronsard that her pain persists nine months after her devastating loss: "Or ma douleur n'est point par le temps divertie, / Et neuf mois sont passés que je n'estois sortie / Du logis pour chercher quelque plaisir nouveau . . ." (12:275, vv. 439-41).

A dedication to ambivalence is equally apparent in the commentary on a portrait in the unusual pseudo-lesbian *Elegie*, "Pour vous montrer que j'ay parfaitte envie." [119] Although published with the 1565 *Elegies, Mascarades et Bergerie*, this piece probably dates from early 1564, when Ronsard joined in the court revelries at Paris and Fontainebleau and became most active as a "poète courtisan" and "fournisseur de vers pour les princes et autres grands seigneurs de la Cour." [120] The portrait in question ostensibly depicts a noblewoman named "Anne," the person alleged to have authored this epistle-like poem in order to describe this artwork and offer it as a token of unswerving love and devotion to another noblewoman, her "Maitresse," a social superior from whom she has been separated, called "Diane."

In the opening stanza the tone is unequivocally laudatory: the picture is ranked among the greatest gifts the lady has to offer as a testimony of fidelity to her beloved:

---

[119] Cf. Pontus de Tyard's *Elegie pour une Dame enamourée d'une autre Dame* in the 1573 *Nouvelles Œuvres Poétiques* (in *Œuvres*, 246-50).

[120] Laumonier, *Œuvres*, 13:viii-x.

> Pour vous montrer que j'ay parfaitte envie
> De vous servir tout le temps de ma vie,
> Je vous supply vouloir prendre de moy
> Ce seul present, le tesmoing de ma foy,
> Vous le donnant d'affection extresme
> Avecq' mon coeur, ma peinture, & moymesme.
>
> (13:170, vv. 1-6)

The high value of the portrait is reaffirmed at the end of the poem, though now as a unit of currency in the economy of emotional compensations. Here Anne wishes that the picture may recompense her mistress' generous "faveur," the affection ("Ce bien") Diane deigns to show despite her admirer's inferior social rank: "Ce bien me vient . . . / De la faveur dont il vous plaist m'user, / Me cognoissant de beaucoup estre moindre: / . . . / C'est la raison pourquoy je vous dedie / Mon sang, mon coeur, ma peinture, & ma vie" (13:175, vv. 127-34).

This compensatory significance stands out again in the sonnet that originally accompanied the elegy in 1565, a poem intended to represent Mistress Diane's reply to her adoring admirer. The quatrains are especially illuminating:

> Anne m'a fait de sa belle figure
> Un beau present que je garde bien cher,
> Cher pour autant qu'on n'en sçauroit cercher
> Un qui passast si belle portraiture.
>   Diane icy redonne sa peinture
> A sa maistresse Anne, pour revancher
> Non le present, mais toujours pour tascher
> Que son service envers son ame dure.
>
> (13:176, vv. 1-8)

Thus we learn that the picture is at least as precious to Diane as it is to Anne. Were it not, Diane's final gesture (which calls to mind Panurge's reaction to the repayment of debts in Rabelais' *Tiers Livre*) would have no basis for success: she would have no grounds for returning the present to prolong Anne's debt and service since the portrait would have failed to satisfy the obligation in the first place. More important, we discover something about the basis for that value. As we may infer from the term "cher" (triadically stressed by the anadiplosis linking verses 2-3 and the harmonic report of the verb "cer*cher*" at the rhyme of verse 3) and the adjectives "belle"/"beau"/"belle" (in verses 1, 2, and 4), the merit of the picture (the reason why it is *cher*) lies in its naturalistic veracity: it is a "beau present" and a "belle portraiture" because it correctly recreates Anne's external "belle figure."

Ronsard underscores the profound affective influence of the portrait as well. In this case, though, the desirability of that impact is distinctly more equivocal than in previous poems. Indeed, for the Pléiade laureate this effect relates directly to one of the most salient and (as we have seen) hotly disputed weaknesses of painting—its muteness: "Dedans la pomme est peinte ma figure / Palle, muëtte, & triste . . ." (13:173, vv. 73-74). As Ronsard emphasizes in so many other instances, the muteness of the picture prevents it from denoting the conceptual and spiritual realities that lie beneath material surfaces:

> Ha! je voudrois que celuy qui l'a faitte
> Pour mon secours ne l'eust point fait muette,
> Elle pourroit vous conter à loysir
> Seulle à par vous, l'extreme desplaisir
> Que je reçoy me voyant separée
> De vous mon tout, demeurant égarée
> De tant de bien qui me souloit venir,
> Ne vivant plus que du seul souvenir,
> Et du beau nom que vous portez, Madame,
> Qui si avant m'est escrit dedans l'ame.
>   Mais quel besoin est il de presenter
> Un portrait mort, qui ne peut contenter?
>   (13:173-74, vv. 77-88)

The portrait is therefore unable to express in full, to "conter à loysir," the hardships and "extreme desplaisir" that Anne endures while separated from Diane. Paradoxically, that flaw is likewise the catalyst of a useful affective consequence. To the degree the painting is physically accurate yet ideationally "mort" it is eminently well suited to move Diane to feel "quelque soucy" whenever Anne and she are apart: "Las! c'est afin qu'en le voyant ainsi / A tout le moins ayez quelque soucy / De moy qui suis en douleur languissante / Pour ne voir point vostre face presente . . ." (13:174, vv. 91-94). It is the ideal souvenir to provoke such a painful response, the perfect mnemonic trace of the longed-for absent essence because the portrait too is always inherently devoid of essence.

On the other hand, by making this point while exposing Anne's deeper wish, her desire that Diane and she be forever as one, Ronsard shows that poetry can do it all. In addition to signifying absence, the poet's art can make whatever is absent fully present. In the last analysis, then, despite its other virtues, the painting needs the poem, the image requires the word, in order to realize the fullest semantic plenitude. This truth is encoded in the strictest literal way at the conclusion of the portrait ekphrasis:

> Puis tellement dedans vous je veux estre
> Qu'autre que vous je ne veux recognoistre:
> Le vers Romain mis autour du portrait
> Declare assez mon desir si parfait,
> *Cest qu'Anne vit en sa Diane mise,*
> *Diane en Anne, & que le temps qui brise*
> *Murs & Chateaux, & qui tout fait plyer,*
> *Deux si beaux noms ne sçauroit deslier.*
>
> (13:174, vv. 97-104: Ronsard's emphasis)

Like the narrative pictures in the *Temple de Messeigneurs*, the portrait is given a verbal supplement, an encircling "vers Romain," that clearly declares what the image should denote—Anne's "desir si parfait" to be conjoined substantially with Diane. Indeed, as if to flaunt the power of words this legend exhibits how language has already made that union a reality, for Anne's name is already effectively inscribed within the verbal signifier "Di/*ane*."

Ronsard presents a comparably ambivalent commentary on portraiture in his *Elegie* to Marie Stuart, "Bien que le trait de vostre belle face," a poem similarly composed during the early 1560s [121] and initially published with the 1567 *Œuvres*, in the third book of *Elegies*. Unlike the previous two pieces, however, the present work seems to register a full awareness and acceptance of its conflicting attitudes toward portrait painting. That impression is poignantly

---

[121] The reference to the Queen's departure from France, "Partant helas! de la belle contrée" (v. 26), makes Marie's departure for Scotland on 14 August 1561 the likeliest *terminus a quo*. For the *terminus ad quem*, Laumonier has suggested the date of Marie's remarriage to Henry Darnley, on 29 July 1565 (13:152, n. 1 and 155, n. 2). Based upon Ronsard's treatment of portraiture, I would further propose that the work was probably written soon after the *Elegie* of Anne for Diane, hence in late 1564 or early 1565.

engendered by the inclusion in the poem of two different portraits, each standing to the other "vis à vis" (v. 53), or "Droit au devant" (in the 1578 edition), in a spatial and qualitative opposition.

Reflecting the positive elements of portraiture is the picture of Marie Stuart. The youthful queen is featured as she appears in François Clouet's *Marie Stuart en deuil blanc* (fig. 12), in the solemn, head-to-waist white mourning gown she donned after the death, in December 1560, of her young husband François II: "Un crespe long, subtil & delié, / . . . / Habit de dueil, vous sert de couverture / Depuis le chef jusques à la ceinture . . ." (14:153, vv. 19-22). The poet insists that the painting not only adorns his personal study ("[Dont mon estude & mes livres je pare]": v. 6), but that it also *honors* the site ("Vostre portrait qui fait honneur au lieu": v. 7). This privilege most likely follows from the extraordinary naturalistic properties of the work detailed in the second stanza:

> Vous n'estes pas en drap d'or habillée,
> Ny les joyaux de l'Inde despouillée,
> Riches d'email & d'ouvrages, ne font
> Luire un beau jour autour de vostre front:
> Et vostre main, sans artifice belle,
> N'a rien sinon sa blancheur naturelle:
> Et voz beaux doids, cinq arbres inegaux,
> Ne sont ornez de bagues ny d'anneaux:
> Et la beauté de vostre gorge vive
> N'a pour carquan que sa couleur naive.
>
> (14:152-53, vv. 9-18)

As in the *Discours amoureux de Geneve* and the *Elegie* from Anne to Diane, the poet applauds the physical resemblance of the image to the real person who sat in the presence of the artist. He further insists that it excludes all "artifice," as if to reassure us that it avoids the "art menteur" twice condemned in the *Elegie à Janet*.

The author emphasizes the ability of the picture to excite the deepest passions as well. This affective power is so great that it touches "la cire mesme" of the wax-drawn second portrait–that of "un Roy . . . / Bien jeune d'ans" (14:154, vv. 54-55), the younger brother and successor to François II, Charles IX, who has fallen hopelessly in love with his beautiful widowed sister-in-law. The painting of Marie has a potent effect on the viewer, even when that viewer is a mere simulacrum of a living human being–a fact that testifies all the more convincingly to its capacity to enthrall:

> Chacun diroit qu'il ayme vostre Image,
> Et qu'allumé des rais de vostre jour
> Il se consume & s'escoule d'amour,
> Dedans la cire, & que la cire mesme
> Sentant sa flame en devient toute blesme.
>   On jugeroit qu'il contemple voz yeux,
> Doux, beaux, courtois, plaisans, delicieux,
> Un peu brunets, où la delicatesse
> Rit . . . .
>
> (14:154-55, vv. 58-66)

Besides stimulating sensual and aesthetic responses like those that gratify the pictorial monarch's contemplations of the painted lady's brownish smiling eyes (vv. 63-66), the portrait emits a unique radiance–"rais de vostre jour"–capable of sparking an all-consuming and overflowing feeling of love, of producing an experience akin to the metamorphosing ekplexis intermittently induced by Denisot's painting of Cassandre.

Opposite this picture, both spatially and qualitatively, is the portrait in wax of Charles IX. Notwithstanding the judgements of "Chacun" (v. 58) and "On" (v. 63), which ascribe a certain emotional verisimilitude to the artwork, the most distinctive feature of this painting is its muteness. In contrast to the illustration of Marie Stuart, the rendering of Charles IX thus serves primarily to call attention to the weaknesses of portraiture–particularly to its expressive limitations–and conversely, as we have now come to expect, to accentuate the complementary strengths of poetry. This purpose becomes apparent as the poet continues describing the painted Charles' reactions to the image of Marie:

> Luy donc, espris d'un visage si beau
> Où vit Amour, son trait & son flambeau,
> En son portrait vous diriez qu'il soupire
> Et que *muet ne vous ose rien dire.*
>   Pource voyant mon maistre en tel ennuy,
> *Je suis contraint de raisonner pour luy,*
> *Parlant ainsi . . . .*
>
> (14:155, vv. 71-77: my emphasis)

Speaking for the muted personage configured in the voiceless painting, the poet launches into a sixty-verse inventory that leaves no
doubt as to the king's innermost thoughts and the ability of Ronsard
and poetry to discern and convey them. Whether it involves Charles'
regret over inheriting so many political "malheurs" at such an early
age (vv. 77-88), or his disappointment at receiving his brother's
scepter but not his brother's wife (vv. 89-100); whether it concerns
his suffering as a premature victim of "Ce grand Amour" (vv. 101-
20), his despair that "La parenté" will forever prevent the satisfaction of his love (vv. 121-28), or his jealousy toward his brother, who
enjoyed the great but brief fortune to have "jouy d'une telle beauté"
(vv. 129-36)–every facet of thought and existence seems to fall within the epistemological and referential reach of the poet and his art.

The most explicit comment on this painting is also the last
major reflection on portraiture of Ronsard's career. It appears immediately after the poet demonstrates his ideational authority (we
cite the 1587 version of the *Elegie* for its singular clarity):

> De tels propos je parle pour mon maistre,
> Qui fait semblant en son Image d'estre
> Plein de souspirs, & voudroit s'efforcer:
> Mais hors des dents la voix ne peut passer:
> Le mort tableau luy oste la parolle,
> Et la peinture en larmes toute molle
> En devient palle, & retient la couleur
> De l'amoureux tout palle de douleur,
> Qui se tourmente, & par souspirs desire
> Estre entendu, & si ne le peut dire.
>
> (14:157-58, vv. 137-46)

However well the portrait may represent the physical symptoms of
Charles' suffering, especially his pallor (thanks to the "couleur" of
the painting), it could never give comprehensible presence to the
depth of his torment without the poet's intervention. In fact Charles
could never express his desire to be heard ("Estre entendu") because the picture has no voice and simply cannot utter it ("hors des
dents la voix ne peut passer . . . & ne le peut dire"). Hence, like the
portrait of Anne in the elegy examined earlier, the painting of the
juvenile king Charles is operatively "mort" in relation to the lifelike
figure presented by the poet.

* * *

Manifestly, the ambivalence toward portrait painting identified in the *Elegie à Janet* is by no means limited to that poem. It pervades all of Ronsard's poetic commentaries on the art of pictorial portraiture. The precise bases for that ambivalence are of greatest significance. Two desirable qualities dominate Ronsard's considerations. One corresponds to the natural-sign aesthetic defined and promoted by all the major painting theorists of the Renaissance: the ability of the portraitist to reproduce a convincing facsimile of the living subject's visible physical appearance. While Ronsard likewise acknowledges the painter's naturalistic aptitudes in his poetic evocations of narrative pictures, he is conspicuously more complimentary toward this virtue in the poems about portraiture. The second and most consequential laudable quality coincides with the emotionalist aesthetic of ekplexis recommended by Longinus in his treatise *On the Sublime*. It concerns the potential of a portrait to induce a profoundly gratifying or torturous experience of enthrallment or transformation in the viewer–whether that experience is intellectual and mnemonic or emotional and spiritual. In an exceptional move that brings him into unexpected agreement with such theoretical arch-adversaries as Alberti and Leonardo, Ronsard takes what once was a fundamentally rhetorical and poetic quality and includes it among the greatest possible achievements of painting, especially portrait painting, by virtue of its exceptional naturalistic accuracy.

On the other hand, Ronsard also continues to criticize portraiture for being semantically *muta*, intrinsically ill-suited to signify a person's essential being, his or her true inner Nature. Notwithstanding its physical accuracy, this art form therefore offers but a "shadow"–a "dead" version–of its living referent in the world. Conversely, the Pléiade laureate once more demonstrates that, because poems can "speak," they have none of the expressive limitations of portraits. Hence poetry again emerges as the winner in Ronsard's paragone with the pictorial arts. Yet unlike narrative painting, which lags far behind in the contest, the art of painted portraiture finishes a surprisingly strong second. The effect is to highlight Ronsard's penetrating understanding of the relations between words and images as well as to underscore his inability–or unwillingness–to escape the influence of the paragone debate's intrinsic double bind.

CONCLUSION

THE AMBIVALENCE RECONSIDERED

> Le maniérisme est une attitude complexuelle à
> l'égard du modèle–certains diront une attitude
> réellement complexée. L'imitation maniériste est
> la résultante d'un conflit: d'un côté, nous avons
> une déférence hyperbolisée à l'égard d'un maître
> (qui pourrait renvoyer à un complexe d'inférior-
> ité), et de l'autre des revendications indirectes
> d'autonomie. . . . (Claude-Gilbert Dubois, *Le
> Maniérisme,* 38)

> Ainsi du bon filz de Latonne
> Je raviray l'esprit à moy,
> Luy, du pouvoir que je luy donne
> Ravira les vostres à soy:
> Vous, par la force Apollinée
> Ravirez les Poëtes saincts,
> Eulx, de vostre puissance attaincts
> Raviront la tourbe estonnée.
>
> (*Ode à Michel de l'Hospital,*
> 3:142, vv. 413-20)

The contention between the "sister" arts of poetry and painting
is nowhere more striking than in the works of Pierre de Ronsard.
The Pléiade laureate's engagement in the paragone between the
rival siblings stands out not only for its duration, spanning virtually
the entire length of his forty-year career, but also for its practical
and philosophical scope, taking on the dominant two pictorial genres of the period, narrative painting and portraiture, while adapting
or challenging the broadest range of semiotic and aesthetic theories
of verbal and visual representation. Most remarkable of all, though,

240

is the ambivalence in Ronsard's deliberations. Certainly, his chief objectives change little throughout his writings. Above all, our poet aspires to confirm the semantic superiority of poems over pictures–the ability of the verbal to outperform the visual in signifying the physical and metaphysical verities of nature, humanity, and God. Thus, too, he seeks to establish the primacy of his art in the hierarchy of creative human endeavors and, in worldly regards, to secure himself and all 'true' poets a life of generous and lasting patronage. In the course of his contest-linked reflections, however, Ronsard also registers equivocations that would compromise the attainment of these goals. He expresses a measure of admiration that would contradict his otherwise consistently negative characterization of the painter's achievements. That esteem is especially salient in the contrasting evocations of narrative pictures and portraits. Whereas Ronsard pays only the most perfunctory tribute to story-based tableaux, preferring first to decry the semantic indeterminacy of those creations, he shows an intermittent willingness to waive that condemnation in the case of people pictures, electing instead to exalt these artworks for their ability to effect *ekplexis,* or enthrallment, in the viewer.

To some extent this ambivalence might relate to the aesthetic discourses of the past. As we have seen, ambiloquy is likewise a regular feature of the art-theoretical considerations of Plato, Aristotle, and their medieval and early modern heirs. Hence perhaps our laureate's vacillation is in part a consequence–whether conscious or unconscious–of his deep intellectual debt to these philosophers and, given that profound affinity, of his irrevocable membership in their august company.

Ronsard's ambivalence might further reflect an assent to the ethos of contradiction, tension, and rebellion against linear rationalism that distinguishes the "mannerist" mentality of the sixteenth century. This concurrence–whether intended or not–manifests particular strength in Ronsard's abiding affection for pictorial ekphraseis. Insofar as every painting description inscribes the contradictory mimetic desire of the word to resemble the natural-sign, *visual* Other while retaining its conventional-sign, *verbal* alterity, every such description precipitates the impulse to rivalry of the Girardian double bind. In turn, then, it would coincide with the "attitude maniériste" defined by Claude-Gilbert Dubois in *Le Maniérisme* (1979), his enduring elaboration on the 'mannerism of unresolved tension' originally advocated in the art-historical and literary-critical essays of Nikolaus Pevsner, Wylie Sypher, and Arnold Hauser.[1] Summoning many of the same socio-psychological principles employed by René Girard in earlier studies of human conflict, Dubois proposes that all true mannerist creation proceeds from the fundamental ambition of mankind—and hence of the artist—to "réfléchir le modèle," to be "un miroir réfléchissant."[2] In mannerism, however, this mimetic pursuit simultaneously inscribes an "allégeance subversive," an unfaithful fidelity wherein the imitator interacts with the imitated as the slave relates to the master (for Hegel) or as the son responds to the father (for Freud)—that is, with feelings of intense veneration countervailed by sentiments of ardent defiance (see our first epigraph, above). Accordingly, whenever Ronsard's painting ekphraseis present detectable equivocations, they may merely bear open the ambivalence that is their irrepressible inner nature. Further, they may thereby show Ronsard for what he truly is (if only throughout his ekphrastic parogone poetry): one of the premier mannerist authors of his day.[3]

On another level, this ambivalence might also be the trace of an irrepressible preference for portraiture over narrative paintings. This deference may be partially explained from various biographical and sociological perspectives. In one respect, for instance, Ronsard's fervent dislike of the Italian expatriates in France might have played a part. After all, unlike the leading portraitists in his country,

---

[1] Nikolaus Pevsner, "The Architecture of Mannerism," *The Mint* 1 (1946): 116-37: republished in *Readings in Art History*, vol. 2, ed. Harold Spencer (New York: Scribner's, 1969), 119-48; Wylie Sypher, *Four Stages of Renaissance Style* (1955; reprint New York: Anchor Books, 1965); Arnold Hauser, *The Social History of Art*, vol. 2 (New York: Vintage Books, 1957), and *Mannerism: The Crisis of the Renaissance and the Origin of Modern Art*, 2 vols., trans. Eric Mosbacher (New York: Alfred A. Knopf, 1965). Useful summaries of these and other essays on 'tension' mannerism appear in James V. Mirollo, *Mannerism*, 1-65, and Franklin W. Robinson and Stephen G. Nichols, Jr., eds., *The Meaning of Mannerism* (Hanover: University Press of New England, 1972).

[2] Dubois, *Le Maniérisme*, 25.

[3] As I have noted in my article, "Mannerist Conflict and the *Paragone* in Ronsard's *Temple de Messeigneurs*" (10), Dubois resists such an assertion about Ronsard in his 1979 book on mannerism. It should be added that he comes only slightly closer to that finding in his 1984 "Problems of 'Representation'." Thanks to the present conclusion, however, we now have a socio-psychological basis for identifying Ronsard as a mannerist that may complement the formalist contention to that effect from critics like Marcel Raymond and R. A. Sayce.

who were typically of French or Flemish origins,[4] the foremost narrative painters of mid-sixteenth-century France were transplants from war-torn Italy. Notwithstanding the contributions to the genre by French masters like Jean Cousin and Antoine Caron, story painting was still the principal province of the Italians who lead the 'school' of artists at Fontainebleau: Il Rosso, Primaticcio, and Nicolò dell'Abate. Their cultural 'invasion' would hardly have left Ronsard indifferent. Despite his deep-seated and often frankly avowed debt to the "divine" poets of Rome and early modern Italy, Ronsard was as much an advocate of *translatio studii* as Guillaume Budé, Jean Lemaire, and Joachim du Bellay.[5] Like his countrymen, the *Gaulois Apollon* held zealously to the fantasy that France was the single proper heir to the paramount human triumphs of the past, and for that reason, France should be the only legitimate beacon of learning and culture (to say nothing of socio-economic, political, and religious authority) for the present and beyond. Although he often expresses his disappointment with the harsh realities of life in his country,[6] Ronsard never abandons the belief, distilled in the 1549 *Hymne de France,* that "Jupiter" loyally preserves the preeminence of the French ancestors of Hector, the one and only "race legitime" (1:30, v. 120).

In addition, Ronsard harbored a singular personal disdain for the Italians who, with the consent or urging of Catherine de Médicis, had come to occupy an unusually prominent place in the courts of Henri II and Charles IX. This sentiment looms especially vitriolic in his *Au Tresorier de l'espargne,* an epistle from the early 1570s that remained unpublished until the *Œuvres* of 1604. Addressing Nicolas Moreau, the treasurer of France from 1571-1586, the poet

---

[4] Although born in France, François Clouet was often associated with the Low Countries, both for his style and because his father, Jean Clouet (the first "Janet"), was born somewhere in Flanders about 1485 and never received formal citizenship, despite a long and distinguished career in the service of François I from 1516 (when his name first appeared on the Royal Accounts) until his death in 1541. For more on the life of Jean Clouet, see Mellen, *Jean Clouet*, 10-16.

[5] For more on this topos and the early modern French authors who sought to deconstruct the "voyage" to Ancient and early modern Rome, see Eric Macphail, *The Voyage to Rome in French Renaissance Literature,* Stanford French and Italian *Studies* 68 (Saratoga: Anma Libri, 1990).

[6] Cf. the two 1562 *Discours des Miseres de ce Temps* (11:19-60), the 1563 *Remonstrance au peuple de France* (11:63-106), and the 1564 *Compleinte à la Royne mere du Roy* (12:172-88).

takes a deliberate swipe at "Les vrays corbeaux ravisseurs de nos biens" (18:301, v. 28), the rapacious Italian courtiers who receive "les plus gras benefices, / Daces, imposts, & les meilleurs offices" (18:302, vv. 41-42) at the expense of the more worthy Frenchmen, who are admonished to take satisfaction in a mere "Attendez" (18:302, v. 44), the hope of a promise deferred. [7]

In a related regard, Ronsard's contrasting attitudes cannot be divorced from the realities of artistic and literary patronage at the time. If the dominant French portrait painters collected respectable incomes and privileges, the major Italian narrative painters, who participated centrally in the planning and adornment of the King's edifices, were all the more liberally remunerated. According to the Royal Accounts of 1540, for example, François Clouet inherited his father's (Jean Clouet's) annual salary of 240 livres, [8] whereas the iconographic designer of the bellifontine Galerie François I, "maistre Rousse de Roux [Il Rosso Fiorentino], paintre, maistre conducteur desdits ouvrages de stucq et painture de ladite grande gallerie," earned 50 livres per month, or an anticipated 600 livres for the year. [9] Likewise, the 1560 ledgers of the royal treasurer Jean Durant record an award to "messire Francisque de Primadicis [Francesco Primaticcio] de Boulongne" totaling "1,200 liv[res]" for his annual "gages." [10] The latter's wages would have been far more apt to pique the vanity of our Pléiade laureate, who received an equivalent income in 1560, than the comparably modest earnings of the portraitists. [11]

The salaries of the Italian narrative painters tell only part of the story. Considerable though these wages may have been, they

---

[7] Cf. *Ronsard au Roy Charles IXe* (18:405, vv. 27-28; 408, vv. 91-92), a satirical ode to Charles IX dating from the same period as the epistle *Au Tresorier*, yet whose publication is delayed nearly three centuries, until Prosper Blanchemain grants it a place in his 1855 *Œuvres inédites de Ronsard*. The laureate's complaints against the Italian courtiers, otherwise designated as "les hommes estrangers," is likewise apparent in the 1564 *Compleinte à la Royne mere du Roy* (12:181, vv. 179-84). Cf. also, the allusion to the profusion of new "potirons" (mushrooms) at court in the 1560 *Elegie au seigneur l'Huillier* (10:296-97, vv. 79-90). The special case of the Italian artists is taken up below.

[8] Mellen, *Jean Clouet*, 13, 80.

[9] Laborde, "Comptes des bâtiments royaux," in *Renaissance*, 1:402.

[10] Laborde, *Renaissance*, 1:484

[11] Cf. Weber, *Création poétique*, 31. Beginning in 1556, the account books of Bertrand Le Picart and Jean Durant report similarly generous salaries and compensations for Nicolò dell'Abate and Ruggiero de Ruggieri (Laborde, *Renaissance*, 1:444 ff).

drained but a fraction of the riches poured into subsidizing the palaces that housed the Italianate pictorial narratives. In yet another account book, Nicolas Picart chronicles a total payment of "448,723 livres 3 sous" for work done at Fontainebleau between January 1540 and September 1550.[12] Thus it is no surprise when, in the epistolary hymn *A tresillustre prince Charles, Cardinal de Lorraine* of the 1556 *Second livre des Hymnes,* Ronsard feels the need to challenge the royal agenda that forgoes his *Franciade,* an "oeuvre laborieux" (8:344, v. 386), and other poetic ambitions in favor of "un tableau basty par un art otieux" (8:344, v. 385) and so many extravagant buildings designed and decorated by the foreign (i.e., Italian) painters: "Je ne scaurois penser que des peintres estranges / Meritent tant que nous, les postes des loüenges . . ." (8:344, vv. 383-84).

Ronsard's resentment scarcely abates with time. Even after Charles IX acquiesces to his appeals for the capital to pursue his promised epic, the poet cannot resist taking the royal family to task for squandering the national treasure on ventures like the Bourbon's castle at Moulins and the Tuileries Palace. Once more his epistle to the King's treasurer, Nicolas Moreau, is revealing. In this instance, Ronsard juxtaposes the abstract idea of material impermanence (in one of the few late reprises of the *exegi monumentum* topos) with charges of cheating by the rival painters and their artisan associates. Assumptions that the Tuileries will be "deshabité" and without "fenestre ny salle, / Leton entier, corniche ny ovalle" before "cent ans" have passed (18:302, vv. 52-53) are adjoined to suspicions that, even as he writes, the "Peintres" of the Tuileries are conspiring with the project's "Maçons, Engraveurs, Entailleurs" to "Succe[r] l'espargne avec leurs piperies . . ." (18:302, vv. 48-49). It is important to recall that the chief paintings for such edifices were primarily of the narrative type that the foremost practitioner of the genre in 1573 was still an Italian: Francesco Primaticcio's colleague and successor, Nicolò dell'Abate. Moreover, even though Ronsard writes this poem some three years after Primaticcio's death (on 14 September 1570), he would hardly have forgotten that the Bolognese had held the prestigious position of "abbé de Saint Martin de Troyes, conseiller et ausmonier ordinaire du Roy et superintendant des bastimens et édiffices de Sa Majesté"

---

[12] Laborde, *Renaissance,* 1:434.

since 1559.[13] In that post, the Italian master played a key role in all
the major building operations in France throughout the 1560s. In
the words of Louis Dimier, "D'une façon générale, comme le Primatice avait la main sur tous les châteaux de la couronnne, on ne
fit rien pendant dix ans dans ces châteaux, dont il n'eût l'ordon-
nance."[14] What is more, Primaticcio was regularly poised to solicit
large sums of money in response to the demands of his work force
and creditors. Appeals like the one to Catherine de Médicis in a
Fontainebleau letter dated 24 April 1565, in which the supervisor
of royal constructions requests a substantial increase in an already
generous building allocation of thirty thousand Francs,[15] would
only have fueled Ronsard's misgivings about the financial dealings
of his Italian painter counterparts.

The poet's preference for portraiture, like his willingness to
multiply all portrait references (favorable and unfavorable), might
also represent a concession to the extraordinary popularity of this
pictorial genre during the second third of the sixteenth century. As
previously mentioned, portraiture had at last regained the ardent
appreciation it knew in Antiquity, and Ronsard would have been
hard-pressed to resist this wave of enthusiasm in his poetry.

But even if he had ignored the tide of public opinion, our laureate could scarcely have disregarded the deference that grew from
his own personal acquaintance with the portraitists and the portrait
pictures of his day. We have witnessed abundant evidence of this fa-

---

[13] Laborde, *Renaissance* 1:530-31.

[14] Louis Dimier, *Le Primatice* (Paris: Albin Michel, 1928), 64.

[15] "Par la lettre de Votre Majesté du 15 de février, j'ai compris que les trente
mille francs étaient pour les bâtiments [all royal edifices], et les dix mille pour la
sépulture [the St-Denis tomb for the Queen, her husband, and her children], bien
qu'à ce que m'a dit le trésorier des Bâtiments, les dix mille de la sépulture ne
doivent être prêts qu'à la fin de l'année; ce qui m'est de grande conséquence, parce
que je me veux mettre en peine non seulement de voir la fin de la dette, mais, s'il
m'était possible, m'y hâter. Un mot de Votre Majesté peut faire que Monsieur de
l'Épargne nous ordonne tout de suite nos paiements; car je ne voudrais pas (comme
il a fallu faire l'an passé) avoir à prendre sur les bâtiments pour donner à la sépulture. Si Votre Majesté savait de combien de côtés il faut que je me tourne et répar-
tisse les dépenses des bâtiments, les trente mille francs ordonnés à cet effet lui
paraîtraient fort peu de chose; car, comme plusieurs fois j'ai dû le lui écrire, il y a
maintenant partout besoin de réparation, et celui qui m'a précédé [Philibert De-
lorme] y a laissé tant de dettes que j'en ai presque honte: lesquelles dettes, moyen-
nant la recommandation de ceux qui y sont propres et la prière de grands personnages, il faut se mettre à même d'éteindre peu à peu, sinon j'irai à la male grâce du
monde, et passerai pour turc ou pour juif": Dimier, *Le Primatice*, 91.

miliarity and (tempered) fondness in the *Elegie à Janet*, sonnet CCVIII of the 1553 *Amours*, the *Elegie* to Marie Stuart, and of course, in the multiple pieces to or about his poet-painter friend Nicolas Denisot du Mans. It is similarly manifest outside of his poetic writings. In his speech "De la joie et de la tristesse," delivered before Henri III during a meeting or banquet of the *Académie du Palais* shortly after the King established that institute (an extension of Baïf's and Courville's *Académie de poésie et de musique*) at the Louvre in 1575,[16] Ronsard alludes approvingly to the "Flaman," the famous Flemish-born portraitist Corneille de Lyon.[17] In terms that parallel his versified praises of portraiture, the author commends "un excellent tableau" by this artist for its symmetrically proportioned colors and lines, and for a resulting "air et perspicacité qui *vous contraint soudain de l'admirer*, et *tout ravy* le contempler et atacher vos yeux sur la peinture, [de sorte que] telle peinture . . . *vous esmeut et agite amyablement et doucement* le sens de la vue" (18:474-75: my emphasis).

Ronsard's knowledge of Corneille was undoubtedly shaped, in part, by the literary and anecdotal testimonies of his contemporaries. As we have seen from sonnet XXXIV of the 1552 *Amours*, for instance, he certainly knew of Pontus de Tyard's reference to this painter in sonnet LXV of the 1549 *Erreurs amoureuses*. Despite the "ombre" remark, which Ronsard revives in his complaints against Denisot's Cassandre portrait, Tyard explicitly ranks the *Flaman* "du nombre / Des plus expers excellens [portraitists] de nostre aage" (vv. 5-6),[18] Concerning the Palace Academy speech in particular, Roger Gaucheron has suggested that our laureate may also have wanted to "faire discrètement allusion" to the reports of Catherine de Médicis' reaction when, during a visit to the painter's

---

[16] Roger Gaucheron, "Un Discours inédit de Ronsard," *Mercure de France* 176 (1924): 604-13. This "Discours" was subsequently reedited by Silver and Lebègue and included in Laumonier's *Œuvres Complètes*, 18:470-79. For more on Ronsard's affiliation with the Palace Academy, see Frances Yates, *The French Academies of the Sixteenth Century* (London: Warburg Institute, 1947), 27-35, 141-42. See also, Binet, *Vie de Ronsard*, 49-50, n. 1.

[17] Corneille de Lyon has been studied, in varying degrees, by a number of art historians. See especially, Dimier, *Peinture*, 1:32-40, 2:58-72; Bouchot, *Les Clouet*, 39-51; Sylvie Béguin, "Corneille de Lyon," in *Le XVIe Siècle Européen: Peintures et Dessins dans les Collections Publiques Françaises*, ed. Roseline Bacou, et al., 2nd edition (Paris: Réunion des Musées Nationaux, 1966), 68-69; Blunt, *Art and Architecture*, 119-20. See also, Laborde, *Renaissance*, 1:76-78, 144-45 (n. 2).

[18] See Chapter Three, 209-10. Cf. Yates, *Academies*, 139.

Lyon studio, she discovered an unsolicited group portrait featuring herself and her three daughters as they appeared in the early 1550s. According to Brantôme's account of the event, the Queen "prit fort grand plaisir à cette veue et . . . s'y ravist en la contemplation si bien qu'elle n'en peust retirer ses yeux de dessus." [19] It is equally likely, however, that Ronsard enjoyed many firsthand encounters with the Flaman's pictures. Given his regular association with the court personnages who comprised the artist's main subjects and most faithful clients, contact with Corneille's paintings and drawings was all but inevitable. [20] And as a reader of Tyard's *Erreurs*, our poet would almost surely have seen and admired the portraitist's medallion engraving of "Pasithée" printed after the title page of the *canzoniere* (fig. 20).

From a properly literary and aesthetic perspective, on the other hand, the complimentary treatment of portraiture may connect, in some measure, to Ronsard's well-known Ovidian and Anacreontic sensualization of the Neoplatonic and Petrarchan topoi of love. Perhaps, that is, Ronsard detected a stronger voluptuousness in early modern figure painting than critics like Plattard have allowed; and because this carnal quality appealed to the sensibilities he sought to privilege in his poetry, he was moved to assign an inalienable worth to portraiture. This conclusion is encouraged in the anti-Neoplatonic sonnet XII of the 1578 *Sonets & Madrigals pour Astree*. While pondering the best means to nurture the bonds of amorous servitude, the poet insists that true satisfaction in love comes only when *agape* is supplemented with a fusion of the flesh.

---

[19] Brantôme writes of this and similar meetings, where the remarks were no less complimentary, in his essay on Catherine de Médicis in the *Vie des Dames illustres* (*Œuvres complètes*, ed. Ludovic Lalanne, vol. 7 [Paris: Mme. Ve. Jules Renouard, 1864], 343-44). Brantôme's comments are repeated in Laborde, *Renaissance*, 1:76-77, and Gaucheron, "Un Discours inédit," 606. Corneille de Lyon's other mid-century venerators include Jean Second (*Iter Gallicum*), Eustorge de Beaulieu (*Divers rapports* [1544], rondeau LXVIII), and Borghini (*Il Riposo* [ed. 1584]): cf. Dimier, *Portrait*, 35, 39.

[20] Dimier notes that, despite his geographical connection to Lyon, the majority of Corneille's known pictures depict court models: "Chose remarquable, on ne voit peindre à Corneille, presque aucun personnage de la société de Lyon, où il vivait établi. Ses modèles sont à la cour." (*Portrait*, 33). Through his dealings with François de Bourbon-Enghien (cf. Chapter Three, 217-21), for example, Ronsard may well have seen Corneille's portrait of François' younger brother, Jean, painted circa 1550, before his death at the battle of Saint-Quentin in 1557 (see Béguin, "Corneille de Lyon," *XVIe Siècle*, 68, fig. 83).

FIG. 20: Corneille de Lyon, *Pasithée* (1549). From Pontus de Tyard, *Erreurs amoureuses* (1555) (verso of the title page), Paris (cliché Bibliothèque Nationale de France)

When this corporal alliance becomes impossible due to the physical absence of the beloved (here the mysterious Astrée [21]), however, a painted portrait may make a contribution toward realizing that end: "Il faut avoir de l'amy le portrait, / Cent fois le jour en rebaiser le traict: / Que d'un plaisir deux ames soient guidees" (17:190, vv. 9-11).

The idea of the portrait as an interim substitute for the beloved also arises in regard to the poet's last mistress, Hélène de Surgères, in sonnet XX of the 1578 *Premier livre des Sonets pour Helene*. Because "l'esprit ne sent rien que par l'ayde du corps" (17:213, v. 14), and all portraits distill the essence of the sitter's visible physicality, the imagined painting would remain a tantalizing proxy empowered to heighten the poet's hope for a carnal union, "un baiser doucement amoureux" (17:212, v. 2), with the emotionally and physically distant *bien-aimée*: "Si j'avois le portrait de vostre belle face, / Las! je demande trop! ou bien de vos cheveux, / Content de mon malheur je serois bienheureux, / Et ne voudrois changer aux celestes de place" (17:213, vv. 5-8).

A revealing though seldom recognized intertext for this poem is Louise Labé's "Oh! si j'étais en ce beau sein ravie," sonnet XIII of the 1555 *Œuvres poétiques*. The resemblances and differences between these sonnets efface all ambiguity about Ronsard's position on love. Like the "Belle Cordière," the Pléiade laureate implicitly repudiates the Neoplatonists and (to a lesser extent) the orthodox Petrarchans by reaffirming the value of the "baiser" in the amorous adventure. For both authors, no real love is possible without a measure of intimate carnal contact. Yet whereas the Lyonnaise continues to consider the physical as a means to an end, a way to procure an "heur" (contentment) that transcends corporeality and presupposes the "mort" of one's individual identity in a Neoplatonic merging of souls, [22] Ronsard views sensuality as an end in itself, as its own reward, because the pleasure of Eros belongs as much to

---

[21] "Astrée" is generally identified as Françoise d'Estrées, the mother of Gabrielle d'Estrées, mistress of the future Henri IV. For more on "Astrée" and Françoise d'Estrées, see Pierre Champion, *Ronsard et son temps* (1925: rpt. Paris: Champion, 1967), esp. 279-84.

[22] "Si, de mes bras le tenant accolé, / Comme du lierre est l'arbre encerclé, / La mort venait, de mon aise envieuse, / Lors que souef plus il me baiserait, / Et mon esprit sur ses lèvres fuirait, / Bien je mourrais, plus que vivante, heureuse": Louise Labé, *Œuvres poétiques*, ed. Françoise Charpentier (Paris: Gallimard, 1983), 121, vv. 9-14.

the physical "corps" as it does to the metaphysical "esprit."[23] It is for this reason that a portrait of Hélène's "belle face" (or her "cheveux" alone) can afford some satisfaction. Indeed, physicality is so desirable that, in the present sonnet, it prompts Ronsard to approve the worthiness of *les yeux* and the experience of visible reality in open disregard for the protests against sight (and the visible *dehors*) that he levels in the majority of paragone commentaries. Lamenting his lack of a tangible memento of Hélène, the poet concedes that something as dear to his eyes as a portrait has the potential to console in a profound degree: "je n'ay rien de vous que je puisse emporter, / Qui soit cher à mes yeux pour me reconforter" (17:213, vv. 9-10).

Notwithstanding this move toward an appreciation of portraiture, Ronsard shows little inclination to mitigate his contempt for narrative painting. While poems such as *A son Luc*, the *Temple de Messeigneurs*, and *La Lyre* plainly attest to his awareness of the sensual triumphs of story pictures, our laureate is tenacious in condemning their overall worth and capabilities. Personal resentments may account for a basic disposition to denounce, but the theoretical and philosophical principles summoned to sustain his attacks signal the overarching influence of a more substantive trepidation.

Without a doubt, Ronsard would have been especially concerned that narrative painting should presume to represent myth and history. This pictorial genre thereby posed a direct threat to the poetry that occupies the summit of his devoutly defended hierarchy of the arts. Similar to the "Theologie allegoricque" and the "Poëme

---

[23] Both the concept of the kiss and the concept of physical love have a common antecedent in the 1539 *Basia* of the Flemish-born poet, Jean Second. Yet where Labé takes primary inspiration from Second's *Basium* II, "Vicina quantum vitis lascivit in ulmo" ("As the vine runs wild with its neighbor the elm"), which stresses the spiritual joy to succeed the kissing lovers' double *death*, Ronsard seems to follow *Basium* XVI, "Latonae niveo sidere blandior" ("More charming than the snowy star of Latona"), a *carpe diem* piece whose focus is the corporeal pleasure that kissing makes possible *in life*. See Jean Second, *Le Livre des baisers*, trans. Thierry Sandre (Paris: Renaudot & Cie., 1989), 28-31, 64-69. As the Webers have noted (*Amours*, 731), Ronsard's explicit validation of the "corps" may also be traced to Marot's 1535 *Blasons du corps féminin* and the final verses of the anonymous poem, "Le Corps": "Car l'esprit, il n'a que le penser, / Sans corps ne peult ou plaire ou offenser / Parquoy le corps est maistre des effectz, / Qui nous font tous parfaictz, ou imparfaictz" (vv. 75-78; in *Poètes du XVIe Siècle*, ed. Albert-Marie Schmidt [Paris: Gallimard, 1953], 347).

Heroïque" perfected by the "divine poets" of Antiquity and resurrected in his own odes, elegies, hymns, and epic *Franciade*, narrative
painting would strive to signify the very mythological and quasi-his-
torical subjects which, by virtue of their prodigious complexity and
profound didactic content, comprise the noblest of all artistic topics. Different from the supreme order of poetry, however, narrative
painting would invariably fall short of realizing its lofty ambition.
For Ronsard, this art form would be overwhelmed by the complexity of its subjects, and so impeded from fulfilling their ideational
promise, by virtue of its vision-bound, synchronic and natural signifiers. At best, then, story painting would achieve a veritable muddle
of meanings, succumb to the chaotic semiosic drift, and in so doing,
invite charges of incompetence, and even negligence and indolence,
against the narrative painter. It is no coincidence that this last reproach is included in the hymn to Charles de Lorraine. To culmi-
nate his complaints against the Italians' unfair advantage in matters
of patronage, Ronsard pointedly contrasts the "tableau basty par un
art *otieux*," the narrative picture constructed by a *lazy* (for Cotgrave, "idle") art, with his "Franciade, oeuvre *laborieux*," a creation
that the posthumous preface to the epic tellingly ascribes to the
"Poëte bien advisé, plein de *laborieuse* industrie"–i.e., to the artist
whose divine talents and powerful verbal medium enable him to
produce a *carefully constructed* work whose "dernier acte . . . se
cole, se lie & s'enchesne si bien & si à propos l'un dedans l'autre,
que la fin se rapporte dextrement & artificiellement au premier
poinct de l'argument." [24] In other terms, narrative painting would
fail to achieve the kind of *copieuse diversité* that Ronsard so strongly
endorses throughout his poetic evocations of story pictures: the
copia of the Neoplatonic *discordia concors* which, like the original
multiple Oneness of God, is simultaneously a discordant multiplicity and a comprehensible harmonious unity. [25]

    Painted portraiture, on the other hand, posed no such threat to
our poet's theoretical creed. It was free from the grandiose aspirations of narrative painting and thus too from the profound short-

---

[24] For more on the *Franciade* preface, see Chapter Two, 135-36. The link between chaos and idleness is more explicitly drawn in Ronsard's love poetry: cf. the
"Chaos otieux" of Amour in sonnet XLII of the 1552 *Amours* (4:45).
    [25] Malcolm Quainton presents an authoritative examination of the cosmic and
social dimensions of Ronsard's *discordia concors* and the concept of an ordered
copia in his *Ronsard's Ordered Chaos* (7-30 and passim).

comings of that art. Indeed, for these reasons and all those stated previously, portrait painting afforded the Pléiade laureate a unique opportunity to advance an essential yet often critically undervalued inflection in his poetic and aesthetic theory. Whereas story painting supplied a foil against which Ronsard could reaffirm his well-known (Neo-)Platonic notion of the *poeta vates*, of the poet as a prophet whose charge to translate and transmit divine truth privileges the *semantic* plenitude of words, portraiture provided an analogue through which to exemplify his less-remembered Longinian tenet of the artist as an *auctor stuporis*, a creator of *ekplexis*, whose obligation to precipitate enthrallment stresses the *affective* capacity of poems and pictures. This connection in no way implies that Ronsard never takes up the emotive capacity of poetry outside of his portrait poems; nor does it deny the fact that, prior to 1554, his emotionalist aesthetic took inspiration from authors other than Longinus. Jupiter's promise to the Muses in Strophe 13 of the 1552 *Ode à Michel de l'Hospital* (vv. 413-20: see the second epigraph, above) clearly shows that the poet's power to "ravir la tourbe estonnée" would occasionally figure as a major theme where painting is of no discernible interest and where the principal subtexts for the idea are still the proto-Longinian concepts of ecstasy (for Plato) and rapture (for the Neoplatonists).[26]

Such noteworthy instances notwithstanding, portraiture would alone bring out the true significance of this inflection in Ronsardian poetics. Only in respect to figure painting does enthrallment man ifest itself as one of our laureate's most enduring preoccupations–if merely because the poems about that art arrive regularly at all stages of his career. Solely in this regard, too, do we fully understand the lofty place of this notion in Ronsard's order of outstanding poetic attributes–particularly as its presence in the verses on portraits invariably elevates it to an equal (but antithetical) footing with the cardinal poetic principles staged in the narrative-painting poems. And only by virtue of its connection with portraiture does ekplexis stand out as the common ground on which Ronsard may ultimately consent to concur with paragone arch-rivals like Leonar-

---

[26] In the first case, see Laumonier's textual note (3:142, n. 2), which identifies the inspiration for Strophe 13 as Plato's remark on the ecstatic impact of artistic madness in the *Ion* (albeit with none of the philosopher's original irony); in both cases, see above, Chapter One, # 72, and Chapter Three, 202-03.

do da Vinci, for whom (we recall) the figure painter's art furnishes a similarly privileged context in which to promote the aesthetic merits of enthrallment. On the basis of the ekplexis invoked in the portrait poems, it appears that Ronsard has taken a step toward accepting the spirit of ut pictura poesis: he seems to have moved closer to recognizing an underlying parity between poetry and painting. But as we have also seen, he never openly embraces that spirit: our poet never candidly admits to an inter-art equivalence. Hence Ronsard's ambivalence toward painting continues, and the tension of his "attitude maniériste" survives in the absence of a lasting truce between his inveterately contentious sisters.

SELECT BIBLIOGRAPHY

(A) EDITIONS OF RONSARD'S WORKS

Ronsard, Pierre de. *Œuvres complètes.* Ed. Paul Laumonier, Isidore Silver and Raymond Lebègue. 20 vols. Paris: Hachette (STFM), 1914-1975.
———. "Un discours inédit de Ronsard." Ed. Roger Gaucheron. *Mercure de France* 636 (December 1924): 604-13.
———. *Œuvres complètes.* Ed. Gustave Cohen. 2 vols. Paris: Gallimard (Pléiade), 1950.
———. *Les Odes de Ronsard.* Ed. Charles Guérin. Paris: Cèdre, 1952.
———. *Les Amours de Pierre de Ronsard.* Ed. Henri Weber and Catherine Weber. Paris: Garnier, 1963.
———. *Les Œuvres de Pierre de Ronsard: Texte de 1587.* Ed. Isidore Silver. 7 vols. Chicago; University of Chicago Press for Washington University Press, 1967.

(B) OTHER EDITIONS

Alberti, Leon Battista. *On Painting and On Sculpture: The Latin Texts of "De Pictura" and "De Statua."* Ed. and trans. Cecil Grayson. London: Phaidon Press Ltd., 1972.
———. *Della pittura.* In *Opere Volgari.* Ed. Cecil Grayson. Vol. 3. Bari: G. Laterza & Figli, 1973.
Anacreon. *The Anacreontea and Principal Remains of Anacreon of Teos.* Trans. and ed. Judson France Davidson. New York: Dutton, 1915.
Aquinas, Thomas. *Summa Theologiae.* Blackfriars. 60 vols. New York: McGraw-Hill Book Co., 1964.
Ariosto, Ludovico. *Orlando Furioso.* Ed. Santorre Debenedetti. Vol. 3. Bari: Gius. Laterza & Figli, 1928.
———. *Sir John Harington's Translation of "Orlando Furioso" by Lodovico Ariosto.* Ed. Graham Hough. Carbondale: Southern Illinois University Press, 1962.
Aristotle. *The "Art" of Rhetoric.* Trans. John Henry Freese. London: William Heinemann, 1926.
———. *The Poetics.* In *Aristotle: "The Poetics"; "Longinus": "On the Sublime"; Demetrius: "On Style."* Trans. W. Hamilton Fyfe. Rev. ed. London: William Heinemann Ltd., 1932.
———. *Politics.* Trans. H. Rackham. London: William Heinemann Ltd., 1932.

Aristotle. *The Poetics*. In *Aristotle's Theory of Poetry and Fine Art, with a Critical Text and Translation of the "Poetics"*. New York: Dover Publications, Inc., 1951.

————. *Parts of Animals*. Trans. A. L. Peck. Cambridge, Mass.: Harvard University Press, 1955.

————. *Posterior Analytics*. Trans. Hugh Tredennick. Cambridge, Mass.: Harvard University Press, 1960.

————. *On the Art of Poetry*. Trans. Ingram Bywater. 1920. Reprint, Oxford: Oxford University Press, 1990.

Baïf, Jean-Antoine de. *Amours de Meline*. In *Evvres en rime de Ian Antoine de Baïf*. Vol. 1. Ed. Charles Marty-Laveaux. Geneva: Slatkine, 1965.

Binet, Claude. *La Vie de P. de Ronsard* (1586). Ed. Paul Laumonier. 1909. Reprint, Geneva: Slatkine, 1969.

Brantôme (Bourdeilles, Pierre de). *Vie des Dames illustres. Catherine de Médicis*. In *Œuvres Complètes*. Ed. Ludovic Lalanne. Vol. 7. Paris: Mme. Ve. Jules Renouard, 1864.

Cellini, Benvenuto. *The Life of Benvenuto Cellini*. Trans. John Addington Symonds. 2nd ed. New York: Charles Scribner's Sons, 1920.

————. *Vita*. Ed. Ettore Camesasca. Milan: Rizzoli, 1954.

Cennini, Cennino. *Il Libro dell'Arte*. Ed. and trans. Daniel V. Thompson, Jr. 2 vols. New Haven: Yale University Press, 1932.

Dante Alighieri. *The Banquet*. Trans. Christopher Ryan. Stanford: Anma Libri, 1989.

————. *Il Convivio*. Ed. Maria Simonelli. Bologna: Casa Editrice Prof. Riccardo Patron, 1966.

————. *The Divine Comedy: Purgatory*. Trans. Louis Biancolli. New York: Washington Square Press, 1966.

————. *The Divine Comedy*. Trans. Charles S. Singleton. Bollingen Series 80. Princeton: Princeton University Press, 1970-75.

————. *Literary Criticism of Dante Alighieri*. Trans. and ed. Robert S. Haller. Lincoln: University of Nebraska Press, 1973.

Da Vinci, Leonardo. *The Literary Works of Leonardo da Vinci*. Ed. Jean Paul Richter. 3rd edition. 2 vols. London: Phaidon Press Ltd., 1970.

————. *The Notebooks of Leonardo da Vinci*. Ed. Jean Paul Richter. 1883. Reprint, New York: Dover, 1970.

Dolce, Lodovico. *Dolce's "Aretino" and Venetian Art Theory of the Cinquecento*. Trans. and ed. Mark W. Roskill. New York: New York University Press, 1968.

Du Bellay, Joachim. *La Deffence et Illustration de la langue francoyse*. Ed. Henri Chamard. Paris: Marcel Didier, 1948.

Ficino, Marsilio. *Marsilio Ficino and the Phaedran Charioteer*. Trans. and ed. Michael J. B. Allen. Berkeley: University of California Press, 1981.

————. *Opera Omnia*. "In Timaeum Commentarium." 1576. Reprint, Turin: Bottega d'Erasmo, 1959, 1983.

The Greek Anthology in France. Trans. W. R. Paton. 5 vols. London: William Heinemann, 1927.

————. Ed. James Hutton. Ithaca: Cornell University Press, 1946.

Hermes Trismegistos. *Hermetica*. Trans. Brian P. Copenhaver. Cambridge: Cambridge University Press, 1992.

The Holy Bible. Ed. Herbert G. May and Bruce M. Metzger. New York: Oxford University Press, 1962.

Homer. *The Iliad*. Trans. and ed. Richmond Lattimore. Chicago: University of Chicago Press, 1951.

Horace (Quintus Horatius Flaccus). *Satires, Epistles and Ars Poetica*. Trans. H. Rushton Fairclough. London: William Heinemann Ltd., 1936.

Horace (Quintus Horatius Flaccus). *The Odes and Epodes*. Trans. Charles E. Bennett. Cambridge, Mass.: Harvard University Press, 1964.

Horapollo. *The Hieroglyphics of Horapollo*. Trans. George Boas. Bollingen Series 23. New York: Pantheon Books Inc., 1950.

Joubert, Laurent. *Traité du ris suivi d'un dialogue sur la cacographie française (1579)*. Geneva: Slatkine Reprints, 1973.

Landino, Christoforo. *Dante con l'espositione di Christoforo Landino, et di Alessandro Vellutello*. Venice: Appresso Giouambattista, Marchio Seba & Fratelli, 1564.

Le Caron, Louis. *Dialogues*. Eds. Joan A. Buhlmann and Donald Gilman. Geneva: Droz, 1986.

Longinus. *On the Sublime*. Ed. W. Rhys Roberts. Cambridge: University Press, 1907.

———. *On the Sublime*. In *Aristotle: "The Poetics"; "Longinus": "On the Sublime"; Demetrius: "On Style."* Trans. W. Hamilton Fyfe. Rev. ed. London: William Heinemann Ltd., 1932.

———. *On the Sublime*. Ed. D. A. Russell. Oxford: Clarendon Press, 1964.

Lucian. *Essays in Portraiture*. In *The Works of Lucian*. Ed. and trans. Austin Morris Harmon. Vol. 4. London: William Heinemann Ltd., 1925.

———. *Essays in Portraiture Defended*. In *The Works of Lucian*. Ed. and trans. Austin Morris Harmon. Vol. 4. London: William Heinemann Ltd., 1925.

Marot, Clément. *Blasons du corps féminin*. In *Poètes du XVIe Siècle*. Ed. Albert-Marie Schmidt. Paris: Gallimard, 1953.

Muret, Marc-Antoine de. *Commentaires au premier livre des "Amours" de Ronsard*. *Travaux d'Humanisme et Renaissance* 207. Eds. Jacques Chomarat, Marie-Madeleine Fragonard, Gisèle Mathieu-Castellani. Geneva: Librairie Droz, 1985.

Navarre, Marguerite de. *Comédie de Mont-de-Marsan*. In *Théâtre Profane*. Ed. V. L. Saulnier. Geneva: Droz, 1963.

Petrarch. *Petrarch's Lyric Poems: The "Rime sparse" and Other Lyrics*. Trans. and ed. Robert M. Durling. Cambridge, Mass.: Harvard University Press, 1976.

Pico della Mirandola, Gianfrancesco. *Of Being and Unity (De ente et uno)*. Trans. and ed. Victor Michael Hamm. Milwaukee: Marquette University Press, 1943.

———. *Heptaplus*. Trans. Douglas Carmichael. In *Pico della Mirandola: On the Dignity of Man*. Ed. Charles Glenn Wallis. New York: Bobbs-Merrill Company, Inc., 1965.

Plato. *Ion*. Trans. W. R. M. Lamb. London: William Heinemann, 1925.

———. *Republic*. Trans. Paul Shorey. 2 vols. Cambridge, Mass.: Harvard University Press, 1935.

Plotinus. *The Enneads*. Trans. Stephen MacKenna. 4th edition. London: Faber and Faber Ltd., 1969.

———. *Enneads*. Trans. A. H. Armstrong. 7 vols. Cambridge, Mass.: Harvard University Press, 1978-88.

Plutarch. *Bellone an Pace Clariores Fuerint Athenienses*. In *Moralia*. Trans. Frank Cole Babbitt. Cambridge, Mass.: Harvard University Press, 1936.

Proclus. *Commentaire sur la République*. Trans. A. J. Festugière. Paris: Librairie Philosophique J. Vrin, 1970.

Propertius. *Propertius*. Trans. H. E. Butler. Cambridge: Harvard University Press, 1952.

Quintilian. *Institutio Oratoria of Quintilian*. Ed. and trans. Harold Edgeworth Butler. 4 vols. London: William Heinemann Ltd., 1933.

Second, Jean. *Le Livre des baisers*. Ed. and trans. Thierry Sandre. Paris: Renaudot & Cie., 1989.

Theocritus. *The Greek Bucolic Poets*. Ed. and trans. J. M. Edmonds. Cambridge: Harvard University Press, 1970.

Tyard, Pontus de. *Œuvres Poétiques Complètes*. Ed. John C. Lapp. Paris: Librairie Marcel Didier, 1966.

Vasari, Giorgio. *Le Vite de' più eccellenti pittori, scultori e architettori*. Eds. Rosanna Bettarini and Paola Barocchi. 6 vols. Florence: Studio per Edizioni Scelte, 1966-87.

———. *Le Vite de' più eccellenti pittori, scultori e architettori*. Ed. Gaetano Milanesi. 9 vols. 1906. Reprint, Florence: G. C. Sansoni, 1981.

Virgil. *The Aeneid of Virgil*. Trans. Allen Mandelbaum. Berkeley: University of California Press, 1971.

———. *Virgil*. Trans. H. Rushton Fairclough. 2 vols. Cambridge: Harvard University Press, 1954.

(C) Ronsard and Pléiade Criticism

Adhémar, Jean. "Ronsard et l'Ecole de Fontainebleau." *Bibliothèque d'Humanisme et Renaissance* 20 (1958): 344-48.

Barron, Brian. "'Ut Pictura poesis': un lieu commun de la Renaissance et son importance dans l'oeuvre de Ronsard." Ph.D. diss., University of Edinburgh, 1981.

Campo, Roberto E. "A Poem to a Painter: The *Elegie à Janet* and Ronsard's Dilemma of Ambivalence." *French Forum* 12 (1987): 273-87.

———. "The Arts in Conflict in Ronsard's *Des peintures contenues dedans un tableau*." *Romance Quarterly* 39 (1992): 411-24.

———. "Pictorial Concerns in the Ronsardian *Exegi Monumentum*." *The Sixteenth Century Journal* 24 (1993): 671-83.

———. "Mannerist Conflict and the *Paragone* in Ronsard's *Temple des Messeigneurs*." *L'Esprit Créateur* 33 (1993): 9-19.

Castor, Grahame. *Pléiade Poetics: A Study in Sixteenth-Century Thought and Terminology*. Cambridge: University Press, 1964.

Cave, Terence. "Ronsard's Mythological Universe." In *Ronsard the Poet*. Ed. Terence Cave. London: Methuen and Co. Ltd., 1973.

———. "*Enargeia*: Erasmus and the Rhetoric of Presence in the Sixteenth Century." *L'Esprit Créateur* 16 (1976): 5-19.

———. *The Cornucopian Text*. Oxford: Clarendon Press, 1979.

Chamard, Henri. *Joachim du Bellay, 1522-1560*. Lille: Université de Lille, 1900.

———. *Histoire de la Pléiade*. 4 vols. Paris: Henri Didier, 1939-40.

Champion, Pierre. *Ronsard et son temps*. Reprint 1925. Paris: Champion, 1967.

Clements, Robert J. *Critical Theory and Practice of the Pléiade*. Cambridge, Mass.: Harvard University Press, 1942.

Creore, Alvin E. *A Word-Index to the Poetic Works of Ronsard*. Leeds: W. S. Maney and Son Ltd., 1972.

Dassonville, Michel. *Ronsard: Etude historique et littéraire*. 5 vols. Geneva: Librairie Droz, 1968-90.

———. "Eléments pour une définition de l'Hymne ronsardien." In *Autour des 'Hymnes' de Ronsard*. Ed. Madeleine Lazard. Paris: Librairie Honoré Champion, 1984.

Delacourcelle, Doris. *Le Sentiment de l'art dans la "Bergerie" de Remy Belleau*. Oxford: Blackwell, 1945.

Demerson, Guy. *La Mythologie classique dans l'oeuvre lyrique de la "Pléiade."* Geneva: Droz, 1972.

Fenoaltea, Doranne. *Du palais au jardin: L'architecture des "Odes" de Ronsard*. *Etudes Ronsardiennes* 3. Geneva: Librairie Droz, 1990.

Ford, Philip. "Ronsard the Painter: a Reading of 'Des Peintures contenues dedans un tableau'." *French Studies* 40 (1986): 32-44
———. "La fonction de l'*ekphrasis* chez Ronsard." In *Ronsard en son IVe Centenaire: L'Art de poésie. Etudes Ronsardiennes 2*. Eds. Yvonne Bellenger, Jean Céard, Daniel Ménager and Michel Simonin. Vol. 2. Geneva: Librairie Droz, 1989.
———. *Ronsard's "Hymnes:" A Literary and Iconographical Study*. Tempe, Arizona: Medieval and Renaissance Texts and Studies, 1997.
Franchet, Henri. *Le Poète et son oeuvre d'après Ronsard*. 1923. Reprint, Geneva: Slatkine Reprints, 1969.
Gendre, André. *Ronsard poète de la conquête amoureuse*. Neuchâtel: Baconnière, 1970.
Joukovsky, Françoise. *La Gloire dans la poésie française et néolatine du XVIe siècle*. Geneva: Librairie Droz, 1969.
———. "L'*Elegie à Janet* de Ronsard, portrait 'mental.'" In *Le Portrait*. Ed. Joseph-Marc Bailbe. Rouen: Université de Rouen, 1987.
———. *Le Bel objet: Les paradis artificiels de la Pléiade*. Paris: Librairie Honoré Champion, 1991.
Laumonier, Paul. *Ronsard poète lyrique*. Paris: Librairie Hachette, 1923.
Lazard, Madeleine, ed. *Autour des 'Hymnes' de Ronsard*. Paris: Librairie Honoré Champion, 1984.
Lebègue, Raymond. "La Pléiade et les Beaux-Arts." In *International Federation for Modern Languages and Literatures: Atti del Quinto Congresso Internazionale di Lingue e Letterature Moderne*. Florence, 1951.
Levi, A. H. T. "The Role of Neoplatonism in Ronsard's Poetic Imagination." In *Ronsard the Poet*. Ed. Terence Cave. London: Methuen and Co. Ltd., 1973.
McGowan, Margaret M. *Ideal Forms in the Age of Ronsard*. Berkeley: University of California Press, 1985.
Mellerio, Louis. *Lexique de Ronsard*. Paris: Plon, 1895.
Stackelberg, Jürgen V. "Ronsard und Aristoteles." *Bibliothèque d'Humanisme et Renaissance*, 25 (1963). 349-61.
Ménager, Daniel. *Ronsard: Le Roi, le poète et les hommes*. Geneva: Droz, 1979.
Nash, Jerry C. " 'Fantastiquant mille monstres bossus': Poetic Incongruities, Poetic Epiphanies, and the Writerly Semiosis of Pierre de Ronsard." *Romanic Review* 84 (1993): 143-62.
O'Brian, John. "Clio's 'Cabinet': Metaphorical Edifices in Ronsard's 'Hymnes' of 1555-1556." *Modern Language Review* 81 (1986): 37-50.
Plattard, Jean. "Les Arts et les artistes de la Renaissance française jugés par les écrivains du temps." *Revue d'Histoire littéraire de la France* 21 (1914): 481-502.
Pot, Olivier. *Inspiration et Mélancolie: L'épistémologie poétique dans les Amours de Ronsard. Etudes Ronsardiennes IV*. Geneva: Droz, 1990.
Quainton, Malcolm. *Ronsard's Ordered Chaos: Visions of Flux and Stability in the Poetry of Pierre de Ronsard*. Manchester: Manchester University Press, 1980.
Raymond, Marcel. *Etre et dire*. Neuchâtel: Editions de la Baconnière, 1970.
———. *L'Influence de Ronsard sur la poésie française (1550-1585)*. 2 vols. 1965. Reprint, New York: Burt Franklin, 1971.
Rochambeau, Achille de. *Famille de Ronsart: recherches généologiques, historiques et littéraires sur P. de Ronsard et sa famille*. 1868. Reprint, Nendeln, Liechtenstein: Kraus Reprint, 1973.
Roellenbleck, Georg. "Les *Hymnes* de 1555-1556: Questions de genre." In *Ronsard en son IVe Centenaire: L'art de poésie*. Eds. Yvonne Bellenger, et al. *Etudes Ronsardiennes*. Vol. 2. Geneva: Librairie Droz, 1989.
Sayce, Richard A. "Ronsard and Mannerism: The Elégie à Janet." *L'Esprit Créateur* 6 (1966): 234-47.

Silver, Isidore. *The Intellectual Evolution of Ronsard*. 2 vols. St. Louis: Washington University, 1969.

———. *Ronsard and the Hellenic Renaissance in France II: Ronsard and the Grecian Lyre*. 3 vols. Geneva: Droz, 1981-87.

Simonin, Michel. *Pierre de Ronsard*. Paris: Fayard, 1990.

Wildenstein, Georges. "La Collection de tableaux d'un admirateur de Ronsard." *Gazette des Beaux-Arts* 51 (1958): 5-8.

Wilson, Dudley. B. *Ronsard Poet of Nature*. Manchester: University Press, 1961.

(D) GENERAL CRITICISM AND LITERARY HISTORY

Allen, Michael J. B. *The Platonism of Marsilio Ficino: A Study of His "Phaedrus" Commentary, Its Sources and Genesis*. Berkeley: University of California Press, 1984.

Atchity, Kenneth John. *Homer's "Iliad": The Shield of Memory*. Carbondale: Southern Illinois University Press, 1978.

Ayim, Maryann. "Semiosis." In *Encyclopedic Dictionary of Semiotics*. Eds. Thomas A. Sebeok, et al. 2 vols. Berlin: Mouton de Gruyter, 1986.

Bassett, Samuel Eliot. *The Poetry of Homer*. Berkeley: University of California Press, 1938.

Bellenger, Yvonne. "Les poètes français et la peinture: la ressemblance comme critère esthétique au XVIe siècle." In *Mélanges à la mémoire de Franco Simone*. Geneva: Slatkine, 1980.

Bergin, Thomas G. *Dante*. New York: Orion Press, 1965.

Bouchot, Henri. *Les Femmes de Brantome*. Paris: Quantin, 1890.

Butcher, Samuel Henry. "Aristotle's Poetics." In *Aristotle's Theory of Poetry and Fine Art, with a Critical Text and Translation of the "Poetics"*. New York: Dover Publications, Inc., 1951.

Casagrande, Gino. "'Esto Visibile Parlare': A Synaesthetic Approach to *Purgatorio* 10.55-63." In *Lectura Dantis Newberryana*. Eds. Paolo Cherchi and Antonio C. Mastrobuono. Vol. 2. Evanston: Northwestern University Press, 1990.

Chastel, André. *Marsile Ficin et l'art*. Geneva: Librairie Droz, 1975.

Chiarenza, Marguerite Mills. *"The Divine Comedy": Tracing God's Art*. Boston: Twayne Publishers, 1989.

Copenhaver, Brian. "Hermes Trismegistus, Proclus, and the Question of a Philosophy of Magic in the Renaissance." In *Hermeticism and the Renaissance: Intellectual History and the Occult in Early Modern Europe*. Eds. Ingrid Merkel and Allen G. Debus. Washington, D. C.: Folger Books, 1988.

Cotgrave, Randle. *A Dictionarie of the French and English Tongues, 1611*. Menston, Eng.: Scolar Press Ltd., 1968.

Curtius, Ernst. *European Literature and the Latin Middle Ages*. Trans. Willard R. Trask. Princeton: Princeton University Press, 1973.

Davis, Michael. *Aristotle's "Poetics": The Poetry of Philosophy*. Lanham, Maryland: Rowman and Littlefield, 1992.

De Bruyne, Edgar. *The Esthetics of the Middle Ages*. Trans. Eileen B. Hennessy. New York: Frederick Ungar, 1969.

Derrida, Jacques. *De la grammatologie*. Paris: Editions de Minuit, 1967.

De Sanctis, Francesco. *History of Italian Literature*. Trans. Joan Redfern. New York: Harcourt Brace, 1931.

Dubois, Claude-Gilbert. *Le Maniérisme*. Paris: Presses Universitaires de France, 1979.

———. "Problems of 'Representation' in the Sixteenth Century." Trans. Monique Briand-Walker. *Poetics Today* 5 (1984): 461-78.

Eco, Umberto. *Art and Beauty in the Middle Ages*. New Haven: Yale University Press, 1986.

———. *The Aesthetics of Thomas Aquinas*. Trans. Hugh Bredin. Cambridge, Mass.: Harvard University Press, 1988.

———. *The Limits of Interpretation*. Bloomington: Indiana University Press, 1990.

Else, Gerald F. *Plato and Aristotle on Poetry*. Ed. Peter Burian. Chapel Hill: University of North Carolina Press, 1986.

Gaucheron, Roger, ed. *Recueil des Dames*. Paris: Payot, 1926.

Galand-Hallyn, Perrine. "'Enargeia' maniériste, 'enargeia' visionnaire des prophéties du Tibre au songe d'océan." *Bibliothèque d'Humanisme et Renaissance* 53 (1991): 305-28.

Gent, Lucy. *Picture and Poetry: 1560-1620: Relations between Literature and the Visual Arts in the English Renaissance*. Lemington Spa: James Hall, 1981.

Girard, René. *Deceit, Desire and the Novel: Self and Other in Literary Structure*. Trans. Yvonne Freccero. Baltimore: Johns Hopkins Press, 1965.

———. *Violence and the Sacred*. Trans. Patrick Gregory. Baltimore: Johns Hopkins University Press, 1977.

Greimas, A. J. *Dictionnaire de l'ancien français*. Paris: Librairie Larousse, 1968.

Hagstrum, Jean H. *The Sister Arts: The Tradition of Literary Pictorialism and English Poetry from Dryden to Gray*. Chicago: University of Chicago Press, 1958.

Halliwell, Stephen. *Aristotle's Poetics*. Chapel Hill: University of North Carolina Press, 1986.

Hatzfeld, Helmut A. *Literature through Art: A New Approach to French Literature*. 1952. Reprint, Chapel Hill: University of North Carolina Press, 1969.

Heffernan, James A. W. *Museum of Words: The Poetics of Ekphrasis from Homer to Ashbery*. Chicago: University of Chicago Press, 1993.

Hopkins, Jasper. *Nicholas of Cusa's Metaphysics of Contradiction*. Minneapolis: Banning, 1983.

Hubert, Henri and Mauss, Marcel. *Sacrifice: Its Nature and Function*. Trans. W. D Halls. London: Cohen & West Ltd., 1964.

Huguet, Edmond. *Dictionnaire de la langue française du seizième siècle*. 8 vols. Paris: Didier, 1925-1966.

Jakobson, Roman. *Essais de linguistique générale*. Trans. and ed. Nicolas Ruwet. Paris: Editions de Minuit, 1963.

———, "Linguistics and Poetics." In *Selected Writings*. Vol. 3. "Poetry of Grammar and Grammar of Poetry." Ed. Stephen Rudy. The Hague: Mouton Publishers, 1981.

Jugé, Clément. *Nicolas Denisot du Mans (1515-1559): Essai sur sa vie et ses oeuvres*. Geneva: Slatkine, 1969.

Kerrigan, William and Braden, Gordon. *The Idea of the Renaissance*. Baltimore: Johns Hopkins University Press, 1989.

Koyré, Alexandre. *From the Closed World to the Infinite Universe*. New York: Harper & Row, 1958.

Krieger, Murray. "The Ekphrastic Principle and the Still Movement of Poetry; or Laokoön Revisited." In *The Play and Place of Criticism*. Baltimore: The Johns Hopkins Press, 1967).

———. *Ekphrasis: The Illusion of the Natural Sign*. Baltimore: Johns Hopkins University Press, 1992.

Kristeller, Paul Oskar. *The Philosophy of Marsilio Ficino*. Trans. Virginia Conant. New York: Columbia University Press, 1943.

Lecercle, François. *La Chimère de Zeuxis: Portrait poétique et portrait peint en France et en Italie à la Renaissance*. Tübingen: Gunter Narr Verlag, 1987.

Mack, Burton. "Religion and Ritual." "Introduction." In *Violent Origins*. Ed. Robert G. Hamerton-Kelly. Stanford: Stanford University Press, 1987.

Macphail, Eric. *The Voyage to Rome in French Renaissance Literature. Stanford French and Italian Studies* 68. Saratoga: Anma Libri, 1990.

McKeon, Richard. "Literary Criticism and the Concept of Imitation in Antiquity." In *Critics and Criticism: Ancient and Modern*. Ed. R. S. Crane. Chicago: University of Chicago Press, 1952.

Merrill, Robert Valentine and Clements, Robert J. *Platonism in French Renaissance Poetry*. New York: New York University Press, 1957.

Mirollo, James V. *Mannerism and Renaissance Poetry: Concept, Mode, Inner Design*. New Haven: Yale University Press, 1984.

Mitchell, W. J. Thomas. *Iconology: Image, Text, Ideology*. Chicago: University of Chicago Press, 1986.

Naïs, Hélène. *Les Animaux dans la poésie française de la Renaissance*. Paris: Didier, 1961.

Norton, Glyn P. "The Horatian Grotesque in Renaissance France: The Genesis of a Poetic Formula." *Romanic Review* 65 (1974): 157-74.

O'Malley, Glenn. "Literary Synaesthesia." *Journal of Aesthetic and Art Criticism* 15 (1957): 391-411.

Reinikka, Merle A. *A History of the Orchid*. Coral Gables: University of Miami Press, 1972.

Riffaterre, Michael. *Fictional Truth*. Baltimore: Johns Hopkins University Press, 1990.

Roberts, W. Rhys. *Greek Rhetoric and Literary Criticism*. New York: Longmans, Green and Co., 1928.

Robinson, Franklin W. and Stephen G. Nichols, Jr., eds. *The Meaning of Mannerism*. Hanover: University Press of New England, 1972.

Rouget, François. *L'Apothéose d'Orphée: l'esthétique de l'ode en France au XVIe siècle, de Sébillet à Scaliger (1548-1561)*. Geneva: Droz, 1994.

Sandys, John Edwin. *A History of Classical Scholarship*. 3 vols. 3rd edition. Cambridge: University Press, 1908-1921.

Saslow, James M. *Ganymede in the Renaissance: Homosexuality in Art and Society*. New Haven: Yale University Press, 1986.

Sayers, Dorothy L. *Introductory Papers on Dante*. New York: Harper and Brothers, 1954.

Scarborough, John. "Hermetic and Related Texts in Classical Antiquity." In *Hermeticism and the Renaissance: Intellectual History and the Occult in Early Modern Europe*. Eds. Ingrid Merkel and Allen G. Debus. Washington, D.C.: Folger Books, 1988.

Schnapp, Jeffrey T. "Introduction to *Purgatorio*." In *The Cambridge Companion to Dante*. Ed. Rachel Jacoff. New York: Cambridge University Press, 1993.

Seznec, Jean. *The Survival of the Pagan Gods*. Trans. Barbara F. Sessions. 1953. Reprint, Princeton: Princeton University Press, 1972.

Singleton, Charles S. *Commedia: Elements of Structure*. Cambridge: Harvard University Press, 1954.

———. "Allegory." In *Critical Essays on Dante*. Ed. Giuseppe Mazzotta. Boston: G. K. Hall and Co., 1991.

Smith, William, ed. *Dictionary of Greek and Roman Mythology*. 3 vols. Boston: Little, Brown and Co., 1859.

Stanley, Keith. *The Shield of Homer: Narrative Structure in the "Iliad"*. Princeton: Princeton University Press, 1993.

Steiner, Wendy. *Pictures of Romance*. Chicago: University of Chicago Press, 1988.

Summers, David. *The Judgment of Sense: Renaissance Naturalism and the Rise of Aesthetics*. Cambridge: Cambridge University Press, 1987.

Sypher, Wylie. *Four Stages of Renaissance Style*. 1955. Reprint, New York: Anchor Books, 1965.

Thurston, Herbert and Attwater, Donald. *Butler's Lives of the Saints*. 3 vols. New York: Kennedy, 1956.

Trimpi, Wesley. "The Meaning of Horace's 'Ut Pictura Poesis'." *Warburg and Courtauld Institutes* 36 (1973): 1-34.

Weber, Henri. *La Création poétique au XVIe siècle en France*. Paris: Librairie Nizet, 1955.

Willcock, Malcolm M. *A Companion to the Iliad*. Chicago: University of Chicago Press, 1976.

Yates, Frances A. *The French Academies of the Sixteenth Century*. London: Warburg Institute, 1947.

——. *Giordano Bruno and the Hermetic Tradition*. Chicago: University of Chicago Press, 1964.

——. *The Art of Memory*. Chicago: University of Chicago Press, 1966.

(E) ART HISTORY AND CRITICISM

Adhémar, Jean. *Le Dessin français au XVIe siècle*. Luzon: Mermod, 1954.

——. *Les Clouet et la cour des rois de France*. Paris: Bibliothèque Nationale, 1970.

Barasch, Moshe. *Theories of Art: From Plato to Winckelmann*. New York: New York University Press, 1985.

Béguin, Sylvie. "Corneille de Lyon." In *Le XVIe Siècle Européen: Peintures et Dessins dans les Collections Publiques Françaises*. Ed. Roseline Bacou, et al. 2nd edition. Paris: Réunion des Musées Nationaux, 1966.

Béguin, Sylvie, et al. *L'Ecole de Fontainebleau*. Paris: Musées Nationaux, 1972.

Blunt, Anthony. *Artistic Theory in Italy 1450-1600*. Oxford: Clarendon Press, 1940.

——. *Art and Architecture in France 1500-1700*. 4th edition. New York: Penguin Books, 1982.

Bouchot, Henri. *Les Clouet et Corneille de Lyon*. Paris: Librairie de l'Art, 1892.

——. *L'Exposition des primitifs français: la peinture en France sous les Valois*. 3 vols. Paris: Librairie Centrale des Beaux-Arts, n.d.

Broglie, Raoul de, "Les Clouet de Chantilly: Catalogue illustré," *Gazette des Beaux-Arts* (May June, 1971): 239-336.

Campbell, Lorne. *Van der Weyden*. New York. Harper and Row, 1980.

——. *Renaissance Portraits: European Portrait-Painting in the 14th, 15th and 16th Centuries*. New Haven: Yale University Press, 1990.

Dimier, Louis. *French Painting in the Sixteenth Century*. Trans. Harold Child. London: Duckworth & Co., 1904.

——. *Histoire de la peinture de portrait en France au XVIe siècle*. 3 vols. Paris: Librairie Nationale d'Art et d'Histoire, 1924-25.

——. *Histoire de la peinture française des origines au retour de Vouet: 1300 à 1627*. Paris: Librairie Nationale d'Art et d'Histoire, 1925.

Fourreau, Armand. *Les Clouet*. Paris: Rieder, 1929.

Golson, Lucile M. "Landscape Prints and Landscapists of the School of Fontainebleau." *Gazette des Beaux-Arts*, 73 (1969): 95-110.

Gombrich, Ernst H. "*Icones Symbolicae*: The Visual Image in Neo-Platonic Thought." *Journal of the Warburg and Courtauld Institutes* 11 (1948): 163-92.

——. *The Heritage of Apelles: Studies in the Art of the Renaissance*. Ithaca: Cornell University Press, 1976.

Gower, Ronald. *Three Hundred French Portraits, Representing Personages of the Courts of Francis I, Henry II, and Francis II*. London: Sampson Low, Marston, Low & Searle, 1875.

Hauser, Arnold. *The Social History of Art*. Vol. 2. New York: Vintage Books, 1957.

Hauser, Arnold. *Mannerism: The Crisis of the Renaissance and the Origin of Modern Art*. Trans. Eric Mosbacher. 2 vols. New York: Alfred A. Knopf, 1965.

Johnson, William McAllister. "Once More the Galerie François Ier at Fontainebleau." *Gazette des Beaux-Arts* 103 (1984): 127-44.

Joxe, Louis, et al. *Fontainebleau*. 2 vols. Ottawa: National Gallery of Canada, 1973.

Kemp, Martin. *Leonardo da Vinci: The Marvellous Works of Nature and Man*. Cambridge, Mass.: Harvard University Press, 1981.

Laborde, Le Comte de. *La Renaissance des arts à la cour de France: Etudes sur le seizième siècle*. 3 vols. 1850. Reprint, New York: Burt Franklin, 1965.

Lee, Rensselaer. *Ut Pictura Poesis: The Humanistic Theory of Painting*. New York: Norton, 1967.

Lévêque, Jean-Jacques. *L'Ecole de Fontainebleau*. Neuchâtel: Editions Ides et Calendes, 1984.

Mellen, Peter. *Jean Clouet: Complete Edition of the Drawings, Miniatures and Paintings*. London: Phaidon Press Ltd., 1971.

Mendelsohn, Leatrice. *Paragoni: Benedetto Varchi's Due Lezzioni and Cinquecento Art Theory*. Ann Arbor: University of Michigan Research Press, 1982

Moreau-Nélaton, Etienne. *Chantilly: crayons français du XVIe siècle*. Paris: Librairie Centrale des Beaux-Arts, 1910.

———. *Catherine de Médicis et les Clouets de Chantilly*. Paris: Firmin-Didot, 1926.

Panofsky, Erwin. *Galileo As a Critic of the Arts*. The Hague: Martinus Nijhoff, 1954.

———. *Idea: A Concept in Art Theory*. Trans. Joseph J. S. Peake. Columbia, S. Carolina: University of South Carolina Press, 1968.

———. *Studies in Iconology: Humanistic Themes in the Art of the Renaissance*. 1939. Reprint, New York: Harper & Row, 1972.

Panofsky, Erwin and Panofsky, Dora. "The Iconography of the Galérie François Ier at Fontainebleau." *Gazette des Beaux-Arts* 52 (1958): 113-90.

———. "La Galerie François Ier au château de Fontainebleau." *Revue de l'Art* 16-17 (1972).

Papillon, Jean-Michel. *Traité historique et pratique de la gravure en bois*. 2 vols. 1766. Reprint, Paris: Editions des Archives Contemporaines, 1985.

Pevsner, Nikolaus. "The Architecture of Mannerism." In *Readings in Art History*. Ed. Harold Spencer. Vol. 2. New York: Scribner's, 1969. First published in *The Mint* 1 (1946): 116-37.

Pope-Hennessy, John. *The Portrait in the Renaissance*. Bollingen Series 35.12. New York: Bollingen Foundation, 1966.

Roussel, Pierre Désiré. *Histoire et description du château d'Anet*. Paris: D. Jouaust, 1875.

Rubin, Patricia Lee. *Giorgio Vasari: Art and History*. New Haven: Yale University Press, 1995.

Salet, Francis. *La Tapisserie française du moyen-âge à nos jours*. Paris: Vincent, 1946.

Swindler, Mary Hamilton. *Ancient Painting from the Earliest Times to the Period of Christian Art*. New Haven: Yale University Press, 1929.

Tatarkiewicz, Wladyslaw. *History of Aesthetics*. Eds. Cyril Barrett and D. Petsch. 3 vols. The Hague: Mouton, 1970-74.

Trinquet, Roger. "L'Allégorie politique au XVIe siècle dans la peinture française, ses Dames au Bain." *BSHAF* (1967): 1-16.

Walker, John. *Portraits: 5,000 Years*. New York: Harry N. Abrams, Inc., 1983.

Zerner, Henri. "Le système décoratif de la Galerie François Ier à Fontainebleau." In *Actes du Colloque International sur l'Art de Fontainebleau*. Ed. André Chastel. Paris: Editions du Centre National de la Recherche Scientifique, 1975.

INDEX OF RONSARD POEMS CITED

GENERAL INDEX

(Asterisks denote illustrations)

NORTH CAROLINA STUDIES IN THE ROMANCE LANGUAGES AND LITERATURES

I.S.B.N. Prefix 0-8078-

Recent Titles

When ordering please cite the ISBN Prefix plus the last four digits for each title.

Send orders to: University of North Carolina Press
P.O. Box 2288
CB# 6215
Chapel Hill, NC 27515-2288
U.S.A.